Incidents of Travel in Yucatan

DISTRIBUIDOR EXCLUSIVO
Distribuidora Británica, S.A. de C.V.
Grecia No. 151
Col. San Alvaro
02090 - Azcapotzalco, D.F.
Tels.: 5341-15-66 • 5341-16-26
Fax: (5) 341-35-58

John L. Stephens

Incidents of Travel in Yucatan

Volumes One and Two
Condensed Edition

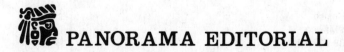 **PANORAMA EDITORIAL**

INCIDENTS OF TRAVEL IN YUCATAN

First edition: 1988
Ninth reprint: 2000
© Copyright Panorama Editorial, S.A. de C.V.
   for the condensed edition based on the
   original text of the first edition published
   by Harper and Brothers, New York, 1843

Tels.: 55-35-93-48 • 55-92-20-19
Fax: 55-35-92-02 • 55-35-12-17
e-mail: panorama@iserve.net.mx
http://www.panoramaed.com.mx

Printed in Mexico
Impreso en México
ISBN 968-38-0198-6

Index

index

index

PREFACE

Between 1839 and 1841, John Lloyd Stephens, a North American traveler, diplomat and keen amateur archeologist, and Frederick Catherwood, an English architect and draughtsman, traveled in and explored a large part of the Maya region on two occasions. They made their impressions and discoveries known by publishing two books that have become classics among the literature on ancient Maya cities: *Incidents of Travel in Central America, Chiapas and Yucatan* (1841), and *Incidents of Travel in Yucatan* (1843), with texts by Stephens and magnificent illustrations by Catherwood.

At that time, when the Maya culture and its archeological remains were practically unknown, Stephens' books, quickly became best-sellers, but their greatest claim to fame is to have aroused interest among the general public and attracted the attention of other explorers and archeologists, who began to take a closer look at this region, leading to a whole new series of investigations.

The two works give a very readable account of the fortunes and adventures of the two explorers during their travels, with detailed and accurate descriptions of the various archeological sites they visited and the works of art they discovered.

Although the main object of the present edition is to condense and comment on the second book, a sketch of the first journey, made between October 1839 and July 1840, is included, since this led to the publication of *Incidents of Travel in Central America, Chiapas and Yucatan*. This will clarify parts of the work in hand, which deals only with Yucatan but where Stephens refers back to persons and events of the first trip. It will also give the reader a more complete picture of the discoveries made by these two explorers.

Both works have become classics over the years; they laid the foundations of American archeology and demonstrated the homogeneity of Maya culture; considered the ruins as works of art for the first time and, finally, insisted that these structures were of American origin, refuting fashionable theories that they had been built by Egyptians, Phoencians or the lost tribes of Israel.

Incidents of Travel in Yucatan, the outcome of the second journey, made between October 1841 and July 1842, describes over forty archeological sites on the Yucatan peninsula, many of which are illustrated by Catherwood's masterly drawings. Some of these sites were undiscovered at the time while others, although visited, were unknown to the world in general. The virtue of these two explorers is not only that they rediscovered these sites, but that they spread their knowledge with their books.

The second book was originally published in two volumes but is here condensed into one. The original text is respected throughout, but long or repeated descriptions of life on haciendas, dances, bullfights, places, countryside, etc., have been omitted. Also, the comparisons made between Maya buildings and those of Egypt, Greece and Rome have been eliminated, as have long arguments where the author tries to demonstrate that these ancient cities were still inhabited when the Spanish arrived in the sixteenth century. This theory has been proved false, so its omission in no way affects the sense and sequence of Stephens' text.

The original titles of each chapter have been shortened so as to reflect only the subjects retained in this condensed version. Texts in *italics* are the notes and comments of the editor.

BIOGRAPHICAL SKETCH OF THE AUTHOR

John Lloyd Stephens was born in Shrewsbury, New Jersey, on November 25, 1805. Soon after he was one year old the family moved to New York, where he later studied at the Classical School and then Columbia Collage.

On leaving Columbia he decided to study law, and was taken on as a clerk in the office of Daniel Lord, one of the most prestigious lawyers of the time. He recommended Trapping Reeve's Law School in Litchfield, Connecticut, where Stephens graduated in 1824.

Before beginning his career as a lawyer properly speaking he traveled with his cousin Charles Hendrickson through the West to Illinois, then to New Orleans. In 1827 he went to Albany, a town in the north of New York State, to be admitted as a lawyer.

At that time, New York was undergoing a series of changes and alterations: houses were being remodeled or else demolished to make way for new ones and gas lighting was being installed. Changes were also happening on the political and cultural fronts, and very soon Stephens entered politics. By 1828 he was more interested in this than in the profession of lawyer, which he practiced from an office in Wall Street.

It was this interest that led him indirectly to his later discoveries: he had to make so many speeches that eventually his throat was affected. The family doctor suggested that he should take a trip to Europe for the sake of his health.

This journey took Stephens to Rome, Naples, Sicily and Greece. Full of curiosity about antiquity, he went on to the Levant.

Stephens first appeared in print in October 1835 when one of his long letters to Fenno Hoffman, editor of the *American Monthly Magazine* was published, ostensibly without his permission although he had jokingly asked his friend not to publish what he had written.

All this seems likely to have been arranged beforehand, since the letter was published in four parts under the title of *Scenes in the Levant,* signed by 'An American'. Stephens followed the Roman road to Ephesus and wandered through the ruins, expressing his pleasure at seeing them in his letter.

He continued to Constantinople, sailing through the Greek islands. On impulse he then went to Russia, where he visited Kiev, Moscow and St. Peterburg (Leningrad). From there he traveled to Warsaw, where he was confined to bed for a few days because of his throat infection.

Later he passed through Vienna, then Germany, and finally reached Paris, ready to return to the United States. However he was not able to obtain a passage, and so had time to browse through the old books sold on stands along the river Seine. Here he discovered several lithographs of a ruined city called Petra, located in Arabia Petrea (Stony Arabia), and decided to go there by way of Egypt.

Stephens was one of the first to sign the visitor's book at the American Consulate in Alexandria, where he met the consul, British-born George Giddon, who was passionately interested in Egyptian archeology. The traveler was disappointed by what he saw in Alexandria in late 1835 since it did not live up to his expectations.

Because Egypt was not very safe at that time, Stephens was advised to see the Pasha, Mehmet Ali, to obtain a safe-conduct that would enable him to travel. The pasha, who seemed to have stepped out of the pages of the *Arabian Nights,* received Stephens well and gave him the safe-conduct that was to be very useful to him on his trip down the Nile.

He set off in January 1836, accompanied by Paolo Nuozzo, an Italian he had met in Constantinople. Sailing beyond Memphis, they visited the pyramids of Giza, then Dendera, the ruins of Thebes, Luxor and the Temples of Ammon. They saw the temples at Karnak and the colossal statue of Memmon, erected by Amenhotep III. There Stephens found the names of other travelers and, if he had paid more attention, would have seen that of Frederick Catherwood.

From there they continued to the island of Elephantine, Aswan and the island of Philae with its temples dedicated to the goddess Hathor and the largest one, dedicated to Isis that Catherwood had drawn in 1833.

In March 1836 Stephens disguised himself as a Cairo merchant for his journey to Petra. Adolphe Linant, co-author of a book about this city, had traveled this same route eleven years earlier, and gave him valuable information. Other experienced travelers warned him of the dangers he could expect.

With a caravan of five camels and a camel driver, Stephens and Nuozzo set out for Mecca. They followed the shores of the Gulf of Suez as far as the foothills of Mt. Sinai, where they rested for a few days in the Orthodox monastery of St. Catherine, presenting a letter from the Greek patriarch of Cairo.

They then continued towards Gaza, taking the road to 'Aqaba, where they took refuge in the ancient fortress, arousing the curiosity of the local inhabitants, who rarely saw strangers. Here Stephens talked with Sheikh Alouin, whom he had met in Cairo. The ruins of Petra were in the territory governed by the sheikh and he agreed to guide Stephens to them.

Once they had reached an agreement they took the old Roman road and in three days reached the mountains of Seir, where Mt. Hor stands. The entrance to Petra was through the Sik, a deep, narrow cleft in Mt. Seir. They rode into it, and soon Stephens could see a temple carved into the rock face: El Khazneh. He was overawed by the superb façade, and as he visited the other buildings he was lost for words to describe the wonder and amazement he felt.

After Petra, Stephens went north along the Roman road to the Holy Land, crossing Edrom, and arrived in Jerusalem on March 12, 1836, where he called on the Turkish governor. At this time Stephens did not know that two years earlier Catherwood had drawn the plan of the Mosque of Omar, but he was to learn this later in London.

He eventually reached Beirut where illness confined him to bed for ten days, finally sailing for England via Alexandria, and arriving in autumn 1836.

BIOGRAPHICAL SKETCH OF THE ARTIST

Frederick Catherwood was born in the East London suburb of Hoxton on February 27, 1799, in a house at 21 Charles Square. He was educated at a local school, which he left, according to his certificate "a perfect grammarian, a good Orator and Poet, well instructed in Latin, Greek and Hebrew".

Catherwood's physical appearance is almost unknown. Although he had various artist friends, it seems nobody ever painted or drew him. He appears in only one of his own drawings, among the ruins of Tulum; a tall, well-built man with light-colored hair.

In 1820 he attended some lectures at the Royal Academy in Somerset House. There he became familiar with the works of Piranesi, and was fascinated by the artist's drawing of Roman ruins. By this time, Catherwood had had served his apprenticeship to an architect, and was attracted to archeology.

Shortly afterward, Joseph Severn invited him to Rome. Severn, a painter, had gone to Italy with the poet Keats, who had died of tuberculosis. Once in Rome, Catherwood was quickly accepted into the Society of Englishmen and began to study classical architecture. He worked with Elizabeth, Duchess of Devonshire in her private excavations of the Roman Forum, and his drawings of the catacombs appeared in the *Dictionary of Architecture*.

He later went to Sicily, traveling down the east coast of the island and making drawings of the ruins, with Mt. Etna in the background. From there he went to Athens, the dream of all architecture students in those days. Unfortunately, his drawings dating from this time have been lost.

In 1824, Henry Parks, Joseph Scoles and Catherwood collected together all the money they had and hired a boat to sail up the Nile. For more than a year they drew, sketched and made plans of the ruins of Egypt.

In October of the same year, Catherwood met Robert Hay, heir of the Earl of Tweedsdale, who showed great interest in his drawings and invited him to take part in an expedition up the Nile with a group of artists, architects and antiquarians to investigate the various ruins. This group laid the foundations of Egyptian archeology with the work they did between 1824 and 1833.

On this second trip up the Nile, Catherwood drew a plan of Thebes in color as well as a general plan of all the ruins and a panoramic view of the Nile Valley which was later reproduced on a larger scale and exhibited in both London and New York as a panorama. He also drew the colossus of Memnon at Thebes, the court of the palace of Ramses, the raised terrace and pillars of Osiris and, further upriver, several temples on the island of Philae.

When the expedition ended almost all its members published something, using Catherwood's work. He himself did not write anything, which is why he is so often held responsible for the fact that so little is known of his personal life. He was an extremely modest man, in spite of his talents.

Later he worked as architectural adviser to Mehmet Ali, who ordered him to repair the mosques in Cairo. The pasha gave him a safe-conduct, and with this he was able to travel wihout any problems through Libya into western North Africa.

In mid 1833, Catherwood, Francis Arundale and Joseph Bonomi disguised themselves as Turkish merchants to travel to Mt. Sinai and Arabia Petrea. Following the caravan route along the Red Sea they reached the Rock of the Inscriptions after seven days, and then went on to visit the ruins of Sabit el Khadin and the ancient mines of Umm Lugma. On September 16 they arrived at the monastery of St. Catherine, guarding Mt. Sinai, and on October 6 entered Jerusalem.

There Catherwood made architectural and archeological investigations and drew a complete plan of El 'Aqsa: the Dome of the Rock and the Mosque of Omar. To draw his panoramic view of the city he used a *camera lucida*, a very popular piece of apparatus in the nineteenth century that through mirrors or prisms projected the outline of objects onto paper, where they could be traced.

The mosaic-covered Dome of the Rock presented certain difficulties: according to tradition, this was where the prophet Mohammed had mounted his winged horse to fly to the seven paradises, and unbelievers were not allowed to enter. Catherwood however, thanks to the decree identifying him as engineer to Mehmet Ali was allowed in and made his drawings safely.

He later visited Geraza where, in spite of the hostility of the local inhabitants he did a ground plan —the first ever to be made— and a drawing of the Temple of Artemis. Continuing his jorney, he went to Baalbek, originally a Phoenician city that was later Greek and then Roman and was still known by its Greek name of Heliopolis, City of the Sun. Here he made drawings of all the architecture and, in March 1834, made preparations to go to the desert city of Palmyra.

In 1835, after nine whole years of investigating the remains of ancient cultures, Frederick Catherwood returned to London. For financial reasons he contacted Robert Burford and was engaged to paint panoramas.

A German artist called Breisig is supposed to have invented the panorama in the late eighteenth century. Following in his footsteps, Robert Baker set one up in Leicester Square, London, where the public could see historical or modern events illustrated on a continuous canvas in a rotunda. In 1826 Baker sold the business to the Burfords, and after that the rotunda was known as 'Burford's Panorama'.

Burford was always looking for new material and made a point of contacting artists returning from abroad. This was how he met Catherwood and introduced him to the business of panoramas. Even if this did not bring Catherwood a reputation as an architect it did bring him money and led to his meeting with John Lloyd Stephens.

FIRST MEETING OF STEPHENS
AND CATHERWOOD

In London Stephens was well received at the American Consulate and there read the issues of the *American Monthly Magazine* where his letters had been printed, signed simply as being by 'An American'. However, his identity had been discovered and he was already a literary figure.

Visiting the sights of London he came to Leicester Square and Burford's Panorama where 'The Ruins of Jerusalem' were announced. He went in to see the circular panoramic view, lit by gas lamps, and there met Catherwood. This meeting was to lead to the revelation of the mysterious civilization of the Mayas.

There is no documentary information about the relations between Stephens and Catherwood in the years immediately following. In 1836 Stephens returned to New York, where he wrote his book on Arabia Petrea. In the same year Burford's Panorama arrived, announced as 'A splendid painting of the largest class, covering a surface of ten thousand square feet, painted from drawings taken by Mr. Catherwood, brilliantly illuminated every night by more than two hundred gas jets'.

The city had changed since Stephens' departure: a fire in the winter of 1835 had caused widespread damage; inflation was rising; credit had been suspended and the whole country was in the grip of depression.

It was probably at Stephens' suggestion that Catherwood moved to New York. The city had to be rebuilt and architecs were in demand, so Catherwood easily found work and soon afterward entered into association with the architect Frederick Diaper. After a few months his income was good enough for him to be able to return to England for his family. They settled in New York in Houston street, and also rented a piece of land on the corner of Broadway and Prince Street. Catherwood was soon able to build his own Panorama here, which became very successful.

Meanwhile, Stephens was writing his *Incidents of Travel in Arabia Petraea*, published in two volumes in 1837. Edgar Allen Poe gave the book a very favorable review that helped toward its great success; in fact, within two years it sold 21,000 copies and earned Stephens a respectable sum of money. This he used for his expedition in search of the Maya civilization.

Catherwood's panorama was also flourishing. Stephens contributed to this to a certain extent, as in the eighth edition of *Arabia Petraea* he mentioned the panorama and urged his readers to visit it. This financial success enabled the artist to dedicate part of his time to the study of the mysterious ruins of Central America that Stephens had talked about.

John Russell Bartlett, who later founded a publishing house and bookstore with Charles Welfod was, according to his diary, the first to show Stephens the book by Jean-Frédéric Waldeck on Yucatan that he had just received from France. He also showed him other works referring to the region, all of which interested Stephens immensely.

He took the books home and spent days reading the descriptions of ruins: the work of Captain Del Río, who had discovered Palenque; the book entitled *Antiquités Mexicaines* that contained accounts based on the reports of Captain Dupaix who had visited these same ruins. In this volume he read an article by the Yucatan-born Lorenzo de Zavala mentioning the existence of Uxmal, another ruined city in his native state. A specialist journal published in the United States contained news of Copán, yet another ruined city, in Honduras.

Then William Leggett, the American minister in Central America died. Stephens applied to the President for the post and was successful. On August 13. 1839 he received instructions from the Secretary of State, John Forsyth: he was to go to Central America, close the legation, send any official papers to the United States, find the government, present his credentials and negotiate a trade treaty. Nobody knew for certain whether a Central American government existed at all, and if it did, where its capital was and who was the president.

Stephens must have already talked with Catherwood about his plans to visit Central America, beause a very short time afterwards, in September 1839, he drew up a contract. This document, now in the Bancroft Library of the University of California, states that Catherwood should accompany Stephens during his diplomatic mission and later go with him to Chiapas and Yucatan to make drawings of the ruins. It also stipulates that Stephens would use these and that Catherwood himself would publish neither the drawings nor any account of the journey, and establishes how much the artist was to receive and the conditions of payment.

Obviously Stephens firmly intended to explore the region for ruins as soon as his diplomatic duties were over.

The
First Journey

Having received instructions on his diplomatic mission, Stephens began to make preparations. Meanwhile Catherwood bought the materials he needed for his drawings: paper, pencils, sepia ink (his favorite for art work), brushes, etc. He also invested in a new camera lucida and surveying and meteorological equipment.

On October 3, 1839, they boarded the British brig Mary Ann, *and after almost a month at sea reached Belize, at the time the only port of entry to Central America. Stephens and Catherwood were invited several times to Government House by his excellency, Colonel Archibald MacDonald. On the day they sailed for Izabal toasts were drunk to Queen Victoria, the President of the United States, Martin Van Buren and to the success of the journey.*

MacDonald also warned them that the region they intended to visit was in upheaval, since several factions were fighting each other, and told Stephens that in the case of danger he hould not hesitate to send word to him immediately. However, by this time the colonel had his own plans. Although he had no official authorization from the British government, he intended to send two men to Palenque: Patrick Walker, who was to write an account of the journey, and Captain John Caddy, to draw the ruins. He did not want an American to be first! So MacDonald's envoys set out on November 13, 1839.

Walker and Caddy reached Palenque first, carried out some explorations and made drawings of the buildings. When they returned to Belize 144 days later they expressed the opinion that the ruins were of 'Egypto-Indian' origin. The British government refused to cover their expenses since no approval had been given, and pointed out that the only motive for the expedition was ". . .that we might not be outstripped in this case in scientific zeal by the Americans".

Stephens and Catherwood, completely unaware of MacDonald's plans, left Belize on a steamship for the lake of Izabal and the port of the same name. Stephens called on the current commandant there, who warned them that the passport he issued to Guatemala City would probably not be respected as a civil war was in progress.

Stephens' main aim was to get to the ruins of Copán as quickly as he could. At dawn, accompanied by Augustin, a 'French Spaniard' they had hired in Belize as guide and servant, they set off on mules to cross the Mico mountain. Deeper and deeper into the jungle they went on a road that was in fact only an appallingly muddy track. Finally they crossed the Motagua river and passed through several small villages, following the old road to Copán.

In the town of Comatán the travelers had an unpleasant experience. Although Stephens showed his American official passport to the alcalde, it was no use. A party of armed men appeared, led by an officer who told them they could not continue their journey. They were eventually allowed to write a note to a general in Chiquimula. After being kept prisoners under guard for several hours they were suddenly informed that they could go on.

On the banks of the Copán river they discovered a stone wall and, cutting through the thick undergrowth, reached the East Court of the ruined city. There they found carved stones, a temple, a stairway, the remains of stone jaguars and a gigantic head of the God of Corn.

In the main court they discovered large carved monoliths, an enormous stone figure and, standing opposite, a block of stone that they called an 'altar'. The site of Copán was a puzzle to them, and they could not help wondering who had built the city.

Of course, they had absolutely no knowledge of certain facts: that the Mayas had a system of hieroglyphic writing and a calendar closely linked to their religious beliefs; that their economy was based on agriculture, chiefly corn, and that their society had been stratified, with priests and nobles forming the most powerful and important class.

We now know that Copán began to rise in 436 A.D. and that the pyramids, stairways and courts were built over the course of three centuries. The pyramids were reconstructed and enlarged, carved monoliths, stelae, were erected at the end of certain periods until, around 810 A.D. the city collapsed. Copán was abandoned and gradually covered by jungle. It remained in this state until the nineteenth century, when Stephens and Catherwood opened it up.

The explorers soon realized that this was a mysterious, unknown world. As they gazed at these silent stone witnesses they were filled with admiration. However, at that moment they were unaware that they were uncovering not only an archaeological site but a whole civilization, one of the greatest of pre-Hispanic times, that had no known history and, at that time, not even a name. Stephens' interesting text and Catherwood's magnificent illustrations made their discoveries known to the world.

So as to be able to work on the site they needed peons to help them cut and clear away the jungle, but in the village of Copán they had certain difficulties, which they finally solved. Fortunately they met the owner of the land on which the ruins stood, Don José María Acevedo. He showed them the title deeds, saying that the 'idols' belonged to him and that no one could go on the land without his permission.

Acevedo's wife was sick and he wanted the explorers to give her some medicine; he also invited them to stay in a hut near the ruins. Stephens later decided to try and buy the ruins, since he intended to remove some of the monuments eventually and take them to New York where they would form the nucleus of a Museum of American Antiquities. In spite of opposition from another important man in the village, after several conversations with Stephens, Acevedo agreed to sell the ruins of Copán for fifty dollars.

On November 17, 1839, work was begun on the site. First Catherwood drew a map and then gradually and with much difficulty started to capture the essence of the intricate designs on the 'idols' on paper.

Copán is a complex formed of three main courts and several pyramids. In one of these courts are tiers of stone benches and, at one side, a platform with large stone jaguars at the ends, and a massive stone head of the Maya god of the harvest, Yum Kax, which Catherwood copied. On one side of the court is a temple that was still buried in Stephen's time and not uncovered until fifty years later.

Stairways join the courts with another part of the site, now known as the Court of the Hieroglyphic Stairway, which was also covered when the two explorers were there, although Stephens did find several figures that were part of the decoration. This great stairway, with 63 steps, is decorated with a large number of hieroglyphics, some of which have been deciphered as dates as late as 756 A. D., showing it to be one of the last structures to be built at Copán. It is, in fact, one of the most impressive achievements of pre-Hispanic America.

Although the majority of the structures were covered by undergrowth at this time, Catherwood was able to distinguish the main architectural elements, observing that they were closely linked to religion.

North of the Court of the Stairway lies the Ball Court, where there ancient inhabitants played the ball game so well-known in Mesoamerica and beyond. After this is the Great Plaza, where the monoliths known as stelae stand. The explorers found a total of eleven and were amazed by their size and rich carving.

The hieroglyphs made Stephens think that the history of the people who had created the city must be engraved on its monuments, and he hoped that one day the key to them would be found.

Over the years, scholars investigating the hieroglyphs believed they referred only to time and dates. In 1958, Heinrich Berlin discovered that the names of places and important people could be identified among them. Tatiana Proskouriakoff analyzed various symbols, deciphering the birth dates of the individuals who had erected the stelae and, according to her system, references to marriages, personal names and allusions to war. Stephens was proved correct.

It is also true, of course, that the Mayas were obsessed by time and its measurement, and at Copán dated monoliths were erected at first every ten years then every five, and the symbolization of time was incorporated into the architecture of all the buildings.

Stephens did not know what the features and elements were of the culture they had discovered; in fact at that time they did not even know the term 'Maya' or the size of the geographical area once occupied by this culture. However, they were absolutely convinced that what they saw at Copán was not the only mark left by this people.

In the West Court Stephens found a square altar standing on four rounded stones, with four human figures on each side. The top was carved with hieroglyphs which the explorer believed to be the records of some important event in the history of this people, and Catherwood undertook the task of copying them.

Stephens believed that the altar showed a meeting or conference, and this was later proved to be correct. We now know that it in fact refers to a meeting of priests that was held at Copán, and the date carved on it is 6 Caban, 10 Mol, corresponding to 765 A. D.

When they returned to New York they compared Catherwood's drawing of the symbols on the altar with hieroglyphs in the Dresden Codex that Alexander Von Humboldt had recently published in part and realized that both works had been produced by the same group of people.

Stephens' books motivated Alfred P. Maudslay to visit Copán in 1882-3, when new buildings were brought to light. In the 1890's the Peabody Museum took over the work of excavation and in this century archeologists from the Carnegie Institution.

After thirteen days exploring Copán, Stephens decided it was time he went to Guatemala City to carry out his duties as a diplomat. Catherwood was to stay behind to complete his drawings and meet up with Stephens later.

On arriving in Guatemala City, Stephens went to see Mr. Hall, the British vice-consul, who told him that there had been a mutiny among the soldiers of Rafael Carrera, the leader of one of the two factions fighting the civil war. Next day he took possession of the house that had been occupied by the American chargé d'affaires and began his search for the government of Guatemala. He learned from other diplomats that there had been a series of revolutions and counter-revolutions. The two sides in the war were led by Rafael Carrera and Francisco Morazán, and it was difficult to say precisely who represented the government. After several days Stephens was able to pay an official visit to Carrera, and was impressed by the young man.

While waiting for Catherwood to arrive from Honduras the American made a short tour that took him to the Pacific coast. Catherwood finally arrived, sick and exhausted, on Christmas Day, but had recovered enough from his ordeals to accompany Stephens as far as the Pacific when he left on January 5 to continue his search for the government of Central

America. On reaching the coast, they separated. Catherwood turned back to spend a month at Antigua, Guatemala's former capital, then visited Copán again and also explored the ruins of Quiriguá, north of this site, on the banks of the Motagua river, where he drew a magnificent stela of red sandstone. Stephens made a long journey that was often difficult and dangerous —but always interesting— through El Salvador, Nicaragua and Costa Rica.

As a result of this twelve hundred mile expedition he wrote a formal report to the authorities in Washington informing them that "after a diligent search, no government found". He now considered himself relieved of his diplomatic duties and free to travel where he wished at his own expense. By this time Catherwood had also returned to Guatemala City and they began to make preparations for their journey to Palenque. Stephens paid another visit to Carrera and obtained a passport personally signed by the general. Armed with this, letters of recommendation from the 'government' to all the magistrates and one from the Vicar General to all the parish priests under his charge the explorers finally left Guatemala City on April 17, 1840.

They followed tracks that led them to the mountains above the beautiful lake of Atitlán. Further on, at Santa Cruz del Quiché, they talked with the rather eccentric priest, who told them he had heard of a place where the Indians still lived as they had in pre-Hispanic times. He seems to have been referring to he Lacandons of eastern Chiapas.

Stephens thought that this place might be found if enough time were dedicated to a search, but time was just what they could not spare; they had to press on to Palenque before the rainy season. They continued to Quezaltenango, where Catherwood painted two fine watercolors, then to Huehuetenango, were they visited the ruins of 'las Cuevas', noting that they were of rough stone cemented together with lime and not of cut stone as at Copán.

To their surprise they met an American here, Henry Pawling, who had been working as superintendent of a cochineal hacienda, where in fact Stephens had met him previously. Pawling had heard, or perhaps read in the Gaceta Oficial *(Official Gazette), of Stephens' journey to Mexico and, tired of the chaos in Guatemala, had decided to join him.*

Pawling was a welcome addition to the party since he spoke Spanish fluently. Stephens found that he could include him under his passport, and appointed him general manager of the expedition. Towards the end of April they crossed into Mexico and reached Comitán, Chiapas. Here they learned that General Santa Anna, President of Mexico, had given orders that no one was to be allowed to visit Palenque. It would have taken too long for Stephens to go to Mexico City and try to obtain a permit, so they decided to continue to the ruins, reasoning that they were not likely to be guarded.

The road through the jungle was atrocious, and the journey was made more difficult and unpleasant by the frequent storms that swept the region. At Ocosingo they found the remains of an ancient city, probably a colony of Palenque, where Catherwood made several drawings. Following the route taken by Dupaix in 1807 they finally arrived at the village of Palenque after ten days.

Stephens presented his passport to the alcalde, who did not show the slightest interest in the visitors. The prefect, on the other hand, received them warmly and said that he had been expecting them because Don Patricio (i.e. Patrick Walker from Belize) had told him they were on their way.

The village of Santo Domingo de Palenque had been founded by a Dominican missionary, Pedro Laurencio, and the ruins took their name from it. In fact, very little was known about them, not even the original Maya name.

The ruined city had been seen by the Indians of the Tumbalá mountains in the eighteenth century, and since then various rumours about it had circulated in the region. In 1773 the canon of Ciudad Real de Chiapas, Father Ramón de Ordoñez y Aguiar, had been carried there in a palanquin. He examined the various buildings and later wrote a Memoria on it.

Three years later the President of the Royal Audience of Guatemala sent instructions to the mayor of Santo Domingo de Palenque, José Antonio de Calderón, to survey the ruins. Calderón did not go until 1784, and his report caused enough interest for the architect Antonio Bernasconi to be sent to make an official survey. The final documents were sent to Spain, where they disappeared.

In 1786, as a result of royal orders, Captain Antonio del Río was commissioned by the government of Guatemala to explore the ruins and took Ricardo Almendariz with him as artist. He had the site cleared, probably causing extensive damage to the buildings in the process. For some reason Del Río's report remained in Guatemala. Many years later it was either sent or taken to London, where it was published in 1822, illustrated with Almendariz' engravings retouched and signed by 'Count' (there is some doubt about his claim to the title) Jean Frédéric Maximilien de Waldeck. This was one of the works that inspired Stephens to make his own expedition.

Even before this book was published the Spanish government had sent Captain Guillelmo Dupaix to Palenque in 1807, accompanied by

Luciano Castañeda as draughtsman. The resulting works lay moldering in Mexico until discovered almost thirty years later. Even then another six or seven years passed before they were published in Paris.

The ruins of Palenque next exerted their fascination on Waldeck, who reached the city in 1832 and lived there for two years. His work on Palenque, not published until 1866, was most imaginative and inaccurate: he drew elephants into the glyphs and tried to demonstrate that the buildings were of Asiatic origin.

Stephens and Catherwood marched towards the ruined city with a string of Indian porters carrying their baggage and equipment. Some three hours out of the village they were alerted by an Indian shouting 'El palacio' —'The palace': they had reached their goal, deep in the rain forest of Chiapas.

The thick-walled Palace, which the explorers chose as their living quarters, had a number of rooms surrounding four courtyards. At the center of the complex was a square, three-stoired building; the main stairway was decorated with bas reliefs, and on the frieze and roof combs fragments of stucco serpents could still be seen.

On the walls they found the names of other travelers who had visited Palenque before them: Waldeck; Noah O. Platt, a New York merchant; Captain John Caddy and Patrick Walker, who had been there only a short time before and, in one of the corridors a verse by William Benham, a young Irishman who had been sent from Tabasco to trade in the jungle.

The Palace complex was the first structure to be explored. Catherwood drew a ground plan, then set up the camera lucida and began to copy the stucco bas reliefs decorating the walls. The artist noted that the art of Palenque was restrained and seemed to date from a later period than that of Copán. It was less intricate, easier to copy, and he happily went on with his work in spite of irritating flies and voracious mosquitoes.

The explorers were not able to sleep much, mainly because of insects, and became weaker and weaker. Stephens was attacked by niguas, tropical fleas, and his foot swelled so much that he had to return to the village for a few days. There he made friends with some priests who were making their annual visit, and took them to see the ruins.

When work on the Palace was finished they hacked a path through the jungle to the building that is now called the Temple of the Inscriptions, but which Stephens named simply Stone House No. 1. The front had five doorways decorated with stucco reliefs and Catherwood drew the figures that time had spared, shading the worn parts. They then went into the dark vault and by the light of a flaming torch examined the interior, discovering two large slabs carved with hieroglyphs. Their *assistant scrubbed the mold off, and they easily recognized the symbols as being just like the ones they had seen at Copán and Quiriguá. Stephens again felt frustrated at not being able to decipher them; he was convinced that they recorded the history of this mysterious people, and had them copied by Catherwood.*

They could never have imagined that they were standing on top of what would be the most spectacular discovery ever made in the world of Maya archeology. More than a century later the Mexican archeologist Alberto Ruz Lhuillier discovered a stone set into the floor of the inner part of the Temple of the Inscriptions that had holes in it by which it could be raised.

After removing the slab he found a narrow flight of stairs filled with rubble. Several seasons of digging eventually revealed that the stairs led down 18 meters (70ft.), at which point a thick wall of cemented rock sealed off a chamber containing six skeletons. Finally, in 1982, he broke into the crypt, where a huge carved stone slab covered most of the floor. This immensely heavy stone, a sarcophagus lid, was carefully raised and under it was found the skeleton of a Maya ruler wearing a mask, necklace and ear ornaments of jade and, near the left foot, a jade statuette of the sun god. This was a remarkable discovery because until then it had always been thought that Maya pyramids had no other function than to support temples, but this one contained the tomb of a ruler.

Without having the slightest idea of what they were leaving behind under their feet, Stephens and Catherwood finished their examination of the temple and went in search of other buildings. Eventually they came to the Temple of the Cross, *which Stephens calls Stone House No. 2. This building had three doorways and a roof crest; the front was covered with stucco decoration. Inside they found the lefthand side of a carving originally made up of three separate tablets. The center was discovered near the river and fragments of the third lay scattered among the ruins. In his usual careful drawing Catherwood restored the center section to its original position. The carving shows a cross with a quetzal perched on the top, standing on a death's head and flanked by two lifesized Indians. The cross, which is actually a stylized tree with its branches at the four points of the compass, was at one time taken as conclusive proof by those who suggested that there had been Christians on the continent of America even before Columbus arrived.*

The next building they came to was a truncated pyramid with a temple standing on top, later named the Temple of the Sun. *The columns at each end of the façade were decorated with glyphs that have been deciphered as 692 A. D. Inside, at the back was a large enclosed altar* with a stone mural set into the rear wall which Stephens called "the most perfect and interesting monument in Palenque." The mural shows two human figures standing at each side of the sun symbol which is backed by two crossed spears. Down each side are rows of hieroglyphs.

The last building to be explored was in very bad condition; the whole of the front part had collapsed, but the inner room contained at least part of an interesting stucco decoration. It originally showed a figure sitting on a couch or throne with a jaguar head at each end, and from this comes the present name of the Temple of the Beau Relief.

After all the wonders they had seen, Stephens came to the conclusion that this people had been "cultivated, polished"; that their art was as important as any in the Old World and that comparisons were unnecessary: it could stand alone.

Other sites lay hidden in the jungle around Palenque that were later discovered thanks to the interest aroused by his books. Stephens and Catherwood had discovered the two extremes of the Maya zone: Copán and Palenque. Between them were many other remains of this mysterious people, and although there were differences from one site to another the inhabitants had undoubtedly spoken the same language and shared similar culture traits and religious beliefs.

Catherwood was sick and they were all exhausted when they left Palenque at the beginning of June, 1840. While Catherwood was recovering in the village Stephens, who had already bought the ruins of Copán and was trying to acquire those of Quiriguá, became interested in the possibility of buying Palenque and had conversations with the prefect about it. However, the transaction was not so simple: according to Mexican law, a foreigner who wished to buy land had to have a Mexican wife. Marriage was not part of Stephens' plans so, after thinking about the complication, he told the prefect that he would buy the land in the name of the American consul at Laguna. Finally in fact deal fell through.

The explorers set off once again, over the plains of Tabasco and Campeche. The first evening they reached the village of Las Playas, where they were allowed to stay in the 'convent', a thatched hut with a mud floor. After two miserably uncomfortable nights they were finally able to leave for the coast by canoe. A few hours later they entered the Río Chico that took them to the great Usumacinta, emptying into the Gulf of Mexico.

Sailing through logwood country they reached the village of Palizada where, after a short stay, they boarded a vessel to take them through the Laguna de Términos to Ciudad del Carmen in Campeche. Here they met Charles Russell, the American consul, who agreed to help Stephens *in buying Palenque: being married to a Mexican he was allowed to buy land.*

It was Stephens' intention to explore the city of Uxmal in Yucatan, but he had to wait to see if Catherwood recovered. The artist's health evidently improved and they boarded the brig Gabrielacho *that would take them to Sisal, the seaport of Merida.*

The morning after landing at Sisal they left for Merida. Stephens writes they reached the village of Hunucama and:

Here we took three fresh horses; and changing them as before, and passing two villages, through a vista two miles long saw the steeples of Merida, and at six o'clock rode into the city. The houses were well built, with balconied windows, and many had two stories. The streets were clean, and many people in them well dressed, animated, and cheerful in appearance; calêches fancifully painted and curtained, having ladies in them handsomely dressed, without hats, and their hair ornamented with flowers, gave it an air of gayety and beauty that, after the sombre towns through which we had passed, was fascinating and almost poetic. No place had yet made so agreeable a first impression; and there was a hotel in a large building kept by Donna Michaele, driving up to which we felt as if by some accident we had fallen upon a European city.

The reader will perhaps be surprised, but I had a friend in Merida who expected me. Before embarking from New-York, I had been in the habit of dining at a Spanish hotel in Fulton-street, frequented principally by Spanish Americans, at which place I had met a gentleman of Merida, and learned that he was the proprietor of the ruins of Uxmal. As yet I knew nothing of the position or character of my friend, but I soon found that everybody in Merida knew Don Simon Peon. In the evening we called at his house. It was a large, aristocratic-looking mansion of dark gray stone, with balconied windows, occupying nearly the half of one side of the plaza. Unfortunately, he was then at Uxmal; but we saw his wife, father, mother, and sisters, the house being a family residence, and the different members of it having separate haciendas. They had heard from him of my intended visit, and received me as an acquaintance. Don Simon was expected back in a few days, but, in the hope of finding him at Uxmal, we determined to go on immediately. Donna Joaquina, his mother, promised to make all necessary arrangements for the journey, and to send a servant with us.

They had arrived on the day before the feast of Corpus Christi.

The city of Merida contains about twenty thousand inhabitants. It is founded on the site of an old Indian village, and dates from a few years after the conquest. In different parts of the city are the remains of Indian buildings. As the capital of the powerful State of Yucatan, it had always enjoyed a high degree of consideration in the Mexican Confederacy, and throughout the republic is famed for its sabios or learned men.

The next day was the fête of Corpus Domini throughout all Spanish America, the greatest in the Catholic Church. Early in the morning, at the tolling of the bell, we went to the Cathedral, which, with the palace of the bishop, occupied one entire side of the plaza. The interior was grand and imposing, having a vaulted roof of stone, and two rows of lofty stone pillars; the choir was in the centre, the altar richly adorned with silver; but the great attraction was in the ladies kneeling before the altars, with white or black veils laid over the top of the head, some of them saintlike purity and beauty, in dress, manners, and appearance realizing the pictures of Spanish romance. Indeed, the Spanish ladies appear nowhere so lovely as in church.

But they were most interested in leaving for the ruined city as soon as possible.

The next morning at half past six we set out for Uxmal on horseback, escorted by a servant of Señor Peon, with Indians before us. At the distance of a league we saw through a vista in the trees a large hacienda belonging to the Peon family, the entrance to which was by a large gate into a cattle-yard. The house was built of stone, and had a front of about one hundred and fifty feet, with an arcade running the whole length. It was raised about twenty feet, and at the foot was a large water-trough extending the whole length, about ten feet wide and of the same depth, filled with water for cattle.

At this place our Indian carriers left us, and we took others from the hacienda, with whom we continued three leagues farther to another hacienda of the family, of much the same character, where we stopped to breakfast. This over, we set out again, and by this time it had become desperately hot.

The road was very rough, over a bed of stone thinly covered, with barely soil enough for the growth of scrubtrees.

Continuing their journey they reached the hacienda of Uayalceh, another property belonging to the Peón family.

We reached another hacienda, a vast, irregular pile of buildings of dark gray stone, that might have been the castle of a German baron in feudal times. Each of these haciendas had an Indian name; this was called the hacienda of Vayalquex, and it was the only one of which Donna Joaquina, in speaking of our route, had made any particular mention. The entrance was by a large stone gateway, with a pyramidal top, into a long lane, on the right of which was a shed, built by Don Simon since his return from the United States as a ropewalk for manufacturing hemp raised on the hacienda; and there was one arrangement which added very much to the effect, and which I did not observe anywhere else: the cattleyard and water-tanks were on one side and out of sight.

We dismounted under the shade of noble trees in front of the house, and ascended by a flight of broad stone steps to a corridor thirty feet wide, with large
mattings, which could be rolled up, or dropped as an awning for protection
against the sun and rain. On one side the corridor was continued around the
building, and on the other it conducted to the door of a church having a large
cross over it, and within ornamented with figures like the churches in towns,
for the tenants of the hacienda. The whole establishment was lordly in its appearance. It had fifteen hundred Indian tenants, bound to the master by a sort
of feudal tenure, and, as the friends of the master, escorted by a household
servant, the whole was ours.

It would have been a great satisfaction to pass several days at this lordly
hacienda; but, not expecting anything to interest us on the road, we had requested
Donna Joaquina to hurry us through, and the servant told us that the señora's
orders were to conduct us to another hacienda of the family, about two leagues
beyond, to sleep. At the moment we were particularly loth to leave, on account
of the fatigue of the previous ride. The servant suggested to the major-domo
llamar un coché; in English, to "call a coach," which the latter proposed to do
if we wished it. We made a few inquiries, and said, unhesitatingly and per-
emptorily, in effect, "Go call a coach, and let a coach be called." The major-
domo ascended by a flight of stone steps outside to the belfry of the church,
whither we followed him; and, turning around with a movement and tone of
voice that reminded us of a Mussulman in a minaret calling the faithful to
prayers, he called for a coach. The roof of the church, and of the whole pile
of buildings connected, was of stone cemented, firm and strong as a pavement.
The sun beat intensely upon it, and for several minutes all was still. At length
we saw a single Indian trotting through the woods toward the hacienda, then
two together, and in a quarter of an hour there were twenty or thirty. These
were the horses; the coaches were yet growing on the trees. Six Indians were
selected for each coach, who, with a few minutes' use of the machete, cut a bundle
of poles, which they brought up to the corridor to manufacture into coaches.
This was done, first, by laying on the ground two poles about as thick as a
man's wrist, ten feet long and three feet apart. These were fastened by cross-
sticks tied with strings of unspun hemp, about two feet from each end; grass-
hammocks were secured between the poles, bows bent over them and covered
with light matting, and the coaches were made. We placed our ponchas at the
head for pillows, crawled inside, and lay down. The Indians took off little cotton
shirts covering the breast, and tied them around their petates as hatbands. Four
of them raised up each coach, and placed the end of the poles on little cushions
on their shoulders. We bade farewell to the major-domo and his wife, and, feet
first, descended the steps and set off on a trot, while an Indian followed leading
the horses. In the great relief we experienced we forgot our former scruples
against making beasts of burden of men. They were not troubled with any

sense of indignity or abasement, and the weight was not much. There were no mountains; only some little inequalities which brought the head lower than the heels, and they seldom stumbled. In this way they carried us about three miles, and then laid us down gently on the ground. Like the Indians in Merida, they were a fine-looking race, with a good expression of countenance, cheerful, and even merry in their toil. They were amused at us because we could not talk with them. There is no diversity of Indian languages in Yucatan; the Maya is universal, and all the Spaniards speak it.

When they arrived at the hacienda of Mukuiché a servant took Stephens to see a cenote. He was so impressed by the beauty of the spot that he sent back for Catherwood, and they were soon enjoying a swim in the crystal clear water. Refreshed, they returned to the hacienda for the night.

At daybreak the next morning, with new Indians and a guide on horseback from the hacienda, we resumed our journey. The surface of the country was the same, limestone with scrub trees. There was not soil enough to absorb the water, which rested in puddles in the hollows of the stones. At nine o'clock we reached another hacienda, smaller than the last, but still having a lordly appearance, where, as before, the women were drawing water by a wheel. The major-domo expressed his sense of the honour conferred upon him by our visit, and his anxiety to serve us, gave us a breakfast of milk, tortillas, and wild honey, and furnished us with other Indians and a guide. We mounted again; very soon the sun became intensely hot; there were no trees to shade us, and we suffered excessively. At half past twelve we passed some mounds of ruins a little off the road, but the sun was so scorching that we could not stop to examine them, and at two o'clock we reached Uxmal.

The hacienda of Uxmal was built of dark gray stone, ruder in appearance and finish than any of the others, with a greater appearance of antiquity, and at a distance looked like an old baronial castle. A year before it had been given to Don Simon by his father, and he was making large repairs and additions to the building, though, as his family never visited it, and he only for a few days at a time, for what purpose I could not conceive. It had its cattle-yard in front, with tanks of water around, some with green vegetation on the top, and there was an unwholesome sensation of dampness. It had, too, its church, which contained a figure of nuestra Señor, "Our Lord", revered by the Indians of all the haciendas around, the fame of which had reached the household servants at Merida, and which was the first object that attracted the attention of our guide. The whole hacienda was immediately at our disposal; but, worn down with heat and fatigue, we took at once to our hammocks.

One of the overseers on this hacienda was a young Spaniard and Stephens was surprised to recognize him as a waiter he had known in Delmonico's of New York. Don Simón Peón had taken him to work on his property at Uxmal, where he felt isolated and lonely, so he was glad of the opportunity to talk with the travelers.

In the afternoon, rested and refreshed, we set out for a walk to the ruins. The path led through a noble piece of woods, in which there were many tracks, and our Indian guide lost his way. Mr. C., being unwell, returned to the hacienda. We took another road, and, emerging suddenly from the woods, to my astonishment came at once upon a large open field strewed with mounds of ruins, and vast buildings on terraces, and pyramidal structures, grand and in good preservation, richly ornamented, without a bush to obstruct the view, and in picturesque effect almost equal to the ruins of Thebes; for these, standing on the flat valley of the Nile, and extending on both sides of the river, nowhere burst in one view upon the sight. Such was the report I made to Mr. Catherwood on my return, who, lying in his hammock unwell and out of spirits, told me I was romancing; but early the next morning we were on the ground, and his comment was that the reality exceeded my description.

The place of which I am now speaking was beyond all doubt once a large, populous, and highly civilized city, and the reader can nowhere find one word of it on any page of history. Who built it, why it was located on that spot, away from water or any of those natural advantages which have determined the sites of cities whose histories are known, what led to its abandonment and destruction, no man can tell. The only name by which it is known is that of the hacienda on which it stands.

They spent the day at the ruins, returning to the hacienda in the evening to make their plans for exploration, but during the night Catherwood had an attack of fever, so they remained on the hacienda next day. Stephens took the opportunity to visit the property and learn of life, work and conditions there.

In the afternoon Mr. Catherwood's fever left him, but in a very low state. The hacienda was unhealthy at this season; the great troughs and tanks of water around the house were green, and, with the regular afternoon rains, induced fatal fevers. Mr. Catherwood's constitution was already severely shattered. Indeed, I became alarmed, and considered it indispensable for him to leave the hacienda, and, if possible, the country altogether. To carry out my other plans, we intended at all events to return. We made a calculation that, by setting out the next morning, we could reach the Spanish brig in time to embark for Havana, and in ten minutes' consultation we determined to break up and go home. Immediately we communicated our purpose to the major-domo, who ascended to the belfry of the church and called a coach, to be ready at two o'clock the next morning.

In the mean time I returned for one more view of the ruins. Mr. Waldeck's work on these ruins had appeared before we left this country. It was brought out in Paris in a large folio edition, with illustrations fancifully and beautifully coloured, and contains the result of a year's residence at Merida and eight days at Uxmal. At the time of his visit the ruins were overgrown with trees, which within the last year had been cleared away, and the whole was laid bare and exposed to view.

When he left the surrounding forest the first building Stephens saw was the towering House of the Dwarf.

Drawn off by mounds of ruins and piles of gigantic buildings, the eye returns and again fastens upon this lofty structure. It was the first building I entered. From its front doorway I counted sixteen elevations, with broken walls and mounds of stones, and vast, magnificent edifices, which at that distance seemed untouched by time and defying ruin. I stood in the dorway when the sun went down, throwing from the buildings a prodigious breadth of shadow, darkening the terraces on which they stood, and presenting a scene strange enough for a work of enchantment.

This building is sixty-eight feet long. The elevation on which it stands is built up solid from the plain, entirely artificial. Its form is not pyramidal, but oblong and rounding, being two hundred and forty feet long at the base, and one hundred and twenty broad, and it is protected all around, to the very top, by a wall of square stones. Perhaps the high ruined structures at Palenque, which we have called pyramidal, and which were so ruined that we could not make them out exactly, were originally of the same shape. On the east side of the structure is a broad range of stone steps between eight and nine inches high, and so steep that great care is necessary in ascending and descending; of these we counted a hundred and one in their places. Nine were wanting at the top, and perhaps twenty were covered with rubbish at the bottom. At the summit or the steps is a stone platform four feet and a half wide, running along the rear of the building. There is no door in the centre, but at each end a door opens into an apartment eighteen feet long and nine wide, and between the two is a third apartment of the same width, and thirty-four feet long. The whole building is of stone; inside, the walls are of polished smoothness; outside, up to the height of the door, the stones are plain and square; above this line there is a rich cornice or moulding, and from this to the top of the building all the sides are covered with rich and elaborate sculptured ornaments, forming a sort of arabesque. The designs were strange and incomprehensible, very elaborate, sometimes grotesque, but often simple, tasteful, and beautiful. Among the intelligible subjects are squares and diamonds, with busts of human beings, heads of leopards, and compositions of leaves and flowers, and the ornaments known everywhere as *grecques*. The ornaments, which succeed each other, are all different; the whole form an extraordinary mass of richness and complexity, and the effect is both grand and curious.

The Indians regard these ruins with superstitious reverence. They will not go near them at night, and they have the old story that immense treasure is hidden among them. Each of the buildings has its name given to it by the Indians. This is called the Casa del Anano, or House of the Dwarf, and it is consecrated by a wild legend, which, as I sat in the doorway, I received from the lips of an Indian, as follows:

There was an old woman who lived in a hut on the very spot now occupied by the structure on which this building is perched, and opposite the Casa del Gobernador (which will be mentioned hereafter), who went mourning that she had no children. In her distress she one day took an egg, covered it with a cloth, and laid it away carefully in one corner of the hut. Every day she went to look at it, until one morning she found the egg hatched, and a criatura, or creature, or baby, born. The old woman was delighted, and called it her son, provided it with a nurse, took good care of it, so that in one year it walked and talked like a man; and then it stopped growing. The old woman was more delighted than ever, and said he would be a great lord or king. One day she told him to go to the house of the gobernador and challenge him to a trial of strength. The dwarf tried to beg off, but the old woman insisted, and he went. The guard admitted him, and he flung his challenge at the gobernador. The latter smiled, and told him to lift a stone of three arrobas, or seventy-five pounds, at which the little fellow cried and returned to his mother, who sent him back to say that if the gobernador lifted it first, he would afterward. The gobernador lifted it, and the dwarf immediately did the same. The gobernador then tried him with other feats of strength, and the dwarf regularly did whatever was done by the gobernador. At length, indignant at being matched by a dwarf, the gobernador told him that, unless he made a house in one night higher than any in the place, he would kill him. The poor dwarf again returned crying to his mother, who bade him not to be disheartened, and the next morning he awoke and found himself in this lofty building. The gobernador, seeing it from the door of his palace, was astonished, and sent for the dwarf, and told him to collect two bundles of cogoiol, a wood of a very hard species, with one of which he, the gobernador, would beat the dwarf over the head, and *afterward* the dwarf should beat him with the other. The dwarf again returned crying to his mother; but the latter told him not to be afraid, and put on the crown of his head a tortillita de trigo, a small thin cake of wheat flour. The trial was made in the presence of all the great men in the city. The gobernador broke the whole of his bundle over the dwarf's head without hurting the little fellow in the least. He then tried to avoid the trial on his own head, but he had given his word in the presence of his officers, and was obliged to submit. The second blow of the dwarf broke his scull in pieces, and all the spectators hailed the victor as their new gobernador. The old woman then died; but at the Indian village of Mani, seventeen leagues distant, there is a deep well, from which opens a cave that leads under ground an immense distance to Merida. In this cave, on the bank of a stream, under the shade of a large tree, sits an old woman with a serpent by her side, who sells water in small quantities, not for money, but only for a criatura or baby to give the serpent to eat; and this old woman is the mother of the dwarf.

Next to this pyramid stood a much lower complex.

It is called Casa de las Monjas, or House of the Nuns, or the Convent. It is situated on an artificial elevation about fifteen feet high. Its forms is quadrangular, and one side, according to my measurement, is ninety-five paces in length. It was not possible to pace all around it, from the masses of fallen stones which encumber it in some places, but it may be safely stated at two hundred and fifty feet square. Like the house of the dwarf, it is built entirely of cut stone, and the whole exterior is filled with the same rich, elaborate, and incomprehensible sculptured ornaments.

The principal entrance is by a large doorway into a beautiful patio or courtyard, grass-grown, but clear of tress, and the whole of the inner façade is ornamented more richly and elaborately than the outside, and in a more perfect state of preservation. On one side the combination was in the form of diamonds, simple, chaste, and tasteful; and at the head of the courtyard two gigantic serpents, with their heads broken and fallen, were winding from opposite directions along the whole façade.

In front, and on a line with the door of the convent, is another building, on a lower foundation, of the same general character, called Casa de Tortugas, from sculptured turtles over the doorway. This building had in several places huge cracks, as if it had been shaken by an earthquake. It stands nearly in the centre of the ruins, and the top commands a view all round of singular but wrecked magnificence.

Beyond this,. a little to the right, approached by passing over mounds of ruins, was another building, which at a great distance attracted our attention by its conspicuous ornaments. We reached it by ascending two high terraces. The main building was similar to the others, and along the top ran a high ornamented wall in this form, from which it was called Casa de Palomos, or House of Pigeons, and at a distance it looked more like a row of pigeon-houses than anything else.

In front was a broad avenue, with a line of ruins on each side, leading beyond the wall of the convent to a great mound of ruins, which probably had once been a building with which it was connected; and beyond this is a lofty building in the rear, to which this seemed but a vestibule or porter's lodge. Between the two was a large patio or courtyard, with corridors on each side and the ground of the courtyard sounded hollow. In one place the surface was broken, and I descended into a large excavation, cemented, which had probably been intended as a granary. At the back of the courtyard, on a high, broken terrace, which it was difficult to climb, was another edifice more ruined than the others, but which, from the style of its remains and its commanding position, overlooking every other building except the house of the dwarf, and apparently having been connected with the distant mass of ruins in front, must have been one of the most important in the city, perhaps the principal temple. The Indians called it quartel or guard-house.

There was one strange circumstance connected with these ruins. No water had ever been discovered; and there was not a single stream, fountain, or well, known to the Indians, nearer than the hacienda, a mile and a half distant. The sources which supplied this element of life had disappeared; the cisterns were broken, or the streams dried up.

While I was making the circuit of these ruins, Mr. Catherwood proceeded to the Casa del Gobernador, which title, according to the naming of the Indians, indicates the principal building of the old city, the residence of the governor, or royal house. It is the grandest in position, the most stately in architecture and proportions, and the most perfect in preservation of all the structures remaining at Uxmal.

The first terrace is six hundred feet long and five feet high. It is walled with cut stone, and on the top is a platform twenty feet broad, from which rises another terrace fifteen feet high. At the corners this terrace is supported by cut stones, having the faces rounded so as to give a better finish than with sharp angles. The great platform above is flat and clear of trees, but abounding in green stumps of the forest but lately cleared away, and now planted, or, rather, from its irregularity, sown with corn, which as yet rose barely a foot from the ground. At the southeast corner of this platform is a row of round pillars eighteen inches in diameter and three or four feet high, extending about one hundred feet along the platform; and these were the nearest approach to pillars or columns that we saw in all our exploration of the ruins of that country. In the middle of the terrace, along an avenue leading to a range of steps, was a broken, round pillar, inclined and falling, with trees growing around it. It was part of our purpose to make an excavation in this platform, from the impression that underneath would be found a vault, forming part of the immense reservoirs for supplying the city with water.

In the centre of the platform, at a distance of two hundred and five feet from the border in front, is a range of stone steps more than a hundred feet broad, and thirty-five in number, ascending to a third terrace, fifteen above the last, and thirty-five feet from the ground, which, being elevated on a naked plain, formed a most commanding position. The erection of these terraces alone was an immense work. On this third terrace, with its principal doorway facing the range of steps, stands the noble structure of the Casa del Gobernador. The façade measures three hundred and twenty feet. Away from the region of dreadful rains, and the rank growth of forest which smothers the ruins of Palenque, it stands with all its walls erect, and almost as perfect as when deserted by its inhabitants. The whole building is of stone, plain up to the moulding that runs along the tops of the doorway, and above filled with the same rich, strange, and elaborate sculpture, among which is particularly conspicuous the ornament before referred to as la grecque. There is no rudeness or barbarity in the design or proportions; on the contrary, the whole wears an air of architectural symmetry and grandeur; and as the stranger ascends the steps and casts a bewildered eye along its open and desolate doors, it is hard to believe that he sees before him the work of a race in whose epitaph, as written by historians, they are called ignorant of art, and said to have perished in the rudeness of savage life.

But there was one thing which seemed in strange want of conformity with all the rest. It was the first object that had arrested my attention in the house of the dwarf, and which I had marked in every other building. I have mentioned that at Ocosingo we saw a wooden beam, and at Palenque the fragment of a wooden pole; at this place *all the lintels had been of wood, and throughout the ruins most of them were still in their places over the doors.* These lintels were heavy beams, eight or nine feet long, eighteen or twenty inches wide, and twelve or fourteen thick. The wood, like that at Ocosingo, was very hard, and rang under the blow of the machete. As our guide told us, it was of a species not found in the neighbourhood, but came from the distant forests near the Lake of Peten. Why wood was used in the construction of buildings otherwise of solid stone seemed unaccountable; but if our guide was correct in regard to the place of its growth, each beam must have been carried on the shoulders of eight Indians, with the necessary relief carriers, a distance of three hundred miles; consequently, it was rare, costly, and curious, and for that reason may have been considered ornamental. The positon of these lintels was most trying, as they were obliged to support a solid mass of stone wall fourteen or sixteen feet high, and three or four in thickness. Once, perhaps, they were strong as stone, but they showed that they were not as durable, and contained within them the seeds of destruction Most, it is true, were in their places, sound, and harder than lignum vitae; but others were perforated by wormholes; some were cracked in the middle, and the walls, settling upon them, were fast overcoming their remaining strength; and others had fallen down altogether. In fact, except in the house of the nuns the greatest destruction was from the decay and breaking of these wooden beams. If the lintels had been of stone, the principal buildings of this desolate city would at this day be almost entire; or, if the edifices had been still occupied under a master's eye, a decaying beam would have been replaced, and the buildings saved from ruin. In the moment of greatness and power, the builders never contemplated that the time would come when their city would be a desolation.

The Casa del Gobernador stands with its front to the east. In the centre, and opposite the range of steps leading up the terrace, are three principal doorways. The middle one is eight feet six inches wide, and eight feet ten inches high; the others are of the same height, but two feet less in width. The centre door opens into an apartment sixty feet long and twenty-seven feet deep, which is divided into two corridors by a wall three and a half feet thick, with a door of communication between of the same size with the door of entrance. The plan is the same as that of the corridor in front of the palace at Palenque, except that here the corridor does not run the whole length of the building, and the back corridor has no door of egress. The floors are of smooth square stone, the walls of square blocks nicely laid and smoothly polished. The ceiling forms a triangular arch without the keystone, as at Palenque ; but, instead of the rough stones overlapping or being covered with stucco, the layers of stone are bevilled as they rise, and present an even and polished surface. Throughout, the laying and polishing of the stones are as perfect as under the rules of the best modern masonry.

When they originally landed at Sisal they thought that their work at Uxmal would take only two or three days, but when they actually saw the ruins they realized from experience that it would take much longer. In addition, they were under the protection of the owner and enjoyed comforts they had not had on other sites.

An important point to note is that Stephens believed that these buildings were "indigenous", built by the original inhabitants of the country. However, his remarks about the antiquity of the ruins were incorrect, as demonstrated by later archeologists.

. . .but I repeat my opinion that we are not warranted in going back to any ancient nation of the Old World for the builders of these cities; that they are not the work of people who have passed away and whose history is lost, but that there are strong reasons to believe them the creations of the same races who inhabited the country at the time of the Spanish conquest, or some not very distant progenitors. And I would remark that we began our exploration without any theory to support. Our feelings were in favour of going back to a high and venerable antiquity. During the greater part of our journey we were groping in the dark, in doubt and uncertainty, and it was not until our arrival at the ruins of Uxmal that we formed our opinion of their comparatively modern date. Some are beyond doubt older than others; some are known to have been inhabited at the time of the Spanish conquest, and others, perhaps, were really in ruins before; and there are points of difference which as yet cannot very readily be explained; but in regard to Uxmal, at least, we believe that it was an existing and inhabited city at the time of the arrival of the Spaniards. Its desolation and ruin since are easily accounted for. Throughout the country the convents are rich in manuscripts and documents written by the early fathers, caciques, and Indians, who very soon acquired the knowledge of Spanish and the art of writing. These have never been examined with the slighest reference to this subject; and I cannot help thinking that some precious memorial is now mouldering in the library of a neighbouring convent, which would determine the history of some one of these ruined cities; moreover, I cannot help believing that the tablets of hieroglyphics will yet be read. No strong curiosity has hitherto been directed to them; vigour and acuteness of intellect, knowledge and learning, have never been expended upon them.

By this time, Catherwood was seriously ill, so they set out for Sisal to sail back to the United States.

At three, by the light of the moon, we left Uxmal by the most direct road for Merida, Mr. Catherwood in a coach and I on horseback, charged with a letter from the junior major-domo to his compatriot and friend, Delmonico's head chocolate-maker. As I followed Mr. C. through the woods, borne on the shoulders of Indians, the stillness broken only by the shuffle of their feet, and under my great apprehensions for his health, it almost seemed as if I were following his bier.

It was half past one when we reached Merida, and we had been up and on the road since two in the morning. Fortunately, with the easy movement of the coach, Mr. C. had suffered but little. I was tired beyond all measure; but I had, what enabled me to endure any degree of fatigue, a good cot, and was soon asleep.

The Spanish vessel was to sail the next day. Toward evening, after a heavy rain, as the dark clouds were rolling away, and the setting sun was tinging them with a rich golden border, we left Merida. At eleven o'clock we reached Hunucama, and stopped in the plaza two hours to feed the horses. An hour before daylight we reached Sisal, at six o'clock we embarked on board the Spanish brig Alexandre for Havana, and at eight we were under way.

It was the twenty-fourth of June; and now, as we thought, all our troubles were ended.

But in fact they were not. When the Alexandre *taking them to Havana had sailed about 150 miles they were becalmed. For two weeks the sea remained like a mirror and the heat was intense. On July 13 the last cask of drinking water was opened, but fortunately a breeze sprang up two days later, then another ship was sighted. This was the* Helen Maria, *bound for New York. The explorers were transferred and landed in New York on July 31, 1840.*

Volume I

CHAPTER I

Embarcation — Arrival at Sisal — Merida

The reader of my "Incidents of Travel in Central America, Chiapas, and Yucatan," may remember that the researches of Mr. Catherwood and myself in the last-mentioned country were abruptly terminated by the illness of the former. During our short sojourn in Yucatan, we received vague, but, at the same time, reliable intelligence of the existence of numerous and extensive cities, desolate and in ruins, which induced us to believe that the country presented a greater field for antiquarian research and discoveries than any we had yet visited. Under these circumstances, it was a severe hardship that we were compelled to leave it, and our only consolation in doing so was the hope of being able to return, prepared to make a thorough exploration of this unknown and mysterious region. In about a year we found ourselves in a condition to do so; and on Monday, the ninth of October, we put to sea on board the bark Tennessee, Scholefield master, for Sisal, the port from which we had sailed on our return to the United States.

We had a valuable addition to our party in Dr. Cabot, of Boston, who accompanied us as an amateur, particularly as an ornithologist.

On the twenty-seventh we furled sails off the port of Sisal. Five vessels were at anchor, an extraordinary circumstance for Sisal, and fortunate for us, because otherwise, as our captain had never been there before, though carefully looking for it, we might not have been able to find it. Our anchorage ground was on the open coast, two or three miles from land, at which distance it was necessary to keep, lest we should be driven ashore in case of a norther. Captain Scholefield, in fact, before he had discharged his cargo, was obliged to slip his cables and put to sea, and did not get back to his anchorage ground in nine days.

It was only four o'clock in the afternoon, but, by the regulations of the port, no passenger could land until the vessel had been visited by the health and custom-house officers. We looked out till dark, and long after the moon rose, but no notice whatever was taken of us, and, with no very amiable feelings toward the lazy officials, we turned in again on board.

Very soon we saw coming off toward us the separate canoas of the health and custom-house officers. The preliminaries, however, were soon settled, and we went ashore. All disposition we might have had to complain the night before ceased on landing. Our former visit was not forgotten. The account of it had been translated and published, and, as soon as the object of our return was known, every facility was given us, and all our trunks, boxes, and multifarious luggage were passed without examination by the custom-house officers.

The little town of Sisal had not increased either in houses or inhabitants, and did not present any additional inducements to remain in it. The same afternoon we sent off our luggage in a carreta for Merida, and the next morning started in calezas ourselves.

We had arrived in the fulness of tropical vegetation; the stunted trees along the road were in their deepest green, and Dr. Cabot opened to us a new source of interest and beauty. In order to begin business at once, he rode in the first caleza alone, and before he had gone far, we saw the barrel of his gun protrude on one side, and a bird fall. He had seen at Sisal, egretes, pelicans, and ducks which were rare in collections at home, and an oscillated wild turkey, which alone he thought worth the voyage to that place; and now, our attention being particularly directed to the subject, in some places the shrubs and bushes seemed brilliant with the plumage and vocal with the notes of birds. On the road he saw four different species which are entirely unknown in the United States, and six others which are found only in Louisiana and Florida, of most of which he procured specimens.

We stopped at Huncuma during the heat of the day; at dark reached Merida, and once more rode up to the house of Doña Micaela.

We had arrived at Merida at an opportune moment. As on the occasion of our first visit, it was again a season of fiesta. The fête of San Cristoval, an observance of nine days, was then drawing to its close, and that evening a grand *function* was to be performed in the church dedicated to that saint. We had no time to lose, and, after a hasty supper, under the guidance of an Indian lad belonging to the house, we set out for the church. Very soon we were in the main street leading to it, along which, as it seemed, the whole population of Merida was moving to the fête. In every house a lantern hung from the balconied windows, or a long candle stood under a glass shade, to light them on their way. At the head of the street was a large plaza, on one side of which stood the church, with its great front brilliantly illuminated, and on the platform and steps, and all the open square before it, was a great moving mass of men, women, and children, mostly Indians, dressed in white.

We waited till the last passed out, and, leaving the empty church blazing with light, with rockets, fireworks, drums, and violins all working away together on the steps, we followed the crowd.

Turning along the left side of the plaza, we entered an illuminated street, at the foot of which, and across it, hung a gigantic cross, also brilliantly illuminated, and apparently stopping the way. Coming as we did directly from the church, it seemed to have some immediate connexion with the ceremonies we had just beheld; but the crowd stopped short of the cross, opposite a large house, also brilliantly illuminated. The door of this house, like that of the church, was open to all who chose to enter, or rather, at that moment, to all who could force their way through.

It was here that they saw the non-religious side of the celebrations: a crowd was gathered to play bingo.

They were grayheads, boys and girls, and little children; fathers and mothers; husbands and wives; masters and servants; men high in office, muleteers and bull-fighters; señoras and señoritas, with jewels around their necks and roses in their hair, and Indian women, worth only the slight covering they had on; beauty and deformity; the best and the vilest in Merida; perhaps, in all, two thousand persons; and this great multitude, many of whom we had seen but a few minutes before on their knees in the church, and among them the fair bevy of girls who had stood by us on the steps, were now assembled in a public gambling-house! a beautiful spectacle for a stranger the first night of his arrival in the capital!

The game which they were engaged in playing is called La Loteria, or the Lottery. It is a favourite amusement throughout all the Mexican provinces, and extends to every village in Yucatan. It is authorized by the government, and, as was formerly the case to a pernicious extent with the lotteries in our own country, is used as an instrument to raise money, either for the use of the government itself, or for other purposes which are considered deserving.

Stephens points out that this was a popular game which, although it involved betting, was important in bringing people together.

The amount played for will give some idea of the character of the game. Before commencing, the boy called out that the stake should in no case exceed two reals. This, however, was considered too high, and it was fixed by general consent at a medio, or six and a quarter cents. The largest amount proclaimed by the boy was twenty-seven dollars and three reals, which, divided among four hundred and thirty-eight players, did not make very heavy gambling. In fact, an old gentleman near whom I was standing told me it was a small affair, and not worth learning; but he added that there was a place in the neighbourhood where they played monté for doubloons. The whole amount circulated during the evening fell far short of what is often exchanged at a small party in a private drawing-room at home, and among those who would not relish the imputation of being accounted gamblers. In fact, it is perhaps but just to say that this great concourse of people was not brought together by the spirit of gambling. The people of Merida are fond of amusements, and in the absence of theatres and other public entertainments, the loteria is a great gathering-place, where persons of all ages and classes go to meet acquaintances. Rich and poor, great and small, meet under the same roof on a footing of perfect equality; good feeling is cultivated among all without any forgetting their place.

At about eleven o'clock we left. On our way down the street we passed the open door of a house in which were tables piled with gold and silver, and men around playing what, in the opinion of my old adviser of the loteria, was a game worth learning. So passed our first night in Merida.

CHAPTER II

A Bullfight — Grand Mass — A grand Procession — The Alameda

That night they decided to rent a house next day, as they expected to stay in Merida for a few days.

Early the next morning the carreta arrived with our luggage, and, to avoid the trouble of loading and unloading, we directed it to remain at the door, and set out immediately to look for a house. We had not much time, and, consequently, but little choice; but, with the help of Doña Micaela, in half an hour we found one that answered our purpose. We returned and started the carreta; an Indian followed, carrying on his head a table, and on the top of it a wash-handbasin; another with three chairs, all Doña Micaela's, and we closed the procession.

In the mean time the fiesta of San Cristoval was going on. Grand mass was over, and the next ceremony in order was a *corrida de toros*, or bull-fight, to commence at ten o'clock.

The Plaza de Toros, or, in English, the bull-ring, was in the square of the church of San Cristoval. The enclosure or place for spectators occupied nearly the whole of the square, a strange and very original structure, which in its principles would astonish a European architect. It was a gigantic circular scaffold, perhaps fifteen hundred feet in circumference, capable of containing four or five thousand persons, erected and held together without the use of a single nail, being made of rude poles, just as they were cut in the woods, and tied together with withes. The interior was enclosed by long poles, crossing and interlacing each other, leaving only an opening for the door, and was divided in like manner by poles into boxes.

The corrida had begun when we arrived on the ground, and the place was already thronged.

A bull was in the ring, two barbed darts trimmed with blue and yellow paper were hanging from his flanks, and his neck was pierced with wounds, from which ran down streams of blood. The picadores stood aloof with bloody spears in their hands; a mounted dragoon was master of ceremonies, and there were, besides, eight or ten vaqueros, or cattletenders, from the neighbouring haciendas, hard riders, and brought up to deal with cattle that run wild in the woods. These were dressed in pink-coloured shirt and trousers, and wore small hats of straw platted thick, with low round crowns, and narrow brims turned up at the side. Their saddles had large leathern flaps, covering half the body of the horse, and each had a lazo, or coil of rope, in his hand, and a pair of enormous iron spurs, perhaps six inches long, and weighing two or three pounds.

The bullfight ended at twelve o'clock, but Stephens and his companions were reminded that there was another one at 4pm, which they also attended.

This was the last corrida of the fiesta, and some of the best bulls had been kept in reserve. The first that was dragged on was received with acclamations, as having distinguished himself before during the fiesta; but he bore an ugly mark for a favourite of the people, having been dragged by the nose till the cartilage was completely torn out by the rope.

The next would have been worthy of the best bull-fights of Old Spain, when the cavalier, at the glance of his lady's eye, leaped into the ring to play the matador with his sword. He was a large black bull, without any particular marks of ferocity about him; but a man who sat in our box, and for whose judgment I had conceived a great respect, lighted a new straw cigar, and pronounced him *"muy bravo"*. There was no bellowing, blustering, or bravado about him, but the showed a calmness and self-possession which indicated a consciousness of strength. The picadores attacked him on horseback, and, like the Noir Faineant, or Sluggish Knight, in the lists at Ashby, for a time he contented himself with merely repelling the attacks of his assailants; but suddenly, as if a little vexed, he laid his head low, looked up at the spears pointed at his neck, and, shutting his eyes, rushed upon a picador on one side, struck his horse in the belly with his horns, lifted him off his feet, and brought horse and rider headlong to the ground. The horse fell upon the rider, rolled completely over him, with his heels in the air, and rose with one of the rider's feet entangled in the stirrup. For an instant he stood like a breathing statue, with nostrils wide and ears thrown back, wild with fright; and then, catching sight of the bull, he sprang clear of the ground, and dashed off at full speed around the ring, dragging after him the luckless picador. Around he went, senseless and helpless, his whole body grimed with dirt, and with no more life in it, apparently, than in a mere log of wood. The picadores extricated their fallen companion, and carried him out. His face was so begrimed with dirt that not a feature was visible; but, as he was borne across the ring, he opened his eyes, and they seemed starting from his head with terror.

He was hardly out of the ring when a hoarse cry ran through the spectators, *"a pie! a pie!"* "on foot! on foot!" The picadores dismounted and attacked the bull fiercely on foot, flourishing their ponchas. Almost at the first thrust he rushed upon one of his adversaries, tumbled him down, passed over his body and walked on without even turning round to look at him. He too was picked up and carried off.

The attack was renewed, and the bull became roused. In a few moments he brought another picador to the ground, and, carried on by his own impetus, passed over the body, but, with a violent effort, recovered himself, and turned short round upon his prostrate prey, glared over him for a moment with a low bellow, almost a howl, and, raising his fore feet a little from the ground, so as to give full force to the blow, thrust both horns into the stomach of the fallen picador. Happily, the points were sawed off; and, furious at not being able to gore and toss him, he got one horn under the picador's sash, lifted him, and dashed him back violently upon the ground.

This man, too, was carried off. The sympathy of the spectators had for a while kept them hushed; but, as soon as the man was out of sight, all their pent-up feelings broke out in indignation against the bull, and there was a universal cry, in which the soft tones of women mingled with the hoarse voices of the men, "*Matálo! matálo!*" "Kill him! kill him!" The picadores stood aghast. Three of their companions had been struck down and carried off the field; the bull, pierced in several places, with blood streaming from him, but fresh as when he began, and fiercer, was roaming round the ring, and they held back, evidently afraid to attack him. The spectators showered upon them the opprobrious name of "*cobardes! cobardes!*" "cowards! cowards!" The dragoon enforced obedience to their voice, and, fortifying themselves with a strong draught of agua ardiente, they once more faced the bull, poised their spears before him, but with faint hands and trembling hearts, and finally, without a single thrust, amid the contemptuous shouts of the crowd, fell back, and left the bull master of the field.

Others were let in, and it was almost dark when the last fight ended.

In the evening we took another hot-bath at the loteria, and the next day was Sunday, the last day of the fiesta, which opened in the morning with grand mass in the church of San Cristobal.

At four o'clock in the afternoon we set out for the procession and paseo. The intense heat of the day was over, there was shade in the streets, and a fresh evening breeze. The streets through which the procession was to pass were adorned with branches, and at the corners were large collections of them, forming groves of green. The balconies of the windows were hung with silk curtains and banners, and in the doorways and along the walks sat rows of ladies simply but beautifully dressed, without hats, their hair adorned with flowers, and their necks with jewels. Near the church of San Cristoval we were arrested by the crowd, and waited till the procession came up.

The procession was led by three priests, followed by musicians, a platform with religious images on it, and a crowd of men and women carrying lighted candles.

When the crowd had passed by we strolled to the Alameda. This is the great place of promenade and paseo in Merida. It consists of a broad paved avenue, with a line of stone seats on each side, and beyond, on both sides, are carriage roads, shaded by rows of trees.

This promenade took place every Sunday, but because of the fiesta it was even more lively and colorful than usual.

The most striking feature, the life and beauty of the paseo, were the calesas. Except one or two gigs, and a black, square box-wagon, which occasionally shame the paseo, the calesa is the only wheeled carriage in Merida. The body is somewhat like that of an oldfashioned gig, only much larger, and resting on the shaft a little in front of the wheels. It is painted red, with light and fancifully coloured curtains for the sun, drawn by one horse, with a boy riding him—simple, fanciful, and peculiar to Yucatan. Each calesa had two, and sometimes three ladies, in the latter case the prettiest sitting in the middle and a little in front, all without hats or veils, but their hair beautifully arranged and trimmed with flowers. We sat down on one of the stone benches in the Alameda, with the young, and gay, and beautiful of Merida. Strangers had not been there to laugh at and break up their good old customs. It was a little nook almost unknown to the rest of the world, and independent of it, enjoying what is so rarely found in this equalizing age, a sort of primitive or Knickerbocker state. The great charm was the air of contentment that reigned over the whole. If the young ladies in the calesas had occupied the most brilliant equipages in Hyde Park, they could not have seemed happier; and in their way, not less attractive were the great crowds of Mestizas and Indian women, some of the former being extremely pretty, and all having the same mild and gentle expression; they wore a picturesque costume of white, with a red border around the neck and skirt, and of that extraordinary cleanness which I had remarked as the characteristic of the poorest in Merida. For an hour, one continued stream of calesas, with ladies, and Mestizas, and Indian women, passed us without any noise, or confusion, or tumult, but in all there was such an air of quiet enjoyment that we felt sad as night came on.

The crowning ceremonies of the fiesta were a display of fireworks in the square of the church, followed by a concert and a ball. The former was for the people, the latter for a select few.

One fiesta was hardly ended when another began. On Monday was the great fête of Todos Santos. Grand mass was said in all the churches, and in every family prayers were offered up for the souls of the dead; and, besides the usual ceremonies of the Catholic Church throughout the world, there is one peculiar to Yucatan, derived from the customs of the Indians, and called Mukbipoyo. On this day every Indian, according to his means, purchases and burns a certain number of consecrated candles, in honour of his deceased relatives, and in memory of each member of his family who has died within the year.

Besides this, they bake in the earth a pie consisting of a paste of Indian corn, stuffed with pork and fowls, and seasoned with chili, and during the day every good Yucateco eats nothing but this. In the interior, where the Indians are less civilized, they religiously place a portion of this composition out of doors, under a tree, or in some retired place, for their deceased friends to eat, and they say that the portion thus set apart is always eaten, which induces the belief that the dead may be enticed back by appealing to the same appetites which govern when living.

The fêtes were now ended, and we were not sorry, for now, for the first time, we had a prospect of having our clothes washed. Ever since our arrival, our linen, &c., accumulated during the voyage, had stood in gaping bundles, imploring us to do something for them, but during the continuance of the fiestas not a lavandera in Merida could be found to take in washing.

CHAPTER III

Brief Account of Yucatan — Expedition of Cordova — Discoveries,
Conquests and Sufferings of Montejo and his Companions.

It may be remembered that Columbus, in his first three voyages, did
not reach the Continent of America. On his fourth, final, and ill-fated expedition, "after sixty days of tempestuous weather, without seeing sun or stars", he
discovered a small island, called by the Indians Guanaja, supposed to be that
now laid down on some maps as the island of Bonaca. While on shore at this
island, we saw coming from the west a canoe of large size, filled with Indians,
who appeared to be a more civilized people than any the Spaniards had yet
encountered. In return to the inquiries of the Spaniards for gold, they pointed
toward the west, and endeavoured to persuade them to steer in that direction.

Four years afterward, in the year 1506, Juan Dias de Solis, in company
with Vincent Yañez Pinzon, on of the companions of Columbus on his last
voyage, held the same course to the island of Guanaja, and then, steering to
the west, discovered the east coast of the province now known by the name of
Yucatan, and sailed along it some distance, without, however, prosecuting
the discovery.

On the eighth of February, 1517, Francisco Hernandez de Cordova, a rich
hidalgo of Cuba, with three vessels of good burden and one hundred and ten
soldiers, set sail from the port now known as St. Jago de Cuba, on a voyage
of discovery. Doubling St. Anton, now called Cape St. Antonio, and sailing
at hazard toward the west, at the end of twenty-one days they saw land which
had never been seen before by Europeans.

On the fourth of March, while making arrangements to land, they saw
coming to the ships five large canoes, with oars and sails, some of them containing fifty Indians; and on signals of invitation being made, above thirty came
on board the captain's vessel. The next day the chief returned with twelve large
canoes and numerous Indians, and invited the Spaniards to his town, promising
them food, and whatever was necessary. The words he used were *Conèx cotoch*,
which, in the language of the Indians of the present day, means, "Come to our
town." Not understanding the meaning, and supposing it was the name of the
place, the Spaniards called it Point or Cape Cotoche, which name it still bears.

The Spaniards accepted the invitation, but, seeing the shore lined with
Indians, landed in their own boats, and carried with them fifteen crossbows
and ten muskets.

After halting a little while, they set out, the chief leading the way; and, passing by a thick wood, at a signal from the chief a great body of Indians in ambush rushed out, poured upon them a shower of arrows, which at the first discharge wounded fifteen, and then fell upon them with their lances; but the swords, crossbows, and firearms of the Spaniards struck them with such terror that they fled precipitately leaving seventeen of their number slain.

The Spaniards returned to their ships, and continued toward the west, always keeping in sight of land. In fifteen days they discovered a large town, with an inlet which seemed to be a river. They went ashore for water, and were about returning, when some fifty Indians came toward them, dressed in good mantas of cotton, and invited them to their town.

Hostile preparations of a formidable character were soon apparent, and the Spaniards, fearing to encounter such a multitude, retired to the shore, and embarked with their water-casks. This place was called Kimpech, and at this day it is known by the name of Campeachy.

Continuing westwardly, they came opposite a town about a league from the coast, which was called Potonchan or Champoton. Being again in distress for water, they went ashore all together, and well armed. The Spaniards were unable to embark their water-casks, and, as it was now nearly night, they determined to remain on shore. At daylight great bodies of warriors, with colours flying, advanced upon them from all sides. The fight lasted more than half an hour; fifty Spaniards were killed; and Cordova, seeing that it was impossible to drive back such a multitude, formed the rest into a compact body and cut his way to the boats. Fifty-seven of their companions were killed, and five more died of their wounds. There was but one soldier who escaped unwounded; all the rest had two, three, or four, and the captain, Hernandez de Cordova, had twelve arrow wounds. In the old Spanish charts this place is called the Bay "de Mala Pelea", or "of the bad fight."

This great disaster determined them to return to Cuba. So many sailors were wounded that they could not man the three vessels, in consequence of which they burned the smaller one, and, dividing the crew between the other two, set sail.

It was not until they reached the coast of Florida that they managed to take on water.

After this the vessel of the captain sprung a leak, but by great exertions at the pumps they kept her from sinking, and brought her into Puerto Carenas, which is now the port of Havana. Three more soldiers died of their wounds; the rest dispersed, and the captain, Hernandez de Cordova, died ten days after his arrival. Such was the disastrous end of the first expedition to Yucatan.

In the same year, 1517, another expedition was set on foot. Four vessels were fitted out, two hundred and forty companions enrolled themselves, and

Juan de Grijalva, "a hopeful young man and well-behaved", was named captain-in-chief.

On the sixth of April, 1518, the armament sailed from the port of Matanzas for Yucatan. Doubling Cape San Antonio, and forced by the currents farther down than its predecessor, they discovered the Island of Cozumel.

Crossing over, and sailing along the coast, they came in sight of Potonchan, and entered the Bay of Mala Pelea, memorable for the disastrous repulse of the Spaniards. The Indians, exulting in their former victory, charged upon them before they landed, and fought them in the water; but the Spaniards made such slaughter that the Indians fled and abandoned the town.

Embarking again, and continuing toward the west, in three days they saw the mouth of a very broad river, which, as Yucatan was then supposed to be an island, they thought to be its boundary, and called the Boca de Terminos. At Tobasco they first heard the famous name of Mexico; and after sailing on to Culua, now known as San Juan de Ulloa, the fortress of Vera Cruz, and some distance beyond along the coast, Grijalva returned to Cuba to add new fuel to the fire of adventure and discovery.

Another expedition was got up on a grand scale. Ten ships were fitted out, and it is creditable to the fame of Juana de Grijalva that all his old companions wished him for their chief; but, by a concurrance of circumstances, this office was conferred upon Hernando Cortez, then alcalde of Santiago de Cuba, a man comparatively unknown, but destined to be distinguished among the daring soldiers of that day as the Great Captain, and to build up a name almost over-shadowing that of the discoverer of America.

Among the principal captains in the expeditions both of Grijalva and Cortez was Don Francisco Montejo, a gentleman of Seville. After the arrival of Cortez in Mexico, and while he was prosecuting his conquests in the interior, twice it was considered necessary to send commissioners to Spain, and on both occasions Don Francisco Montejo was nominated, the first time with one other, and the last time alone. On his second visit, besides receiving a confirmation of former grants and privileges, and a new coat of arms, as an acknowledgment of his distinguished services rendered to the crown in the expeditions of Grijalva and Cortez, he obtained from the king a grant for the pacification and conquest of the islands (as it is expressed) of Yucatan and Cozumel, which countries, amid the stirring scenes and golden prospects of the conquest of Mexico, had been entirely overlooked.

This grant, dated December 8, 1526, also stipulated that he should be Adelantado (governor of the province and captain-general) for life, and that this position would be hereditary.

In the year 1527 (the month is not known) the armament sailed from Seville, touching at the islands for supplies.

The fleet stopped at the island of Cozumel, where the adelantado had great difficulty in communicating with the Indians from want of an interpreter. Taking on board one of them as a guide, the fleet crossed over to the continent, and came to anchor off the coast. All the Spaniards went on shore, and, as the first act, with the solemnities usual in the new conquests, took formal possession of the country in the name of the king.

As yet the adelantado had only touched along the coast, and knew nothing of the interior. Experiencing great difficulty from the want of an interpreter, he commenced his march along the coast under the guidance of Indian from Cozumel. The country was well peopled, and without committing any violence upon the inhabitants, or suffering any injury from them, the Spaniards proceeded from town to town until they arrived at Conil. At this place, the Indians being apparently friendly, the Spaniards were thrown off their guard; and on one occasion, an Indian, who came to pay a visit, snatched a hanger from a little negro slave, and attempted to kill the adelantado. The latter drew his sword to defend himself, but the soldiers rushed foward and killed the Indian on the spot.

The adelantado now determined to march from Conil to the province of Choaca, and from this time they began to experience the dreadful hardships they were doomed to suffer in subduing Yucatan. There were no roads; the country was stony, and overgrown with thick woods. Fatigued with the difficulties of their march, the heat, and want of water, they arrived at Choaca, and found it deserted: the inhabitants had gone to join other Indians who were gathering for war.

Setting out again, still under the guidance of the Cozumel Indian, they reached a town named Aké. Here they found themselves confronted by a great multitude of Indians, who had lain in ambush, concealed in the woods.

The adelantado encouraged the Spaniards by relating his experience of war with the Indians, and a fearful battle commenced, which lasted all that day. Night came to put an end to the slaughter, but the Indians remained on the ground. The Spaniards had time to rest and bind up their wounds, but kept watch all night, with the dismal prospect of being destroyed on the next day.

At daylight the battle began again, and continued fiercely till midday, when the Indians began to give way. The Spaniards, encouraged by hope of victory, pressed them till they turned and fled, hiding themselves in the woods; but, ignorant of the ground, and worn out with constant fighting, the victors could only make themselves masters of the field.

In the beginning of the year 1528, the adelantado determined again, by slow marches, to reconnoiter the country; and, having discovered the warlike character of the inhabitants, to avoid as much as possible all conflict with them. With this resolution, they set out from Aké in the direction of Chichen Itza, where, by kindness and conciliation, they got together some Indians, and built houses of wood and poles covered with palm leaves.

Disheartened by not seeing any signs of gold, and learning from the Indians that the glittering metal was to be found in the province of Ba Khalal, the adelantado determined to send the Captain Davila to found in the province a town of Spaniards. Davila set out with fifty foot-soldiers and sixteen horsemen, and from the time of this separation difficulties and dangers accumulated upon both. All efforts to communicate with each other proved abortive. After many battles, perils, and sufferings, those in Chichen Itza saw themselves reduced to the wretched alternative of dying by hunger or by the hands of the Indians. An immense multitude of the latter having assembled for their destruction, the Spaniards left their fortifications, and went out on the plain to meet them. The most severe battle ever known in wars with the Indians took place. Great slaughter was made among them, but a hundred and fifty Spaniards were killed; nearly all the rest were wounded, and, worn down with fatigue, the survivors retreated to the fortifications. The Indians did not follow them, or, worn out as they were, they would have perished miserably to a man. At night the Spaniards escaped. From the meager and unsatisfactory notices of these events that have come down to us, it is not known with accuracy by what route they reached the coast; but the next that we hear of them is at Campeachy.

The fortunes of Davila were no better. Arrived at the province of Ba Khalal, he sent a message to the Lord of Chemecal to inquire about gold, and requesting a supply of provisions; the fierce answer of the cacique was, that he would send fowls on spears, and Indian corn on arrows. With forty men and five horses left, Dávila struggled back to the coast, and, two years after their unfortunate separation, he joined the adelantado in Campeachy.

Roused by the arrival of Davila, the adelantado determined to make another attempt to penetrate the country. For this purpose he again sent off Davila with fifty men, himself remaining in Campeachy with but forty soldiers and ten horsemen. As soon as the Indians discovered his small force, an immense multitude gathered round the camp. Hearing a tumult, the adelantado went out on horseback, and, riding toward a group assembled on a little hill, cried out, endeavouring to pacify them; but the Indians, turning in the direction of the voice, and recognising the adelantado, surrounded him, laid hands upon the reins of his horse, and tried to wrest from him his lance. The adelantado spurred his horse, and extricated himself for a moment, but so many Indians came up that they held his horse fast by the feet, took away his lance, and endeavoured to carry him off alive, intending, as they afterward said, to sacrifice him to their gods. Blas Gonzales was the only soldier near him, who, seeing his danger, threw himself on horseback, cleared a way through the Indians with his lance, and, with others who came up at the moment, rescued the adelantado. Both himself and the brave Gonzales were severely wounded, and the horse of the latter died of his wounds.

About this time the fame of the discovery of Peru reached these unlucky conquerors, and, taking advantage of the opportunity afforded by their proximity to the coast, many of the soldiers deserted. To follow up the conquest of Yucatan, it was indispensable to recruit his forces, and for this purpose the adelantado determined on going to New Spain.

He had previously sent information to the king of his misfortunes, and the king had despatched a royal parchment to the audiencia of Mexico, setting forth the services of the adelantado, the labours and losses he had sustained, and charging them to give him assistance in all that related to the conquest of Yucatan. With this favour and his rents in New Spain, he got together some soldiers, and bought vessels, arms, and other munitions of war, to prosecute his conquest. Unluckily, as Tobasco belonged to his government, and the Indians of that province, who had been subdued by Cortez, had revolted, he considered it advisible first to reduce them.

But the adelantado found it much more difficult than the expected to reduce the Indians of Tobasco; and while he was engaged in it, the Spaniards in Campeachy, instead of being able to penetrate into the country, were undergoing great sufferings. The Indians cut off their supplies of provisions, and, being short of sustenance, nearly all became ill. Finding it impossible to hold out any longer, they determined to abandon the place. Gonzales Nieto, who first planted the royal standard on the shores of Yucatan, was the last to leave it, and in the year 1535 not a single Spaniard remained in the country.

We return now to the adelantado, whom we left at Tobasco. Severe wars with the Indians, want of arms and provisions, and, above all, desertions instigated by the fame of Peruvian riches, had left him at a low ebb. In this situation he was joined by Captain Gonzalo Nieto and the small band which had been compelled to evacuate Yucatan, and by the presence of these old companions his spirits were again roused.

But the pacification of Tobasco was much more difficult than was supposed. By communication with the Spaniards, the Indians had lost their fears of them. The country was bad for carrying on war, particularly with cavalry, on account of the marshes and pools; their provisions were again cut off; many of the soldiers went away disgusted, and others, from the great humidity and heat, sickened and died.

While they were in this extremity, the Captain Diego de Contreras, with no fixed destination, and ready to embark in any of the great enterprises which at that time attracted the adventurous soldier, arrived at the port. He had with him a vessel of his own, with provisions and other necessaries, his son, and twenty Spaniards. The adelantado represented to him the great service he might render the king, and by promises of reward induced him to remain. With this assistance he was enabled to sustain himself in Tobasco until, having received additional reenforcements, he effected the pacification of the whole of that country.

The adelantado now made preparations to return to Yucatan. Champoton was selected as the place of disembarcation. According to some of the historians, he did not himself embark on this expedition, but sent his son. It seems more certain, however, that he went in person as commander-in-chief of the armada, and leaving his son, Don Francisco de Montejo, in command of the soldiers, returned to Tobasco, as being nearer to Mexico, from which country he expected to receive and send on more recruits and necessaries. The Spaniards landed some time in the year 1537, and again planted the royal standard in Yucatan. The Indians allowed them to land without noise or opposition, but they were only lying in wait for an opportunity to destroy them. In a few days a great multitude assembled, and at midnight they crept silently up the paths and roads which led to the camp of the Spaniards, seized one of the sentinels, and killed him; but the noise awoke the Spaniards, who, wondering less at the attack than at its being made by night, rushed to their arms. Ignorant as they were of the ground, in the darkness all was confusion. On the east, west, and south they heard the clamour and outcries of the Indians. Nevertheless, they made great efforts, and the Indians, finding their men falling, and hearing the groans of the wounded and dying, relaxed in the fury of their attack, and at length retreated. The Spaniards did not pursue them, but remained in the camp, keeping watch till daylight, when they collected and buried the bodies of their own dead.

For some days the Indians did not make any hostile demonstrations, but they kept away or concealed as much as possible all supplies of provisions. The Spaniards were much straitened, and obliged to sustain themselves by catching fish along the shores. On one occasion two Spaniards, who had straggled to some distance from the camp, fell into the hands of the Indians, who carried them away alive, sacrificed them to their idols, and feasted upon their bodies.

During this time the Indians were forming a great league of all the caciques in the country, and gathered in immense numbers at Champoton. As soon as all the confederates were assembled, they attacked with a horrible noise the camp of the Spaniards, who could not successfully contend against such a multitude. Many Indians fell, but they counted as well lost a thousand of their own number for the life of one Spaniard. There was no hope but in flight, and the Spaniards retreated to the shore. The Indians pursued them, heaping insults upon them, entered their camp, loaded themselves with the clothing and other things, which in the hurry of retreat they had been obliged to leave behind, put on their dresses, and from the shore mocked and scoffed at them, pointing with their fingers, taunting them with cowardice, and crying out, "Where is the courage of the Spaniards?" The latter, hearing from their boats these insults, resolved that death and fame were better than life and ignominy, and, wounded and worn out as they were, took up their arms and returned to the shore.

Another fierce battle ensued; and the Indians, dismayed by the resolution with which these vanquished men again made front against them, retired slowly, leaving the Spaniards masters of the field. The Spaniards cared for no more, content to recover the ground they had lost.

The Indians, seeing that they could not be driven out of the country, and did not intend to leave it, contracted a sort of friendship them, but they were not able to make any advances into the interior. On every attempt they were so badly received that they were compelled to return to their camp in Champoton, which was, in fact, their only refuge.

So many abandoned the expedition that at one time there were only nineteen Spaniards in Champoton.

Again they were relieved, and again their force dwindled away. The fame of the riches of Peru was in every mouth. The poverty of Yucatan was notorious. There were no mines; there was but little encouragement for others to join the expedition, and those in Champoton were discouraged. Struggling with continual hardships and dangers, they made no advance toward the conquest of the country; all who could, endeavoured to get away, some going in canoes, others by land, as occasion offered. In order to confer upon some means of bettering the condition of things, it was necessary for the son of the adelantado to visit his father at Tobasco, and he set out, leaving the soldiers at Champoton under the command of his cousin, a third Don Francisco.

During his absence matters became worse. The people continued going away, and Don Francisco knew that if they lost Champoton, which had cost them so much, all was lost. Consulting with a few who were most desirous of persevering in the enterprise, he brought together those who were suspected of meditating desertion, and told them to go at once, and leave the rest to their fate. The poor soldiers, embarrassed, and ashamed at being confronted with companions whom they intended to desert, determined to remain.

But the succour so earnestly hoped for was delayed. All the expedition which the son of the adelantado could make was not sufficient for those who remained in Champoton. They had been nearly three years without making any advances or any impression upon the country. Despairing of its conquest, and unable to exist in the straits in which they found themselves, they talked openly of disbanding, and going where fortune might lead them. The captain did all that he could to encourage them, but in vain. All had their luggage and ship-stores ready to embark, and nothing was talked of but leaving the country. Juan de Contreras was sent with the despatches, who gave the adelantado, besides, a full account of the desperate condition in which they remained at Champoton.

His intelligence gave the adelantado much anxiety. All his resources were exhausted; he had been unable to procure the succour necessary, and he knew that if the Spaniards abandoned Champoton, it would be impossible to prosecute the conquest of Yucatan.

It does not appear whether the adelantado went to Champoton in person, but vessels arrived carrying soldiers, provisions, clothing, and arms, and toward the end of the year 1539 his son returned, with twenty horsemen, from New Spain. The drooping spirits of the Spaniards were revived, and again they conceived hopes of achieving the conquest of the country.

About this time, too, the adelantado, grieving over the common misfortune of himself and those who had been constant and enduring, but doubting his own fortune, and confiding in the valour of his son Don Francisco, determined to put into the hands of the latter the pacification of Yucatan. He was at that time settled in the government of Chiapas, to which place he summoned his son, and by a formal act substituted him in all the powers given to himself by the king. The act of substitution is creditable alike to the head and heart of the adelantado. It begins with an injunction "that he should strive that the people under his charge should live and be as true Christians, separating themselves from vices and public sins, not permitting them to speak ill of God, nor his blessed mother, nor the saints;" and it concludes with the words, "because I know that you are a person who will know how to do it well, putting first God our Lord, and the service of his majesty, and the good of the country, and the execution of justice."

Within a month from the time when he was called away by his father, Don Francisco returned to Champoton with all the provisions necessary for prosecuting, on his own account, the conquest of Yucatan. From this time the door of better fortune seemed opened to the Spaniards.

Don Francisco determined forthwith to undertake the march to Campeachy. At short distance from Champoton they encountered a large body of Indians, routed them, and, determined not to make any retrograde movement, encamped upon the spot.

Here, again, the history fails, and it does not appear how they were received in Campeachy; but it is manifest from other authorities that in the year 1540 they founded a city under the name of San Francisco de Campeche.

Remaining in this place till things were settled, Don Francisco, in pursuance of his father's instructions, determined on descending to the province of Quepech, and founding a city in the Indian town of Tihoo. Knowing that delay was dangerous, he sent forward the Captain Francisco de Montejo, his cousin, with fifty-seven men. He himself remained in Campeachy to receive and organize the soldiers, who, stimulated by the tidings of his improving fortunes, were every day coming in from his father.

Don Francisco set out for Tihoo, and in all the accounts there is a uniform correspondence in regard to the many dangers they encountered on that journey.

Arriving at a town called Pokboc, they pitched and fortified their camp, with the intention of making a halt, but at night they were roused by finding the camp on fire. The whole camp, and almost everything that they had, were burned up. But they were not dismayed. The captain gave notice of this misfortune to his cousin in Campeachy, and resumed his march. In the year 1540 he arrived at Tihoo.

In a few days he was joined by forty other Spaniards, who were sent on by Don Francisco Montejo, and at this time some Indians came to them and said, "What are you doing here, Spaniards? more Indians are coming against you, more than there are hairs on the skin of a deer." The Spaniards answered that they would go out to seek them; and, leaving the guard in the camp, the Captain Don Francisco Montejo immediately set out, came upon them at a place five leagues distant, and attacked them with such vigour, that, though they at first defended themselves bravely, the Spaniards gained upon them, and killing many, the rest became disheartened and took to flight.

In the mean time the son of the adelantado arrived from Campeachy; and being now all united, and the Indians at first withholding all supplies, they very soon began to suffer from want of provisions. While in this condition, unexpectedly a great cacique from the interior came to them voluntarily (the circumstances will appear hereafter) and made submission. Some neighbouring caciques of Tihoo, either moved by this example, or finding that, after so many years of war, they could not prevail against the Spaniards, also submitted. Encouraged by the friendship of these caciques, and believing that they might count upon their succour until they had finished the subjection of the country, the Spaniards determined to found a city on the site occupied by Tihoo; but in the mean time a terrific storm was gathering over their heads. All the Indians from the east of Tihoo were drawing together; and in the month of June, toward the evening of the feast of Barnaby the apostle, an immense body, varying, according to manuscript accounts, from forty to seventy thousand, came down upon the small band of a little more than two hundred then in Tihoo. The following day they attacked the Spanish camp on all sides. The most terrible battle the Spaniards had ever encountered ensued. The battle lasted the greater part of the day. Many Indians were killed, but immediately others took their places, for they were so many that they were like the leaves on the trees. The arquebuses and crossbows made great havoc, and the horsemen carried destruction wherever they moved, cutting down the fugitives, trampling under foot the wounded and dying. Piles of dead bodies stopped the Spaniards in their pursuit. The Indians were completely routed, and for a great distance the ground was covered with their dead.

The fame of the Spaniards rose higher than before, and the Indians never rallied again for a general battle. All this year the invaders were occupied in drawing to them and conciliating the neighbouring caciques, and on the sixth of January, 1542, they founded, with all legal formalities, on the site of the Indian town of Tihoo, the "very loyal and noble" city of Merida.

CHAPTER IV

Political State of Yucatan — Presentation to the Governor — General
Aspect of Merida

*Stephens continues his description of Yucatan with notes on the political
situation in later times.*

From the time of the conquest, Yucatan existed as a distinct captain-
generalcy, not connected with Guatimala, nor subject to the viceroy of Mexico.
So it continued down to the Mexican revolution. The independence of Yucatan
followed that of Mexico without any struggle, and actually by default of the
mother-country in not attempting to keep it in subjection.

Separated from Spain, in an evil hour Yucatan sent commissioners to Mexico to deliberate upon forming a government; and on the return of these commissioners, and on their report, she gave up her independent position, and
entered into the Mexican confederation as one of the states of that republic.
Ever since she had been suffering from this unhappy connexion, and a short
time before our former visit, a revolution broke out all over the country; in
the successful progress of which, during that visit, the last Mexican garrison was
driven out of Yucatan. The state assumed the rights of sovereignty, asserting
its independent powers, at the same time not disconnecting itself entirely from
Mexico, but declaring itself still a component part of that republic upon certain
conditions. The declaration of its independence was still a moot question. The
assembly had passed a bill to that effect, but the senate had not yet acted upon
it, and its fate in that body was considered doubtful. In the mean time, a com-
missioner had been sent to Texas, and two days after our arrival at Merida
the Texan schooner of war San Antonio arrived at Sisal, bringing a proposition
for Yucatan to pay $8000 per month toward the support of the Texan navy,
and for the Texan vessels to remain upon the coast of Yucatan and protect it
against invasion by Mexico. This proposition was accepted immediately, and
negotiations were pending for farther co-operation in procuring a recognition
of their mutual independence. Thus, while shrinking from an open declaration of
independence, Yucatan was widening the breach, and committing an offence
which Mexico could never forgive, by an alliance with a people whom that
government, or rather Santa Ana, regarded as the worst of rebels, and whom
he was bent upon exerting the whole power of the country in an effort to

reconquer. Such was the disjointed and false position in which Yucatan stood at the time of our presentation to the governor.

One of the first things Stephens and his companions had done when they reached Merida was to visit their old friend Don Simón Peón and his mother, Doña Joaquina. Just as on his previous journey, they offered to do all they could to help, and it was Don Simón himself who introduced them to the governor.

After describing his visit to the governor in his private residence and mentioning other foreigners in Merida at the time, Stephens turns to the city itself.

The population of Merida is probably about twenty-three thousand. The city stands on a great plain, on a surface of limestone rock, and the temperature and climate are very uniform. During the thirteen days that we were in Merida the thermometer varied but nine degrees; and, according to a table of observations kept for many years by the much-esteemed Cura Villamil, it appears that during the year beginning on the first of September, 1841, which included the whole time that we were in the country, the greatest variation was but twenty-three degrees Fahrenheit.

The general aspect of the city is Moorish, as it was built at a time when the Moorish style prevailed in Spanish architecture. The houses are large, generally of stone, and one story in height, with balconies to the windows and large courtyards. In the centre of the city stands the plaza major, a square of about six hundred feet. The whole of the east side is occupied by the cathedral and the bishop's palace. On the west stand the house of the municipality and that of the Doña Joaquina Peon. On the north is the place of the government, and on the south a building which on our first visit arrested our attention the moment we entered the plaza. It is distinguished by a rich sculptured facade of curious design and workmanship. In it is a stone with this inscription:

Esta obra mando hacerla el
Adelantado D. Francisco de Montejo
Año de MDXLIX.

The Adelantado Don Francisco Montejo caused this to be made
in the year 1549.

The subject represents two knights in armour, with visors, breastplates, and helmets, standing upon the shoulders of crushed naked figures, probably intended to represent the conquering Spaniard trampling upon the Indian. Mr. Catherwood attempted to make a drawing of it, and, to avoid the heat of the sun, went into the plaza at daylight for that purpose; but he was so annoyed by the crowd that he was obliged to give it up. There is reason to believe that it is a combination of Spanish and Indian art.

The streets are distinguished in a manner peculiar to Yucatan. In the angle of the corner house, and on the top, stands a painted wooden figure of an elephant, a bull, a flamingo, or some other visible object, and the street is called by the name of this object. On one corner there is the figure of an old woman with large spectacles on her nose, and the street is called la Calle de la Vieja, or the Street of the Old Woman. That in which we lived had on the corner house a flamingo, and was called the Street of the Flamingo; and the reason of the streets being named in this way gives some idea of the character of the people. The great mass of the inhabitants, universally the Indians, cannot read. Printed signs would be of no use, but every Indian knows the sign of an elephant, a bull, or a flamingo.

The great distinguishing feature of Merida, as of all the cities of Spanish America, is in its churches. The great Cathedral; the parish church and convent of San Cristoval; the church of the Jesuits; the church and convent of the Mejorada; the chapels of San Juan Bautista; of Our Lady of Candelaria, of the Santa Lucia and the Virgin, and the convent de las monjas, or the nunnery, with it church and enclosures occupying two whole squares, are all interesting in their history. Some are of good style in architecture, and rich in ornaments; but there is one other, not yet mentioned, which I regard as the most interesting and remarkable edifice in Merida. It is the old Franciscan convent. It stands on an eminence in the eastern part of the city, and is enclosed by a high wall, with turrets, forming what is now called the Castillo. These walls and turrets are still erect, but within is ruin irretrievable.

In 1820 the new constitution obtained by the patriots in Spain reached the colonies, and on the 30th of May Don Juan Rivas Vertiz, then Gefe Politico, and now living in Merida, a fine memorial of the olden time, published it in the plaza. The church sustained the old order of things, and the Franciscan friars, confident in their hold upon the feelings of the populace, endeavoured to put down this demonstration of liberal feeling. A mob gathered in the plaza; friars appeared among them, urging them on; field-pieces were brought out, the mob dispersed, and Don Juan Rivas marched to the Franciscan convent, opened the doors, drove out the monks, above 300 in number, at the point of the bayonet, and gave up the building to destruction.

But this convent contains one memorial far more interesting than any connected with its own ruin; one that carries the beholder back through centuries of time, and tells the story of a greater and a sadder fall.

In one of the lower cloisters going out from the north, and under the principal dormitory, are two parallel corridors. The outer one faces the principal patio, and this corridor has that peculiar arch so often referred to in my previous volumes, two sides rising to meet each other, and covered, when within about a foot of forming an apex, by a flat layer of stones.

The arch particularly interested Stephens because it confirmed the obser-
vations he had made in his book on Central America, Chiapas and Yu-
catan that the ruins in the region had been built by the natives them-
selves.

When I wrote the account of my former journey, the greatest difficulty attending the consideration of this subjects was the absence of all historical record concerning the places visited. Copan had some history, but it was obscure, uncertain, and unsatisfactory. Quirigua, Palenque, and Uxmal had none whatever; but a ray of historic light beams upon the solitary arch in the ruined convent of Merida.

In the account of the conquest of Yucatan by Cogolludo it is stated, that on the arrival of the Spaniards at the Indian town of Tihoo, on the site of which, it will be remembered, Merida now stands, they found many cerros hechos a mano, *i. e.*, hills made by hand, or artificial mounds, and that on one of these mounds the Spaniards encamped.

In the history of the construction of the Franciscan convent, which was founded in the year 1547, five years after the arrival of the Spaniards in Tihoo, it is expressly stated that it was built upon a small artificial mound, one of the many that were then in the place, on which mound, it is added, were *some ancient buildings*. Now we must either suppose that the Spaniards razed these buildings to the ground, and then constructed this strange arch themselves, which supposition is, I think, utterly untenable, or that this corridor formed part of the ancient buildings which, according to the historical account, stood on this artificial mound, and that for some purpose or other the monks incorporated it with their convent.

CHAPTER V

Set up as Ladies' Daguerrotype Portrait Takers — Operation for
Strabismus

But the reader must not suppose that our only business in Merida
was the investigation of antiquities; we had other operations in hand which gave
us plenty of employment. We had taken with us a Daguerreotype apparatus, of
which but one specimen had ever before appeared in Yucatan. Having received
assurances that we might do a large business in that line, we were induced to
set up as ladies' Daguerreotype portrait takers.

Having made trials upon ourselves until we were tired of the subjects, and
with satisfactory results, we considered ourselves sufficiently advanced to begin;
and as we intended to practice for the love of the art, and not for lucre, we
held that we had a right to select our subjects. Accordingly, we had but to
signify our wishes, and the next morning put our house in order for the reception of our fair visiters.

*Three young ladies, chaperoned by their parents, soon arrived, and the
portraits were very successful.*

We continued practising a few days longer; and as all our good results were
extensively shown, and the poor ones we took care to keep out of sight, our
reputation increased, and we had abundance of applications.

There is no immediate connexion between taking Daguerreotype portraits
and the practice of surgery, but circumstances bring close together things entirely
dissimilar in themselves, and we went from one to the other. Secluded as Merida is, and seldom visited by strangers, the fame of new discoveries in science
is slow in reaching it, and the new operation of Mons. Guerin for the cure of
strabismus had not been heard of. In private intercourse we had spoken of this
operation, and, in order to make it known, and extend its benefits, Doctor Cabot
had offered to perform it in Merida. The Merida people have generally fine
eyes, but, either because our attention was particulary directed to it, or that is
really the case, there seemed to be more squinting eyes, or biscos, as they are
called, than are usually seen in any one town.

We had fixed the day for our departure; and the evening but one before,
a direct overture was made to the doctor to perform the operation. The subject

was a boy, and the application in his behalf was made by a gentleman who formed one of a circle in which were in the habit of visiting, and whom we were all happy to have it in our power to serve.

The time was fixed at ten o'clock the next day.

At ten o'clock the doctor's subject made his appearance. He was the son of a widow lady of very respectable family, about fourteen years old, but small of stature, and presenting even to the most casual glance the stamp of a little gentleman. He had large black eyes, but, unluckily, their expression was very much injured by an inward squint.

Modern science has discovered that the eye is retained in its orbit by six muscles, which pull it up and down, inward and outward, and that the undue contraction of either of these muscles produces that obliquity called squinting, which was once supposed to proceed from convulsions in childhood, or other unknown causes. The cure discovered is the cutting of the contracted muscle, by means of which the eye falls immediately into its proper place. It requires a knowledge of the anatomy of the eye, manual dexterity, fine instruments, and Mr. Catherwood, and myself for assistants.

Our patient remained perfectly quiet, with his little hands folded across his breast; but while the knife was cutting through the muscle he gave one groan, so piteous and heart-rending, that it sent into the next room all who were not immediately engaged. But before the sound of the groan had died away the operation was over, and the boy rose with his eye bleeding, but perfectly straight. A bandage was tied over it, and, with a few directions for its treatment, amid the congratulations and praises of all present, and wearing the same smile with which he had entered, the little fellow walked off to his mother.

They had so many applicants for the operation that they stayed in Merida a day longer than they had intended, and even so had to turn many hopeful patients away.

The news of these successes flew like wild-fire, and a great sensation was created throughout the city. All the evening Doctor Cabot was besieged with applications, and I could but think how fleeting is this world's fame! At first my arrival in the country had been fairly trumpeted in the newspapers; for a little while Mr. Catherwood had thrown me in the shade with the Daguerreotype, and now all our glories were swallowed up by Doctor Cabot's cure of strabismus. Nevertheless, his fame was reflected upon us. All the afternoon squint-eyed boys were passing up and down the street, throwing slanting glances in at the door, and toward evening, as Mr. Catherwood and I were walking to the plaza, we were hailed by some vagabond urchins with the obstreperous shout. "There go the men who cure the biscos."

CHAPTER VI

Departure from Merida — Timucui — Tekoh — Ruins of Mayapan

On Thursday, the twelfth day of November, we rose for our departure from Merida. The plan of our route, and all the arrangements for our journey, were made by our friend Don Simon Peon. Early in the morning our luggage was sent forward on the backs of mules and Indians, and we had only to take leave of our friends.

It was our intention to resume our explorations at Uxmal, the point where we were interrupted by the illness of Mr. Catherwood. We had received intelligence, however, of the ruins of Mayapan, an ancient city which had never been visited, about eight leagues distant from Merida, and but a few leagues aside from the road, by the haciendas, to Uxmal. The accounts which we could obtain were meager, and it was represented as completely in ruins; but, in fulfillment of the purpose we at that time entertained of going to every place of which we heard any account whatever, we determined to visit this on our way to Uxmal. It was for Mayapan, therefore, that we were now setting out.

Our saddles, bridles, holsters, and pistols, being entirely different from the mountings of horsemen in that country, attracted all eyes as we rode through the streets. A friend accompanied us beyond the suburbs, and put us into a straight road, which led, without turning, to the end of our day's journey. Instead of the ominous warnings we were accustomed to receive in Central America, his parting words were, that there was no danger of robbers, or of any other interruptions.

Under these favourable circumstances, in good health and spirits, with recommendations from the government to its officers in different sections of the country, and through the newspapers to the hospitality of citizens in the interior, we set out on our journey.

I would remark that no map of Yucatan at all to be depended on has ever been published. The Doña Joaquina Peon had one in manuscript, which she was so kind as to place at our disposal, but with notice that it was not correct; and, in order to keep a record of our own track from the time we left Merida until we returned to it, we took the bearings of the roads, noted the number of hours on each day's journey, and the pace of our horses, and at some places Mr. Catherwood took an observation for latitude. From these memoranda our map is prepared. It is correct so far as regards our route, but does not fix accurately the location of places which we did not visit.

At the distance of a league we passed a fine cattle hacienda, and at twenty minutes past one reached Timucui, a small village five leagues from Merida. This village consisted of a few Indian huts, built around a large open square, and on one side was a sort of shed for a casa real. It had no church or cura, and already we experienced a difficulty which we did not expect to encounter so soon. The population consisted entirely of Indians, who in general throughout the country speak nothing but the Maya; there was not a white man in the place, nor any one who could speak in any tongue that we could comprehend. Fortunately, a muleteer from the interior, on his way to Merida, had stopped to bait his mules under the shade of a large tree, and was swinging in a hammock in the casa real. He was surprised at our undertaking alone a journey into the interior, seeing that we were brought to a stand at the first village from the capital; but, finding us somewhat rational in other respects, he assisted us in procuring ramon leaves and water for the horses.

At three o'clock we left the hamlet, and at a little after four we saw the towers of the church of Tekoh.

The village consisted of a long, straight street, with houses or huts almost hidden by foliage, and inhabited exclusively by Indians. We rode up to the plaza without meeting a single person. At one side of the plaza, on a high stone platform, stood a gigantic church, with two lofty towers, and in front and on each sides was a broad flight of stone steps. Crossing the plaza we saw an Indian woman, to whom we uttered the word *convento*, and, following the direction of her hand, rode up to the house of the cura. It was in the rear of the church, and enclosed by a large wall. The gate was closed, but we opened it without knocking. The convent stood on the same platform with the church, and had a high flight of stone steps. A number of Indian servants ran out to the corridor, to stare at such strange-looking persons, and we understood that the padre was not at home; but we were too well pleased with the appearance of things to think of going elsewhere. We tied our horses in the yard, ascended the steps, and strolled through the corridor of the convent and along the platform of the church, overlooking the village.

The ministro, or assistant, soon joined them, who explained that the cura (priest) was officiating at a burial and would receive them as soon as it was over.

In the mean time, under his escort, we ascended to the top of the church.

The ascent was by a large stone staircase within one of the towers. The top commanded a view of a great plain, covered by an almost boundless forest, extending on one side to the sea, and on the other to the sierra which crosses the peninsula of Yucatan, and runs back to the great traversing range in Guatimala, broken only by a high mound, which at three leagues' distance towered above the plain, a mourning monument of the ruins of Mayapan, the capital of the fallen kingdom of Maya.

On our return we found the cura, Don José Canuta Vela, waiting to receive us; he had been notified of our coming, and had expected us the day before.

He relieved us of all difficulty arising from the want of an interpreter, and, sending for the Indian alcaldes, made immediate arrangements to forward our luggage, and to accompany us himself the next day to the ruins of Mayapan.

The road upon which we entered turned off abruptly from the camino real. This royal road itself, like most of the others which bore that name, would not be considered, in other countries, as indicating a very advanced state of internal improvement, but the one into which we now struck was much rougher and more stony, entirely new, and in some places still unfinished. It had been but lately opened, and the reason of its being opened at all illustrates one striking feature in the character of the Indians. The village to which it leads was under the pastoral charge of our friendly companion, and was formerly reached by a road, or rather path, so circuitous and difficult that, on account of his other duties, he was obliged to give notice that he would be compelled to give it up. To prevent this calamity, all the Indians, in a body, turned out and made this new road, being a straight cut through the woods, two leagues in length.

The priest told them that there were many ruins of ancient buildings in the area, and in fact they saw the remains of a rampart and a large, dried-up reservoir which he called an aguada.

At ten o'clock we reached the small village ot Telchaquillo, containing a population of six hundred souls, and these, again, were all Indians. It was they who had made the road we had travelled over, and the church was under our friend's pastoral charge. We rode to the convent, and dismounted.

In the square of this little village was a great senote, or subterraneous well, which supplied all the inhabitants with water. At a distance the square seemed level and unbroken; but women walking across it with cantaros or water-jars suddenly disappeared, and others seemed to rise out of the earth. On a nearer approach, we found a great orifice or opening in the rocky surface, like the mouth of a cave. The descent was by irregular steps cut and worn in the rocks. Over head was an immense rocky roof, and at a distance of perhaps five hundred feet from the mouth was a large basin or reservoir of water. Directly over the water the roof was perhaps sixty feet high; and there was an opening above which threw down a strong body of light. The water had no current, and its source was a mystery. During the rainy season it rises a little, but never falls below a certain point and at all times it is the only source of supply to the inhabitants. Women, with their water-jars, were constantly ascending and descending; swallows were darting through the cave in every direction, and the whole formed a wild, picturesque, and romantic scene.

At this village we found waiting for us the major domo of the hacienda of San Joaquín, on which stand the ruins of Mayapan. Leaving the senote, we mounted and followed him.

After a short distance they stopped at a large cave that had been dis-
covered recently by the steward who was with them. He told them that
it was so large that he had explored it for four hours without finding
any end. The travelers would have liked to see more of it than just the
cavern at the entrance, but continued. On their way they found ruined
walls and carved stones that showed that they were near an ancient city.
Soon after that they reached the hacienda and the ruins of Mayapan.

The hacienda, or rather rancho, of San Joaquin, on which the ruins of Mayapan lie scattered, is ten leagues south from Merida. It forms part of the great hacienda of Xcanchakan, the property of Don José María Meneses, the venerable cura of San Cristoval, formerly provesor of the Church of Yucatan. We had made the acquaintance of this gentleman at the house of his friend Señor Rejon, secretary of state, and he had sent instructions to his major domo, the same who met us at the last village, to place at our command all the disposable force of the hacienda.

The ruins of Mayapan cover a great plain, which was at that time so overgrown that hadly any object was visible until we were close upon it, and the undergrowth was so thick that it was difficult to work our way through it. Our's was the first visit to examine these ruins. For ages they had been unnoticed, almost unknown, and left to struggle with rank tropical vegetation; and the major domo, who lived on the principal hacienda, and had not seen them in twenty-three years, was more familiar with them than any other person we could find. He told us that within a circumference of three miles, ruins were found, and that a strong wall once encompassed the city, the remains of which might still be traced through the woods.

At a short distance from the hacienda, but invisible on account of the trees, rises the high mound which we had seen at three leagues' distance, from the top of the church at Tekoh, and which is represented in Figure 1. It is sixty feet high and one hundred feet square at the base; and, like the mounds at Palenque and Uxmal, it is an artificial structure, built up solid from the plain. Four grand staircases, each twenty-five feet wide, ascended to an esplanade within six feet of the top. This esplanade was six feet in width, and on each side was a smaller staircase leading to the top. These staircases are in a ruinous condition; the steps are almost entirely gone, and we climbed up by means of fallen stones and trees growing out of its sides.

The summit was a plain stone platform, fifteen feet square. It had no structure upon it, nor were there vestiges of any. Probably it was the great mound of sacrifice, on which the priests, in the sight of the assembled people,

FIG. 1

FIG. 2

cut out the hearts of human victims. The view commanded from the top was a great desolate plain, with here and there another ruined mound rising above the trees, and far in the distance could be discerned the towers of the church at Tekoh.

Around the base of this mound, and throughout the woods, wherever we moved, were strewed sculptured stones. Most of them were square, carved on the face, and having a long stone tenon or stem at the back; doubtless they had been fixed in the wall, so as to form part of some ornament, or combination of ornaments, in the façade, in all respects the same as at Uxmal.

Besides these, there were other and more curious remains. These were representations of human figures, or of animals, with hideous features and expressions, in producing which the skill of the artist seems to have been expended. The sculpture of these figures was rude, the stones were timeworn, and many were half buried in the earth. Figure 2 represents two of them. One is four, and the other three feet high. The full length seems intended to represent a warrior with a shield. The arms are broken off, and to my mind they conveyed a lively idea of the figures or idols which Bernal Dias met with on the coast, containing hideous faces of demons. Probably, broken and half buried as they lie, they were once objects of adoration and worship, and now exist as mute and melancholy memorials of ancient paganism.

At a short distance from the base of the mound was an opening in the earth, forming another of those extraordinary caves before presented to the reader. The cura, the major domo, and the Indians called it a senote, and said that it had supplied the inhabitants of the old city with water.

Leaving the cave or senote, we continued rambling among the ruins. The mounds were all of the same general character, and the buildings had entirely disappeared on all except one; but this was different from any we had at that time seen, though we afterward found others like it.

It stood on a ruined mound about thirty feet high. What the shape of the mound had been it was difficult to make out, but the building was circular. Figure 3 represents this edifice, with the mound on which it stands. The exterior is of plain stone, ten feet high to the top of the lower cornice, and fourteen more to that of the upper one. The door faces the west, and over it is a lintel of stone. The outer wall is five feet thick; the door opens into a circular passage three wide, and in the centre is a cylindrical solid mass of stone, without any doorway or opening of any kind. The whole diameter of the building is twenty-five feet, so that, deducting the double width of the wall and passage, this centre mass must be nine feet in thickness. The walls had four or five coats of stucco, and there were remains of painting, in which red, yellow, blue, and white were distinctly visible.

On the southwest side of the building, and on a terrace projecting from the

FIG. 3

side of the mound, was a double row of columns eight feet apart, of which only eight remained, though probably, from the fragments around, there had been more, and, by clearing away the trees, more might have been found still standing. In our hurried visit to Uxmal, we had seen objects which we supposed might have been intended for columns, but were not sure; and though we afterward saw many, we considered these the first decided columns we had seen. They were two feet and a half in diameter, and consisted of five round stones, eight or ten inches thick, laid one upon another. They had no capitals, and what particular connexion they had with the building did not appear.

So far, although the fragments of sculpture were of the same general character as at Uxmal, we had not found any edifice sufficiently entire to enable us to identify that peculiar arch which we had found in all the ruined buildings of this country; but it was not wanting. At some distance from this place, and on the other side of the hacienda, were long ranges of mounds. These had once been buildings, the tops of which had fallen, and almost buried the structures.

The day was now nearly spent; with the heat and labour we were exceedingly fatigued, and the Indians insisted that we had seen all the principal remains.

Fortunately, at this place again we have a ray of historic light. According to the best accounts, the region of country now called Yucatan was known to the natives, at the time of the Spanish invasion, by the name of Maya, and before that time it had never been known by any other. The name of Yucatan was given to it by the Spaniards. It is entirely arbitrary and accidental, and its origin is not known with certainty.

One language, called the Maya, extended throughout the whole peninsula; and though the Spaniards found the country parcelled into different governments, under various names and having different caciques, hostile to each other, at an earlier period of its history the whole land of Maya was united under one head or supreme lord. This great chief or king had for the seat of his monarchy a very populous city called Mayapan, and had under him many other lords and caciques, who were bound to pay him tribute of cotton clothes, fowls, cacao, and gum or resin for incense; to serve him in wars, and day and night in the temples of the idols, at festivals and ceremonies. These lords, too, had under them cities and many vassals. Becoming proud and ambitious, and unwilling to brook a superior, they rebelled against the power of the supreme lord, united all their forces, and besieged and destroyed the city of Mayapan. This destruction took place in the year of our Lord 1420, about one hundred years, or, according to Herrera, about seventy years, before the arrival of the Spaniards in Yucatan; and, according to the computation of the ages of the Indians, two hundred and seventy years from the foundation of the city. The account of all the details is confused and indistinct; but the existence of a principal city called Mayapan, and its destruction by war at about the time indicated, are mentioned by every historian. This city was occupied by the same race of people who inhabited the country at the time of the conquest, and its site is identified as that which has just been presented to the reader, retaining, through all changes and in its ruins, its ancient name of Mayapan.

The city of Mayapán was very important in pre-Hispanic times since, together with Chichén Itzá and Uxmal, it ruled the peninsula for more than two centuries. This site has not been restored but according to some investigators the city, whose name means 'Maya Banner' covered a large area. It is surrounded by a wall and contains the remains of a large num-

ber of constructions, among which the most outstanding are the Temple of the Warriors *and the* Temple of Sacrifice, *where there is a mask of Chaac, the god of rain. There are also remains of an observatory with a stela of a warrior and another with inscriptions.* The Pyramid of Kukulcán, *uncovered by archeologists from the Carnegie Institution, is 55 meters high, and near it is the now dry* Cenote of Chumul, *which supplied the city with water.*

CHAPTER VII

Hacienda of Xcanchakan — Hacienda of Mucuyché — Arrival at Uxmal
— Changes since last Visit.

After leaving Mayapán they went on to the hacienda of Xcanchakán.

It was late when we left the hacienda. Our road was a mere bridle-path through a wilderness. At some distance we crossed a broken range of stones, rising on each side to a wall, which the major domo said was the line of wall that encompassed the ancient city.

It was nearly dark when we reached the stately hacienda of Xcanchakan, one of the three finest in Yucatan, and containing nearly seven hundred souls. Plate I represents the front of this hacienda. The house is perhaps one of the best in the country, and being within one day's ride of the capital, and accessible by calesa, it is a favourite residence of its venerable proprietor.

Our friend the cura of Tekoh was still with us, and the Indians of the hacienda were within his curacy. Again immediately upon our arrival the bell of the church was tolled to announce his arrival to the sick, those who wished to confess, marry, or be baptized. This over, it struck the solemn note of the *oracion*, or vesper prayers. All rose, and, with uncovered heads stood silent till the last note died away, all, according to the beautiful injunction of the Catholic Church, breathing an inward prayer. Then they bade each other a *buenas noches*, each kissed the cura's hand, and then, with his petata, or straw hat, in his hand, came to us, bowing respectfully, and wishing each of us also the good night.

While they were on the hacienda they saw a native dance called El Toro
(The Bull), a performance that was organized by the cura for the enter-tainment of the visitors.

Early in the morning we were roused by loud bursts of music in the church. The cura was giving them the benefit of his accidental visit by an early mass.

After breakfast the cura left us to return to his village, and we set out to continue our journey to Uxmal. Our luggage was sent off by Indians of the hacienda, and the major domo accompanied us on horseback. Our road was by a bridle path over the same stony country, through thick woods. The whole way it lay through the lands of the provisor, all wild, waste, and desolate, and showing the fatal effects of accumulation in the hands of large landed propri-

PLATE I

FIG. 4

etors. In two hours we saw rising before us the gate of the hacienda of Mucuy-ché (Figure 4). To the astonishment of the gaping Indians, the doctor, as he wheeled his horse, shot a hawk that was hovering over the pinnacle of the gateway, and we rode up to the house.

We were once more on the hands of our old friend Don Simon Peon. The whole hacienda, horses, mules, and Indians, were at our disposal.

Stephens and Catherwood had stayed at this hacienda during their previous journey and had fond memories of it. They lost no time in going back to the cenote to bathe, as they had done before, and were not disappointed by its beauty. That night they slept at the hacienda.

The next day we rode on to the hacienda of San José, where we stopped to make some preparations, and on the fifteenth, at eleven o'clock, we reached the hacienda of Uxmal.

It stood in its suit of sombre gray, with cattle-yard, large trees, and tanks, the same as when we left, it, but there were no friends of old to welcome us. We determined to pass on and take up our abode immediately in the ruins. Stopping but a few minutes, to give directions about the luggage, we mounted again, and in ten minutes, emerging from the woods, came out upon the open field in which, grand and lofty as when we saw it before, stood the House of the Dwarf; but the first glance showed us that a year had made great changes. The sides of the lofty structure, then bare and naked, were now covered with high grass, bushes, and weeds, and on the top were bushes and young trees

FIG. 5

twenty feet high. The House of the Nuns was almost smothered, and the whole field was covered with a rank growth of grass and weeds, over which we could barely look as we rode through. The foundations, terraces, and tops of the buildings were overgrown, weeds and vines were rioting and creeping on the façades, and mounds, terraces, and ruins were a mass of destroying verdure. A strong and vigorous nature was struggling for mastery over art, wrapping the city in its suffocating embraces, and burying it from sight. It seemed as if the grave was closing over a friend, and we had arrived barely in time to take our farewell.

Amid this mass of desolation, grand and stately as when we left it, stood the Casa del Gobernador, but with all its terraces covered, and separated from us by a mass of impenetrable verdure. Helped by the overseer of the hacienda of Uxmal they cut their way through the undergrowth. We moved directly to the wall at the east end, and entered the first open door. Here the mayoral wished us to take up our abode; but we knew the localities better than he did, and, creeping along the front as close to the wall as possible, cutting some of the bushes, and tearing apart and trampling down others, we reached the centre apartment. Here we stopped. Swarms of bats, roused by our approach, fluttered and flew through the long chamber, and passed out at the doors.

The appearance of things was not very promising for a place of residence. There were two salas, each sixty feet long; that in front had three large doors, opening upon the encumbered terrace, and the other had no windows and but one door. In both there was an extreme sensation of closeness and dampness, with an unpleasant smell, and in the back room was a large accumulation of dirt and rubbish.

Throughout Yucatan "el campo", or the country, is considered unhealthy in the rainy season. We had arrived in Yucatan counting upon the benefit of the whole dry season, which generally begins in November and lasts till May; but this year the rains had continued longer than usual, and they were not yet over. Among all the haciendas, Uxmal had a reputation pre-eminent for its un-healthiness. Every person who had ever been at work among the ruins had been obliged by sickness to leave them. Mr. Catherwood had had sad experience, and this unhealthiness was not confined to strangers. The Indians suffered every season from fevers; many of them were at that time ill, and the major domo had been obliged to go away. All this we had been advised of in Merida, and had been urged to postpone our visit; but as this would have interfered materially with our plan, and as we had with us a "medico" who could cure "biscos", we determined to risk it. On the spot, however, perceiving the dampness of the apartments and the rankness of vegetation, we felt that we had been imprudent; but it was too late to draw back, even if we had wished to do so. We agreed that we were better on this high terrace than at the hacienda, which stood low, and had around it great tanks of water, mantled with green, and wearing a very fever-and-aguish aspect. We therefore set to work immediately to make the best of our condition.

They also had an Indian boy with them, who first cleared a space in front of the main entrance and then, slowly and patiently built a fire to counteract the dampness of the room. Finally their baggage arrived, carried by a long line of Indians, who were put to work clearing the terrace and sweeping out the rooms. When this was done the travelers put their beds in the back room and their hammocks in the front.

We had reached the first point of our journey; we were once more at the ruins of Uxmal. It was nearly two years since we originally set out in search of

American ruins, and more than a year since we were driven from this place. The freshness and enthusiasm with which we had first come upon the ruins of an American city had perhaps gone, but our feelings were not blunted, and all the regret which we had felt in being obliged to leave was more than coun- terbalanced by satisfaction of returning.

As a measure of precaution, and in order to have the full benefit of a medical man's company, we began immediately upon a course of preventive treatment, by way of putting ourselves on the vantage ground against fever. As we were all in perfect health, Dr. Cabot thought such a course could not hurt us. This over, we threw more wood upon the pile and went to bed.

As the fire died down during the night they were attacked by swarms of mosquitoes, which made them think that it would be impossible to spend another night there.

CHAPTER VIII

Household Wants — Description of the ruins

The first morning, they realized that they needed a cook. They had, in fact, asked the overseer to find one for them, but this was not easy. However, while they were still preparing their meal, they saw him arriving with the only woman on the hacienda who had agreed to go, on condition that she did not remain at the ruins at night, but could go home every evening. Her name was Chepa Chí, and they estimated her to be a little over fifty. With her she brought her grandson, José.

Before we were in a condition to begin an examination and exploration of the ruins, we had a serious business before us in making the necessary clearings. These were not required for picturesque effect; indeed, overgrown as the ruins were, they addressed themselves more powerfully to the imagination than if the whole field and every stone lay bare; but facilities of moving from place to place were indispensable, and for this purpose we determined first to clear the terrace of the Casa del Gobernador, and cut roads from ruin to ruin, until we had a complete line of communication; and that we might know exactly our whereabout, Mr. Catherwood took an observation, by which he found the latitude of Uxmal to be 20° 27' 30" N.

Among the Indians who arrived to work next day was a boy about fifteen years old called Bernaldo. He spoke Spanish, so he was hired immediately as interpreter and, after showing suprising talent in the kitchen was made head cook, while Chepa Chí simply made the tortillas.

In Stephens' opinion, the brief description given in his first book did not do justice to the ruins, so he describes them again at length.

The first ruin which I shall present is that in which we lived, called the Casa del Gobernador, with the three great terraces on which it stands. This front is three hundred and twenty-two feet long.

This building was constructed entirely of stone. Up to the cornice, which runs round it the whole length and on all four of its sides, the façade presents a smooth surface; above is one solid mass of rich, complicated, and elaborately sculptured ornaments, forming a sort of arabesque.

The grandest ornament, which imparts a richness to the whole façade, is

PLATE II

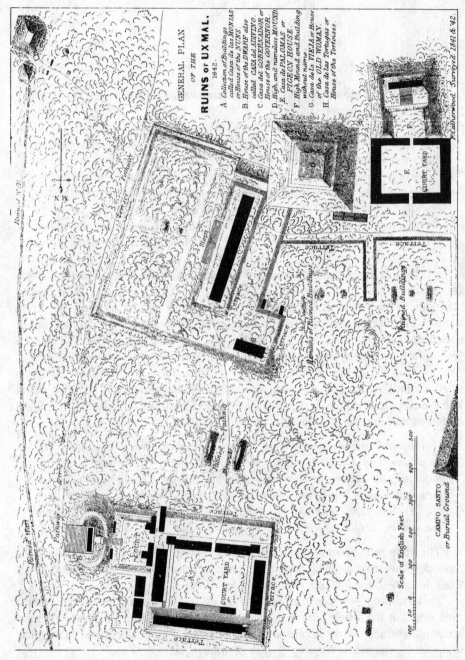

GENERAL PLAN
OF THE
RUINS OF UXMAL.
1842.

A. Collection of Buildings
   called Casa de las MONJAS
   or House of the NUNS.
B. House of the DWARF also
   called CASA del ADIVINO.
C. Casa del GOBERNADOR or
   House of the GOVERNOR.
D. High and nameless MOUND.
E. Casa de PALOMAS or
   PIGEON HOUSE.
F. High Mound and Building.
G. Casa de la VIEJA or House
   of the OLD WOMAN
   without name.
H. Casa de las Tortugas or
   House of the Tortoises.

F. Catherwood Surveyed 1841 & '42

Scale of English Feet.

CAMPO SANTO
or Burial Ground

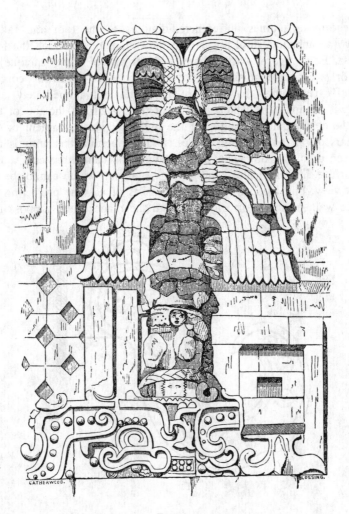

FIG. 6

over the centre doorway. Around the head of the principal figure are rows of characters, which, in our first hurried visit, we did not notice as essentially different from the other incomprehensible subjects sculptured on the façade; but we now discovered that these characters were hieroglyphics. We had ladders made, by means of which Mr. Catherwood climbed up and made accurate drawings of them.

Figure 6 represents the part immediately over the doorway. It shows the remaining portion of a figure seated on a kind of throne. This throne was formerly supported by a rich ornament, still forming part of similar designs over other doorways in this building. The headdress is lofty, and from it proceed enormous plumes of feathers, dividing at the top, and falling symmetrically on each side, until they touch the ornament on which the feet of the statue rest. Each figure was perhaps the portrait of some cacique, warrior, prophet, or priest, distinguished in the history of this unknown people.

Plate III represents that part of the ornament immediately above the preceding; it occupies the whole portion of the wall from the top of the headdress to the cornice along the top of the building. This ornament or combination appears on all parts of the edifice, and throughout the ruins is more frequently seen than any other. In the engraving the centre presents a long, flat, smooth surface. This indicates a projecting ornament, which cannot be exhibited in a front view; but, as seen in profile, consists of a stone projecting from the face of the wall, as shown in Figure 7; and the reader must suppose this stone

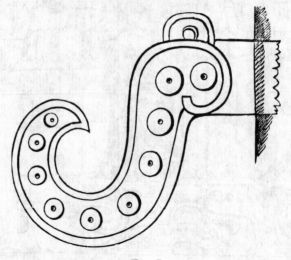

FIG. 7

projecting in order clearly to understand the character of the ornament last presented. It measures one foot seven inches in length from the stem by which it is fixed in the wall to the end of the curve, and resembles somewhat an elephant's trunk, which name has, perhaps not inaptly, been given to it by Waldeck, though it is not probable that as such the sculptor intended it, for the elephant was unknown on the Continent of America. This projecting stone appears with this combination all over the façade and at the corners; and throughout all the buildings it is met with, sometimes in a reversed position, oftener than any other design in Uxmal. It is a singular fact, that though entirely out of reach, the ends of nearly all of them have been broken off; and among the many remains in every part of the walls throughout the whole ruins, there are but three that now exist entire. The reader will percieve how utterly unprof-

Plate III

UXMAL

Ornament of the Casa del Gobernador.

Decoration on the
Nunnery Quadrangle,
Uxmal.

itable it would be to attempt a verbal description of such a façade, and the lines in the engraving show that, as I remarked in my former account, there is no tablet or single stone representing separately and by itself an entire subject, but every ornament or combination is made up of separate stones, each of which had carved on it part of the subject, and was then set in its place in the wall. Each stone by itself is an unmeaning fractional portion, but, placed by the side of others, makes part of a whole, which without it would be incomplete.

The rear elevation of the Casa del Gobernador is a solid wall, without any doorways or openings of any kind. Like the front, above the cornice it was ornamented throughout its whole length with sculptured stone. The subjects, however, were less complicated, and the sculpture less gorgeous and elaborate; and on this side, too, a part of the façade has fallen.

The two ends are thirty-nine feet each. Figure 8 represents the southern end. It has but one doorway, and of this, too, the sculptured subjects were more simple.

The roof is flat, and had been covered with cement; but the whole, is now overgrown with grass and bushes.

Its distinguishing features are, that it was long, low, and narrow; below the cornice plain, and ornamented with sculpture all around. Mr. Catherwood made minute architectural drawings of the whole, and has in his possession the materials for erecting a building exactly like it; and I would remark that, as on our former expedition, he made all his drawings with the camera lucida, for the purpose of obtaining the utmost accuracy of proportion and detail. Besides which, we had with us a Daguerreotype apparatus, the best that could

FIG. 8

Governor's Palace, Uxmal.

be procured in New-York, with which, immediately on our arrival at Uxmal, Mr. Catherwood began taking views; but the results were not sufficiently perfect suit his ideas. At times the projecting cornices and ornaments threw parts of the subject in shade, while others were in broad sunshine; so that, while parts were brought out well, other parts required pencil drawings to supply their defects. They gave a general idea of the character of the buildings, but would not do to put into the hands of the engraver without copying the views on paper, and introducing the defective parts, which would require more labour than that of making at once complete original drawings. He therefore completed everything with his pencil and camera lucida, while Doctor Cabot and myself took up the Daguerreotype; and, in order to ensure the utmost accuracy, the Daguerreotype views were placed with the drawings in the hands of the engravers for their guidance.

The ground plan of the Casa del Gobernador is represented in Figure 9. It has eleven doorways in front and one at each end. The doors are all gone, and the wooden lintels over them have fallen. The interior is divided longitudi-

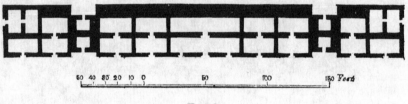

FIG. 9

nally by a wall into two corridors, and these again, by cross walls or partitions, into oblong rooms. Every pair of these rooms, the front and back, communicate by a doorway exactly opposite a corresponding doorway in front.

The principal apartments in the centre, with three doorways opening upon the terrace, are sixty feet long. The one in front is eleven feet six inches wide, and the inner one thirteen feet. The former is twenty-three feet high to the top of the arch, and the other twenty-two feet. The latter has but one door of entrance from the front room, and except this it has no door or aperture of any kind, so that at the ends it is dark and damp, as is the case with all the inner rooms. In these two apartments we took up our abode.

The walls are constructed of square, smooth blocks of stone, and on each side of the doorway are the remains of stone rings fixed in the walls with shafts, which no doubt had some connexion with the support of the doors. The floors were of cement, in some places hard, but, by long exposure, broken, and now crumbling under the feet.

The ceiling forms a triangular arch, as at Palenque, without the keystone. The support is made by stones overlapping, and bevilled so as to present a smooth surface, and within about a foot of the point of contact covered by a layer of flat stones. Across the arch were beams of wood, the ends built in the wall on each side, which had probably been used for the support of the arch while the building was in progress.

For the rest, I refer to the plan, mentioning only one circumstance. In working out the plan on the spot, it was found that the back wall, throughout its whole length of two hundred and seventy feet, was nine feet thick, which was nearly equal to the width of the front apartment. Such thickness was not necessary for the support of the building, and, supposing it might contain some hidden passages, we determined to make a breach through the wall, and to do this in the centre apartment.

Over the cavity left in the mortar by the removal of the stone were two conspicuous marks, which afterward stared us in the face in all the ruined buildings of the country. They were the prints of a red hand with the thumb and fingers extended, not drawn or painted, but stamped by the living hand, the pressure of the palm upon the stone. He who made it had stood before it alive as we did, and pressed his hand, moistened with red paint, hard against the stone. The seams and creases of the palm were clear and distinct in the impression. There was something lifelike about it that waked exciting thoughts, and almost presented the images of the departed inhabitants hovering about the building.

The stones with this red hand upon them were the first that fell as we commenced our breach into the wall. There were two crowbars on the hacienda, and working nearly two days, the Indians made a hole between six and seven feet deep, but throughout the wall was solid, and consisted of large stones imbedded in mortar, almost as hard as rock. The reason of this immense back wall, where everything else had a certain degree of fitness and conformity, we did not discover, and we had this huge hole staring us reproachfully in the face during all the remainder of our residence.

Next to the great building of the Casa del Gobernador, and hardly less extraordinary and imposing in character, are the three great terraces which hold it aloft, and give it its grandeur of position; all of them artificial, and built up from the level of the plain.

The lowest of these terraces is three feet high, fifteen feet broad, and five hundred and seventy-five feet long; the second is twenty feet high, two hundred and fifty wide, and five hundred and forty-five feet in length; and the third, on which the building stands, is nineteen feet high, thirty feet broad, and three hundred and sixty feet in front. They were all supported by substantial stone walls; that of the second terrace is still in a good state of preservation, and at the corners the stones which support it are still in their places, with their outer surfaces rounded, instead of presenting sharp angles.

The platform of this terrace is a noble terra plana, five hundred and forty-five feet long and two hundred and fifty feet wide, and, from the remains still visible upon it, once contained structures and ornaments of various kinds, the character of which it is now difficult to make out. On our first arrival the whole was covered with a rank growth of bushes and weeds ten or twelve feet high, on clearing which away these remains were brought to light.

As Stephens says, the House of the Governor *stands on three terraces, the first of which is one of the largest constructions in the northern Maya area. It has sloping walls and a wide stairway on the eastern side. From this same side starts the 'white road', sacbé in Maya, that connected this site to Kabah.*

The House or Palace properly speaking stands on two smaller terraces, also with sloping sides. The central part of the building has five rooms, and the wings on each side three each. In the frieze on the eastern side is the relief of a dignitary, and all along the frieze are masks of the god of rain, Chaac. The corners of the three sections are finished off with columns of five masks that give the impression of undulating serpents. The frieze also contains five human figures, but the one over the central entrance of the middle section, wearing a feather headdress and sitting on a throne, is the most outstanding.

During explorations made between 1951 and 1952 under the direction of Alberto Ruz Lhuillier the Late Classic frieze with the principal motif of a thatched Maya hut was reconstructed.

Near the centre of the platform, at a distance of eighty feet from the foot of the steps, is a square enclosure, consisting of two layers of stones, in which stands, in an oblique position, as if falling, or perhaps, as if an effort had been made to throw it down, a large round stone, measuring eight feet above the ground and five feet in diameter. This stone is striking for its uncouth and irregular proportions, and wants conformity with the regularity and symmetry of all around. The Indians call this stone the Picote, or whipping-post.

At a distance of sixty feet in a right line beyond this was a rude circular mound, about six feet high. We had used it as a position from which to take a Daguerreotype view of the front of the building, and, at the instance of the Cura Carrillo, who came to pay us a visit, we determined to open it. It was a mere mass of earth and stones; and, on digging down to the depth of three or four feet, a sculptured monument was discovered, which is represented in Figure 10. It was found standing on its feet, in the position represented in the engraving. It is carved out of a single block of stone, and measures three feet two inches in length and two feet in height. It seems intended to represent a double-headed cat or lynx, and is entire with the exception of one foot, which is a little broken. The sculpture is rude. It was too heavy to carry away. We had it raised to the side of the mound for M. Catherwood to draw, and prob-

FIG. 10

ably it remains there still. The *picote*, or great stone, before referred to, appears in Figure 10 in the distance.

> *This sculpture now stands on a small platform at the foot of the great terrace of the Governor's Palace.*

At a distance of 130 feet from this mound was a square stone structure, six feet high and twenty feet at the base, in which we made an excavation, and discovered two sculptured heads, no doubt intended as portraits.

From the centre of this great platform a grand staircase 130 feet broad, which once contained 35 steps, rises to the third terrace, on which the building stands; besides this there is no staircase connected with either of

PLATE IV

UXMAL

Front of the Casa de las Tortugas.

Jaguars platform, Uxmal.

The House of Turtles after reconstruction, Uxmal.

the three terraces, and the only ascent to the platform of the second is by an inclined plane 100 feet broad, at the south end of the building, which makes it necessary for all approaching from the north to pass the whole length of the lower terrace, and, ascending by the inclined plane, go back to reach the steps. The probability is, that the labour of this was not regarded by the ancient inhabitants, and that all visiters or residents in the building passed in and out on the shoulders of Indians in coches, as the rich do now.

There remains to be noticed one important building on the grand platform of the second terrace. It stands at the northwest corner, and is represented in Plate IV. It is called the Casa de las Tortugas, or the House of the Turtles, which name was given to it by a neighbouring cura, from a bead or row of turtles which goes round the cornice, indicated in the engraving.

This building is 94 feet in front and 34 feet deep, and in size and ornaments contrasts strikingly with the Casa del Gobernador. It wants the rich and gorgeous decoration of the former, but is distinguished for its justness and beauty of proportions, and its chasteness and simplicity of ornament. Throughout there is nothing that borders on the unintelligible or grotesque, nothing that can shock a fastidious architectural taste; but, unhappily, it is fast going to decay.

The House of the Turtles was later restored.

Such is a brief description of the Casa del Gobernador, with its three great terraces, and the buildings and structures upon the grand platform of the second. From the place which we had fixed upon as our residence, and the constant necessity of ascending and descending the terraces, it was with these that we became the soonest familiar.

CHAPTER IX

Journey to Jalacho — Village of Becal — Arrival at Jalacho — A Great
Fair — Hacienda of Sijoh — Mounds of Ruins — Hacienda of
Tankuché — More Ruins — Return to the Village

*While Catherwood stayed at Uxmal to make drawings Stephens left to
meet Don Simon Peón and visit some other ruins.*

Having made such advances in the clearing that Mr. Catherwood had
abundance of occupation, on Thursday, the 18th of November, I set out, under
the guidance of the mayoral, on an excursion to meet Don Simon Peon at the
fair of Jalacho, and visit some ruins on another hacienda of his in that neighbourhood. The road was the worst I had found in the country, being simply a
wet and very muddy path for mules and horses to the fair. My horse sunk up
to his saddle-girths, and it was with great exertion that he dragged himself
through.

In half an hour we came into a clear and open country, and at ten we
entered the camino real for Jalacho, a broad and open road, passable for calesas.
Up to this time we had not seen a single habitation or met a human being, and
now the road was literally thronged with people moving on to the fair, with
whose clean garments my mud-stained clothes contrasted very unfavourably.
There were Indians, Mestizoes, and white people on horseback, muleback and
on foot, men, women, and children, many carrying on their backs things to sell,
in petaquillas, or long baskets of straw; whole families, sometimes half a village
moving in company.

*In the village of Becal, Stephens stopped to have breakfast with the cura,
who told him about some other ruins and invited him to visit them on
his way back. However, he was unable to because he took a different
road back to Uxmal.*

In an hour I reached Jalacho, where I met Don Simon and two of his
brothers, with whom I was not yet acquainted; Don Lorenzo, who had a hacienda in that neighbourhood, and Don Alonzo, then living in Campeachy, who
was educated in New York, and spoke English remarkably well.

The village of Jalacho lies on the main road from Merida to Campeachy,
and, next to that of Yzamal, its fair is the greatest in Yucatan, while in some
respects it is more curious. It is not attended by large merchants with foreign

goods, nor by the better classes from Merida, but it is resorted to by all the Indians from the haciendas and villages. It is inferior in one respect: gambling is not carried on upon so large a scale as at Yzamal.

The fair of Halachó lasted eight days. It celebrated the feast of St. James the Apostle and the church was well attended. There were also bullfights and dances, which the author mentions later. He also visited the horse market, as he wanted to buy horses for their journey into the interior. That night on the main square he saw the gambling tables (cards and dice) and the food stands, and was interested to note that the Indians still used cacao beans as currency.

In a casual conversation, Stephens learned that there were some ruins at the village of Maxcanú not far away. He decided to visit them on his way back to Uxmal, and so brought forward his trip to the ruins on the hacienda of Sihó, belonging to the Peón family.

In one building he noted that the inside was very similar to those he had seen at Uxmal, with the same type of arch. From the top of another building, only a mass of fallen stones, he saw two others of nearly the same height, and with difficulty reached them; they were almost completely ruined. However, as he passed between them he realized that there were three others, forming the corners of a square, where he found some huge stones that reminded him of the monuments of Copán, although he says that they were even more extraordinary and incomprehensible. They were of different shapes and sizes and, as they had no carvings on them, he compares them to 'unlettered headstones in a churchyard'.

At this time my visit was merely intended as preliminary, for the purpose of judging whether there were any subjects for Mr. Catherwood's pencil, and it was now about one o'clock. The heat was intense, and sweating and covered with briers and burrs, which stuck to every part of my clothes, I came out into the open road, where my Indian was waiting for me with the horses. We mounted immediately, and continued on a gallop to the hacienda of Tankuché, two leagues distant.

In five minutes after leaving the hacienda, we passed between two mounds of ruins, and, from time to time having glimpses of other vestiges in the woods, in twenty minutes we came to a mound about thirty feet high, on the top of which was a ruined building. Here we dismounted, tied our horses, and ascended the mound. The whole of the front wall had fallen, together with the front half of the arch; the interior chamber was filled with dirt and rubbish nearly up to the cornice, and the arch of the back wall was the only part above ground; but this, instead of being of smooth stones, like all the others we had seen in Yucatan, was plastered and covered with paintings, the colours of which were still bright and fresh. The principal colours were red, green, yellow, and blue, and at first the lines and figures seemed so distinct, that I thought I could make out the subjects. The apartment being filled up with dirt, I stood above the objects, and it was only by sitting, or rather lying down, that I could examine them. One subject at first sight struck me as being a representation of the mask found at Palenque. I was extremely desirous to get this off entire, but found, by experiments upon other parts of the plaster with the machete, that it would be impossible to do so, and left it untouched.

In the interest of the work, I did not discover that thousands of garrapatas were crawling over me. These insects are the scourge of Yucatan, and altogether they were a more constant source of annoyance and suffering than any we encountered in the country. I had seen something of them in Central America, but at a different season, when the hot sun had killed off the immensity of their numbers, and those left had attained such a size that a single one could easily be seen and picked off. These, in colour, size, and numbers, were like grains of sand. They disperse themselves all over the body, get into the seams of the clothes, and, like the insect known among us as the tick, bury themselves in the flesh, causing an irritation that is almost intolerable. The only way to get rid of them effectually is by changing all the clothes. In Uxmal we had not been troubled with them, for they are said to breed only in those woods where cattle pasture, and the grounds about Uxmal had been used as a milpa, or plantation of corn. It was the first time I had ever had them upon me in such profusion, and their presence disturbed most materially the equanimity with which I examined the paintings In fact, I did not remain long on the ground.

It was now nearly dark. My day's work had been a severe one. I was tired and covered with garrapatas, but the next day was Sunday, the last of the fiesta, and I determined on returning to the village that night. There was a brilliant moonlight, and, hurrying on, at eleven o'clock I saw, at the end of a long straight road, the illuminated front of the church of Jalacho. Very soon, amid the shining lights and congregated thousands, I forgot desolations and ruins, and my sympathies once more moved with the living.

CHAPTER X

Cave of Maxcanú — Village of Opocheque — Return to Uxmal

The church was thronged for grand mass; candles were burned, and offerings were made to the amount of many medios, and at nine o'clock the bells tolled for the procession, the crowning scene of the fiesta. The church was emptied of its votaries, and the plaza was alive with people hurrying to take a place in the procession, or to see it pass. I climbed up into the Plaza de Toros, and had a whole box to myself.

At four o'clock I set off with Don Lorenzo Peon, a brother of Don Simon, for Maxcanú. Our mode of conveyance, much used in Yucatan, but new to me, was called a caricoché. It was a long wagon, on two large wheels, covered with cotton cloth as a protection against the sun, and on the bottom was stretched a broad mattress, on which two persons could recline at full length. If they would sit up, it was large enough for three or four. It was drawn by one horse, with a driver riding as postillion, and another horse followed to change. The road was broad, even, and level. It was the camino real between Merida and Campeachy, and would pass in any country for a fair carriage road. All along we passed parties of Indians returning from the fair. In an hour we came in sight of the sierra which traverses at that point the whole peninsula of Yucatan from east to west. The sight of hills was cheering, and with the reflection of the setting sun upon them, they presented almost the first fine scenery I had encountered in the country. In an hour and ten minutes we reached Maxcanú, twelve miles distant, being by far the greatest speed at which I ever travelled in Yucatan.

The hacienda of Don Lorenzo was in this neighbourhood, and he had a large house in the village, at which we stopped. My object in coming to this place was to visit La Cueva de Maxcanú, or the Cave of Maxcanú.

I had before heard so much of caves, and had been so often disappointed, that I did not expect much from this; but the first view satisfied me in regard to the main point, viz., that it was not a natural cave, and that, as had been represented to me, it was hecha à mano, or made by hand.

La Cueva de Maxcanú, or the Cave of Maxcanú, has in that region a marvellous and mystical reputation. It is called by the Indians Satun Sat, which means in Spanish. El Laberinto or El Perdedero, the Labyrinth, or place in which one may be lost.

My retinue consisted of eight men, who considered themselves in my employ, besides three or four supernumeraries, and all together formed a crowd around the door. Except the mayoral of Uxmal, I had never seen one of them before, and as I considered it important to have a reliable man outside, I stationed him at the door with a ball of twine. I tied one end round my left wrist, and told one of the men to light a torch and follow me, but he refused absolutely, and all the rest, one after the other, did the same.

The entrance faces the west. The mouth was filled up with rubbish, scrambling over which, I stood in a narrow passage or gallery, constructed, like all the apartments above ground, with smooth walls and triangular arched ceiling. This passage was about four feet wide, and seven feet high to the top of the arch. It ran due east, and at the distance of six or eight yards opened into another, or rather was stopped by another crossing it, and running north and south. I took first that on the right hand, running south. At the distance of a few yards, on the right side of the wall, I found a door, filled up, and at the distance of thirty-five feet the passage ended, and a door opened at right angles on the left into another gallery running due east. Following this, at the distance of thirteen feet I found another gallery on the left, running north, and beyond it, at the end, still another, also on the left, and running north, four yards long, and then walled up, with only an opening in it about a foot square.

Turning back, I entered the gallery which I had passed, and which ran north eight or ten yards; at the end was a doorway on the right, opening into a gallery that ran east. At the end of this were six steps, each one foot high and two wide, leading to another gallery, which ran north twelve yards. At the end there came another gallery on the left, which ran west ten yards, and at the end of this another on the right running north about sixty feet. This passage was walled up at the north end, and at the distance of five yards from this end another doorway led into a passage running to the east. At the distance of four yards a gallery crossed this at right angles, running north and south, forty-five feet long, and walled up at both ends; and three or four yards farther on another gallery crossed, it, also running nort and south. This last was walled up at the south, and on the north led to still another gallery, which ran east, three yards long. This was stopped by another gallery crossing it, running to the south three yards, when it was walled up, and to the north eight yards, when it turned to the west.

In utter ignorance of the ground, I found myself turning and doubling along these dark and narrow passages, which seemed really to have no end, and justly to entitle the place to its name of El Laberinto.

I was not entirely free from the apprehension of starting some wild animal, and moved slowly and very cautiously. In the mean time, in turning the corners, my twine would be entangled, and the Indians, moved by the probability of getting no pay, entered to clear it, and by degrees all came up with me in a body. I got a glimpse of their torches behind me just as I was turning into a new passage, and at the moment I was startled by a noise which sent me back rather quickly, and completely routed them. It proceeded from a rushing of bats, and, having a sort of horror of these beastly birds, this was an ugly place to meet them in, for the passage was so low, and there was so little room for a flight over head, that in walking upright there was great danger of their striking the face. It was neccesary to move with head bent down, and protecting the lights from the flapping of their wings.

They continued into the cave until they came to a place where the roof had fallen in and completely blocked the passage.

In a spirit of utter disappointment, I pointed out to the Indians the mass of earth that, as it were, maliciously cut off all my hopes, and told them to put an end to their lying stories about the Laberinto and its having no end; and in my disappointment I began to feel most sensibly the excessive heat and closeness of the place, which I had hardly perceived before, and which now became almost insufferable from the smoke of the torches and the Indians choking the narrow passage.

All that I could do, and that was very unsatisfactory, was to find out the plan of this subterraneous structure. I had with me a pocket compass, and, notwithstanding the heat and smoke, and the little help that the Indians afforded me, under all annoyances, and with the sweat dropping on my memorandum book, I measured back to the door.

Having heard the place spoken of as a subterraneous construction, and seeing, when I reached the ground, a half-buried door with a mass of overgrown earth above it, it had not occurred to me to think otherwise; but on examining outside, I found that what I had taken for an irregular natural formation, like a hill-side, was a pyramidal mound of the same general character with all the rest we had seen in the country. Making the Indians clear away some thorn-bushes, with the help of the branches of a tree growing near I climbed up it. On the top were the ruins of a building, the same as all the others. The door of El Laberinto, instead of opening into a hill-side, opened into this mound, and, as near as I could judge from the ruins along the base, was ten feet high, and the Laberinto, instead of being subterraneous, or, rather, under the surface of the earth, was in the body of this mound. Heretofore it had been our impression that these mounds were solid and compact masses of stone and earth, without any chambers or structures of any kind, and the discovery of this gave rise to the exciting idea that all the great mounds scattered over the country contained secret, unknown, and hidden chambers, presenting an immense field for exploration and discovery, and, ruined as the buildings on their summits were, perhaps the only source left for acquiring knowledge of the people by whom the cities were constructed.

At three o'clock I resumed my journey toward Uxmal. For a short distance the road lay along the ridge of the sierra, a mere bed of rock, on which the horse's hoofs clattered and rang at every step. Coming out upon the brow of the sierra, we had one of those grand views which everywhere present themselves from this mountain range; an immense wooded plain, in this place broken only by a small spot like a square on a chessboard, the clearing of the hacienda of Santa Cruz. We descended the sierra, and at the foot of it struck the camino real.

At half past six we reached the village of Opocheque. In the centre of the plaza was a large fountain, at which women were drawing water, and on one side was a Mestizo family, with two men playing the guitar. We stopped for a cup of water, and then, pushing on by a bright moonlight, at nine o'clock reached the village of Moona.

Early the next morning we resumed our course. Immediately behind the village we crossed the sierra, the same broken and stony range, commanding on both sides the same grand view of a boundless wooded plain. In an hour we saw at a distance on our left the high mound of ruins visible from the House of the Dwarf, known under the Indian name of Xcoch. About five miles before arriving at Uxmal, I saw on the right another high mound. The intervening space was covered with trees and thorn-bushes, but I reached it without dismounting. On the top were two buildings about eighteen feet each, with the upper part of the outer walls fallen. Of both, the inner part was entire.

At twelve o'clock I reached Uxmal.

The ruins of Uxmal presented themselves to me as a home, and I looked upon them with more interest than before. I had found the wrecks of cities scattered more numerously than I expected, but they were all so shattered that no voice of instruction issued from them; here they still stood, tottering and crumbling, but living memorials, more worthy than ever of investigation and study, and as I then thought, not knowing what others more distant, of which we had heard, might prove, perhaps the only existing vestiges that could transmit to posterity the image of an American city.

As I approached, I saw on the terrace our beds, with moscheto-nets fluttering in the wind, and trunks and boxes all turned out of doors, having very much the appearance of a forcible ejectment or ouster for non-payment of rent; but on arriving I found that my companions were *moving*. In the great sala, with its three doors, they had found themselves too much exposed to the heavy dews and night air, and they were about removing to a smaller apartment, being that next to the last on the south wing, which had but one door, and could more easily be kept dry by a fire.

During my absence an addition had been made to our household in a servant forwarded from Merida by the active kindness of the Doña Joaquina Peon. He was a dark Mestizo named Albino, short and thick, and so near being squint-eyed that at the first glance I thought him a subject for Doctor Cabot to practise on.

In the afternoon we were comfortably settled in our new quarters. We continued the precaution of kindling a fire in one corner, to drive away malaria, and at night we had a bonfire out of doors.

CHAPTER XI

Arrival of Don Simon — Subterraneous Chambers — More Practice
in Surgery

The next day I resumed my occupation of superintending the Indians.
It was, perhaps, the hardest labour I had in that country to look on and see
them work, and it was necessary to be with them all the time; for if not watched,
they would not work at all.

The next day opened with a drizzling rain, the beginning of the prevailing
storm of the country, called El Norte. This storm, we were told, rarely occurred
at this season, and the mayoral said that after it was over, the regular dry season
would certainly set in. The thermometer fell to fifty-two, and to our feelings
the change was much for the better. In fact, we had begun to feel a degree
of lassitude, the effect of the excessive heat, and this change restored and
reinvigorated us.

This day, too, with the beginning of the storm, Don Simon arrived from
Jalacho, according to promise, to pay us a visit. He was not in the habit of
visiting Uxmal at this season, and though less fearful than other members of his
family, he was not without apprehensions on account of the health of the place.
In fact, he had suffered much himself from an illness contracted there.

Throughout the ruins circular holes were found at different places in the
ground, opening into chambers underneath, which had never been examined,
and the character of which was entirely unknown. We had noticed them, at the
time of our former visit, on the platform of the great terrace; and though this
platform was now entirely overgrown, and many of them were hidden from
sight, in opening a path to communicate with the hacienda we had laid bare
two. The mayoral had lately discovered another at some distance outside the
wall, so perfect at the mouth, and apparently so deep on sounding it with a
stone, that Don Simon wished to explore it.

The next morning he came to the ruins with Indians, ropes, and candles,
and we began immediately with one of those on the platform before the Casa
del Gobernador. The opening was a circular hole, eighteen inches in diameter.
The throat consisted of five layers of stones, a yard deep, to a stratum of solid
rock. As it was all dark beneath, before descending, in order to guard against
the effects of impure air, we let down a candle, which soon touched bottom.
The only way of descending was to tie a rope around the body, and be lowered

by the Indians. In this way I was let down, and almost before my head had passed through the hole my feet touched the top of a heap of rubbish, high directly under the hole, and falling off at the sides. Clambering down it, I found myself in a round chamber, so filled with rubbish that I could not stand upright. With a candle in my hand, I crawled all round on my hands and knees. The chamber was in the shape of a dome, and had been coated with plaster, most of which had fallen, and now encumbered the ground. The depth could not be ascertained without clearing out the interior. In groping about I found pieces of broken pottery, and a vase of terra cotta, about one foot in diameter, of good workmanship, and having upon it a coat of enamel, which, though not worn off, had lost some of its brightness. It had three feet, each about an inch high, one of which is broken. In other respects it was entire.

The discovery of this vase was encouraging. Not one of these places had ever been explored. Neither Don Simon nor any of the Indians knew anything about them, and, entering them now for the first time, we were excited by the hope that we had discovered a rich mine of curious and interesting fabrics wrought by the inhabitants of this ruined city. Besides this, we had already ascertained one point in regard to which we were doubtful before. This great terrace was not entirely artificial.

Descending the terrace, and passing behind the high and nameless mound which towers between the Casa del Gobernador and Casa de Palomos, the Indians cleared away some bushes, and brought us to another opening, but a few feet from the path we had cut through, entirely hidden from view until the clearing was made. The mouth was similar to that of the first; the throat about a yard deep, and the Indians lowered me down, without any obstruction, to the bottom.

The Indians looked upon our entering these places as senseless and foolhardy, and, besides imaginary dangers, they talked of snakes, scorpions, and hornets, the last of which, from the experience we had had of them in different parts of the ruins, were really objects of fear; for a swarm of them coming upon a man in such a place, would almost murder him before he could be hauled out.

It did not, however, require much time to explore this vault. It was clear of rubbish, perfect and entire in all its parts, without any symptoms of decay, and to all appearances, after the lapse of unknown years, fit for the uses to which it was originally applied. Like the one on the terrace, it was domeshaped, and the sides fell in a little toward the bottom, like a well-made haystack. The height was ten feet and six inches directly under the mouth, and it was seventeen feet six inches in diameter. The walls and ceiling were plastered, still in a good state of preservation, and the floor was of hard mortar. Don Simon and Dr. Cabot were lowered down, and we examined every part thoroughly.

Leaving this, we went on to a third, which was exactly the same, except it was a little smaller, being only five yards in diameter.

The fourth was the one which had just been discovered, and which had excited the curiosity of the mayoral. It was a few feet outside of a wall which, as Don Simon said, might be traced through the woods, broken and ruined, until it met and enclosed within its circle the whole of the principal buildings. The mouth was covered with cement, and in the throat was a large stone filling it up, which the mayoral, on discovering it, had thrown in to prevent horses or cattle from falling through. A rope was passed under the stone, and it was hauled out. The throat was smaller than any of the others, and hardly large enough to pass the body of a man. In shape and finish it was exactly the ame as the others, with perhaps a slight shade of difference in the dimensions. The smallness of this mount was, to my mind, strong proof that these subterraneous chambers had never been intended for any purposes which required men to descend into them.

We were extremely disappointed in not finding any more vases or relics of any kind. We could not account for the one found in the chamber under the terrace, and were obliged to suppose that it had been thrown in or got there by accident.

These subterraneous chambers are scattered over the whole ground covered by the ruined city. There was one in the cattleyard before the hacienda, and the Indians were constantly discovering them at greater distances.

That they were constructed for some specific purpose, had some definite object, and that that object was uniform, there was no doubt, but what it was, in our ignorance of the habits of the people, it was difficult to say. Don Simon thought that the cement was not hard enough to hold water, and hence that they were not intended as cisterns or reservoirs, but for granaries or store-houses of maize, which, from our earliest knowledge of the aborigines down to the present day, has been the staff of life to the inhabitants. In this opinion, however, we did not concur, and from what we saw afterward, believe that they were intended as cisterns, and had furnished, in part at least, a supply of water to the people of the ruined city.

That afternoon they went with Don Simon to watch the corn being harvested in a large field in front of the Governor's Palace of Uxmal.

The next day we had another welcome visiter in our fellow-passenger, Mr. Camerden, who was just from Campeachy, where he had seen New-York papers to the third of November. Knowing our deep interest in the affairs of our country, and postponing his own curiosity about the ruins, he hastened to communicate to us the result of the city elections, viz., a contest in the sixth ward and entire uncertainty which party was uppermost.

Mr. Camerden and Don Simon returned to the hacienda for the night. The explorers joined them next day as Dr. Cabot's services were needed.

The next day Doctor Cabot had a professional engagement at the hacienda. In both my expeditions into that region of country our medical department was incomplete. On the former occasion we had a medicine-chest, but no doctor, and this time we had a doctor, but no medicine-chest. This necessary appendage had been accidentally left on board the ship, and did not come to our hands till some time afterward. We had only a small stock purchased in Merida, and on this account, as well as because it interfered with his other pursuits, the doctor had avoided entering into general practice. He was willing to attend to cases that might be cured by a single operation, but the principle diseases were fevers, which could not be cut out with a knife. The day before, however, a young Indian came to the ruins on an errand to Don Simon, who had a leg swollen with varicose veins. He stood at that time in an interesting position, being about to be married. Don Simon had had him at Merida six months, under the care of a physician, but without any good result, and the young man was taking his chance for better or worse, almost with the certainty of becoming in a few years disabled, and a mass of corruption. Doctor Cabot undertook to perform an operation, for which purpose it was necessary to go to the hacienda; and, that we might return with Mr. Camerden, we all went there to breakfast.

Breakfast over, the doctor's patient was brought forward. He was not consulted on the subject of the operation, and had no wish of his own about it, but did as his master ordered him.

The disease was in his right leg, which was almost as thick as his body, covered with ulcers, and the distended veins stood out like whipcords. Doctor Cabot considered it necessary to cut two veins. The Indian stood up, resting the whole weight of his body on the diseased leg, so as to bring them out to the fullest, and supporting himself by leaning with his hands on a bench. One vein was cut, the wound bound up, and then the operation was performed on the other by thrusting a stout pin into the flesh under the vein, and bringing it out on the other side, then winding a thread round the protruding head and point, and leaving the pin to cut its way through the vein and fester out. The leg was then bound tight, and the Indian laid upon the bed. During the whole time not a muscle of his face moved, and, except at the moment when the pin was thrust under the vein, when his hand contracted on the bench, it could not have been told that he was undergoing an operation of any kind.

This over, we set out on our return with Mr. Camerden to the ruins, but hardly left the gate of the cattle-yard, when we met an Indian with his arm in a sling, coming in search of Doctor Cabot. A death-warrant seemed written in his face. His little wife, a girl about fourteen years old, soon to become a mother, was trotting beside him. A few days before, by some awkwardness, he had given his left arm a severe cut near the elbow with a machete. To stop the bleeding, his wife had tied one string as tightly as possible around the wrist, and another in the hollow of the arm, and so it had remained three days. The treatment had been pretty effectual in stopping the bleeding, and it had very nearly stopped the circulation of his blood forever. The hand was shrunken to nothing, and seemed withered; the part of the arm between the two ligatures was swollen enormously, and the seat of the wound was a mass of corruption.

The man had cut an arterial vein. Doctor Cabot had no instruments with him with which to take it up, and, grasping the arm with a strong pressure on the vein, so as to stop the flow of blood, he transferred the arm to me, fixing my fingers upon the vein, and requesting me to hold it in that position while he ran to the ruins for his instruments. This was by no means pleasant. If I lost the right pressure, the man might bleed to death; and, having no regular diploma warranting people to die on my hands, not willing to run the risk of any accident, and knowing the imperturbable character of the Indians, I got the arm transferred to one of them, with a warning that the man's life depended upon him. Doctor Cabot was gone more than half an hour, and during all that time, while the patient's head was falling on his shoulder with fainting fits, the Indian looked directly in his face, and held up the arm with a fixedness of attitude that would have served as a model for a sculptor. I do not believe that, for a single moment, the position of the arm varied a hair's breadth.

Doctor Cabot dressed the wound, and the Indian was sent away, with an even chance, as the doctor considered, for life or death. The next that we heard of him, however. he was at work in the fields; certainly, but for the accidental visit of Doctor Cabot, he would have been in his grave.

CHAPTER XII

Aguadas — Manner of Living at the Ruins — Visit from the Cura of
Ticul — A painful Journey — Arrival at the Convent

In the account of my former visit to the ruins of Uxmal, I mentioned
the fact that this was entirely destitute of apparent means for obtaining water.
Within the whole circumference there is no well, stream, or fountain, and nothing which bears the appearance of having been used for supplying or obtaining
water, except the subterraneous chambers before referred to; which, supposing
them to have been intended for that purpose, would probably not have been
sufficient, however numerous, to supply the wants of so large a population.

Very soon after our arrival our attention and inquiries were directed particularly to this subject, and we were not long in satisfying ourselves that the
principal supply had been drawn from aguadas, or ponds, in the neighbourhood.
These aguadas are now neglected and overgrown, and perhaps, to a certain
extent, are the cause of the unhealthiness of Uxmal.

> They climbed to the top of the House of the Dwarf, and from there saw
> the main aguada, which they visited with Indians cutting a way through
> the undergrowth. The mayoral told them that this aguada was connected
> to others further south.
>
> They were also interested in the aguada for another reason: they
> needed a bath. So, chosing a small cove shaded by a large tree, they had
> a space cleared and a good path cut all the way to the Governor's Palace.

The general opinion with regard to these aguadas is the same with that
expressed by the cura of Tekoh respecting that near Mayapan; viz., that they
were "hechas á mano," artificial formations or excavations made by the ancient
inhabitants as reservoirs for holding water. The mayoral told us that in the dry
season, when the water was low, the remains of stone embankments were still
visible in several places. As yet we were incredulous as to their being at all
artificial, but we had no difficulty in believing that they had furnished the inhabitants of Uxmal with water.

Up to this time our manner of living at the ruins had been very uniform,
and our means abundant. All that was on the hacienda belonging to the master
was ours, as were also the services of the Indians, so far as he had a right to
command them. The property of the master consisted of cattle, horses, mules,

Fig. 11

and corn, of which only the last could be counted as provisions. Some of the Indians had a few fowls, pigs, and turkeys of their own, which they were in general willing to sell, and every morning those who came out to work brought with them water, fowls, eggs, lard, green beans, and milk. Occasionally we had a haunch of venison, and Doctor Cabot added to our larder several kinds of ducks, wild turkeys, chachalachas, quails, pigeons, doves, parrots, jays, and other smaller birds. Besides these, we received from time to time a present from the Doña Joaquina or Don Simon, and altogether our living was better than we had ever known in exploring ruins. Latterly, however, on account of the thickness of the woods, Doctor Cabot had become disgusted with sporting; having no dog, it was sometimes impossible to find one bird out of six, and he confined his shooting to birds which he wanted for dissection. At this time, too, we received intelligence that the fowls at the hacienda were running short, and the eggs gave out altogether.

There was no time to be lost, and we forthwith despatched Albino with an Indian to the village of Moona, twelve miles distant, who returned with a back-load of eggs, beans, rice, and sugar, and again the sun went down upon us in the midst of plenty.

On a line with the back of the Casa del Gobernador rises a high and nameless mound forming one of the grandest and most imposing structures among all the ruins of Uxmal. It was at that time covered with trees and a thick growth of herbage, which gave a gloominess to its grandeur of proportions, and, but for its regularity, and a single belt of sculptured stones barely visible at the top, it would have passed for a wooded and grass-grown hill. Taking some Indians with me, I ascended this mound, and began clearing it for Mr. Catherwood to draw. I found that its vast sides were all incased with stone, in some places richly ornamented, but completely hidden from view by the foliage.

The height of this mound was sixty-five feet, and it measured at the base three hundred feet on one side and two hundred on the other. On the top was a great platform of solid stone, three feet high and seventy-five feet square, and about fifteen feet from the top was a narrow terrace running on all four of the sides. The walls of the platform were of smooth stone, and the corners had sculptured ornaments. The great structure seemed raised only for the purpose of holding aloft this platform. Probably it had been the scene of grand religious ceremonies, and stained with the blood of human victims offered up in sight of the assembled people.

Around the top of the mound was a border of sculptured stone ten or twelve feet high. The principal ornament was the Grecque, and in following it round, and clearing away the trees and bushes, on the west side, opposite the courtyard of the Casa de Palomos, my attention was arrested by an ornament, the lower part of which was buried in rubbish fallen from above.

Stephens gave the Indians instructions to clear away the earth and stones that covered the lower part of the ornament.

The ornament proved to be the same hideous face, with the teeth standing out, before presented, varying somewhat in detail, and upon a grander scale. Throwing up the dirt upon the other side of them, the Indians had made a great pile outside, and stood in a deep hole against the face of the ornament. At this depth the stones seemed hanging loosely over their heads, and the Indians intimated that it was dangerous to continue digging, but by this time my impatience was beyond control. I had from time to time assisted in the work, and, urging them to continue, I threw myself into the hole, and commenced digging with all my strength. The stones went rolling and crashing down the side of the mound, striking against roots and tearing off branches. The perspiration rolled from me in a stream, but I was so completely carried away by the idea that had taken possession of me, so sure of entering some chamber that had been closed for ages, that I stopped at nothing. Before getting below the cornice I thrust the machete through the earth, and found no opening, but a solid stone wall. The ground of my hope was gone, but still I kept the Indians digging, unconsciously, and without any object. In the interest of the moment I was not aware that the clouds had disappeared, and that I had been working in this deep hole, without a breath of air, under the full blaze of a vertical sun. The disappointment and reaction after the high excitement, co-operating with the fatigue and heat, prostrated all my strength. I felt a heaviness and depression, and was actually sick at heart. With great difficulty I dragged myself to our apartments. My thirst was unquenchable, I threw myself into my hammock, and in a few moments a fiery fever was upon me. Our household was thrown into consternaton. Disease had stalked all around us, but it was the first time it had knocked at our door.

On the third day, while in the midst of a violent attack, a gentleman arrived whose visit I had expected, and had looked forward to with great interest. It was the cura Carillo of Ticul, a village seven leagues distant. A week after our arrival at the ruins, the mayoral had received a letter from him, asking whether a visit would be acceptable to us. We had heard of him as a person who took more interest in the antiquities of the country than almost any other, and who possessed more knowledge on the subject. His first words to me were, that it was necessary for me to leave the place and go with him to Ticul. I was extremely reluctant to do so, but it was considered advisable by all. He would not consent to my going alone, or with his servant, and the next morning, instead of a pleasant visit to the ruins, he found himself trotting home with a sick man at his heels. In consequence of some misunderstanding, no coché was in readiness, and I set out on horseback. In the beginning of our ride, I listened with much interest to the cura's exposition of different and localities but by degrees my attention flagged, and finally my whole soul was fixed on the sierra, which stood out before us at a distance of two leagues from San José. My pains increased as we advanced, and I dismounted at the hacienda in a state impossible to be described. The mayoral was away, the doors were all locked, and I lay down on some bags in the corridor. Rest tranquillized me. There was but one Indian to be found, and he told the cura that there were none to make a coché. Those in the neighbourhood were sick, and the others were at work more than a league away. It was impossible to continue on horseback, and, fortunately, the mayoral came, who changed the whole face of things and in a few minutes had men engaged in making a coché. The cura went on before to prepare for my reception. In an hour my coché was ready, and at five o'clock I crawled in. My carriers were loth to start, but, once under way, they took it in good part, and set off on a trot. Changing shoulders frequently, they never stopped till they carried me into Ticul, three leagues or nine miles distant, and laid me down on the floor of the convent. The cura was waiting to receive me. Albino had arrived with my catre, which was already set up, and in a few minutes I was in bed.

For three days I did not leave my bed; but on the fourth I breathed the air from the balcony of the convent. It was fresh, pure, balmy, and invigorating.

In the afternoon of the next day I set out with the cura for a stroll. We had gone but a short distance, when an Indian came running after us to inform us that another of the caballeros had arrived sick from the ruins. We hurried back, and found Doctor Cabot lying in a coché on the floor of the corridor at the door of the convent. He crawled out labouring under a violent fever, increased by the motion and fatigue of his ride. He had been attacked the day after I left, and the fever had been upon him, with but little intermission, ever since. All night, and all the two ensuing days, it continued rising and decreasing, but never leaving him. It was attended with constant restlessness and delirium, so that he was hardly in bed before he was up again, pitching about the room.

The next day Mr. Catherwood forwarded Albino, who, with two attacks, was shaken and sweated into a dingy-looking white man. Mr. Catherwood wrote that he was entirely alone at the ruins, and should hold out as long as he could agains fever and ghosts, but with the first attack should come up and join us.

The cura watched the doctor carefully, but without venturing to offer advice to a medico who could cure biscos, but the third day he alarmed me by the remark that the expression of the doctor's face was *fatál*. In Spanish this only means very bad, but it had always in my ears an uncomfortable sound. I inquired of the cura about the mode of treatment in the country, and whether he could not prescribe for him. Doctor Cabot had never seen anything of this disease, particularly as affected by climate. Besides, he was *hors de combat* on account of the absence of our medicine-chest, and in such constant pain and delirium that he was in no condition to prescribe for himself.

The cura was the temporal as well as spiritual physician of the village; there were daily applications to him for medicine, and he was constantly visiting the sick. Doctor Cabot was willing to put himself entirely into his hands, and he administered a preparation which I mention for the benefit of future travellers who may be caught without a medicine-chest. It was a simple decoction of the rind of the sour orange flavoured with cinnamon and lemon-juice, of which he administered a tumblerful warm every two hours. At the second draught the doctor was thrown into a profuse perspiration. For the first time since his attack the fever left him, and he had an unbroken sleep. On waking, copious draughts of tamarind water were given; when the fever came on again the decoction was repeated, with tamarind water in the intervals. The effect of this treatment was particularly happy, and it is desirable for strangers to know it, for the sour orange is found in every part of the country, and from what we saw of it then and afterward, it is, perhaps, a better remedy for fever in that climate than any known in foreign pharmacy.

Stephens was struck by the peace and charm of the place.

The village of Ticul, to which we were thus accidentally driven, was worthy of the visit, once in his life, of a citizen of New-York. The first time I looked upon it from the balcony of the convent, it struck me as the perfect picture of stillness and repose. The plaza was overgrown with grass; a few mules, with their fore feet hoppled, were pasturing upon it, and at long intervals a single horseman crossed it. The balcony of the convent was on a level with the tops of the houses, and the view was of a great plain, with houses of one story, flat roofs, high garden walls, above which orange, lemon, and plantain trees were growing, and, after the loud ringing of the matin and vesper bell was over, the only noise was the singing of birds.

Like all the Spanish villages, it was laid out with its plaza and streets running at right angles, and was distinguished among the villages of Yucatan for its casas de piedra, or stone houses. These were on the plaza and streets adjoining; and back, extending more than a mile each way, were the huts of the Indians.

The church and convent occupy the whole of one side of the plaza. Both were built by the Franciscan monks, and they are among the grandest of those gigantic buildings with which that powerful order marked its entrance into the country.

The convent is connected with the church by a spacious corridor. It is a gigantic structure, built entirely of stone, with massive walls, and four hundred feet in length. The entrance is under a noble portico, with high stone pillars, from which ascends a broad stone staircase to a spacious corridor twenty feet wide. This corridor runs through the whole length of the building, with a stone pavement, and is lighted in two places by a dome. On each side are cloisters, once occupied by a numerous body of Franciscan friars.

In the pavement of the great corridor, in the galleries, walls, and roof, both of the church and convent, are stones from ancient buildings, and no doubt both were constructed with materials furnished by the ruined edifices of another race, but when, or how, or under what circumstances, is unknown. On the roof the cura had discovered, in a situation which would hardly have attracted any eyes but his own, a square stone, having roughly engraved on it this inscription:

26
Marzo,
1625.

Perhaps this had reference to the date of the construction, and if so, it is the only known record that exists in relation to it; and the thought almost unavoidably occurs, that where such obscurity exists in regard to a building constructed by the Spaniards but little more than two hundred years ago, how much darker must be the cloud that hangs over the ruined cities of the aborigines, erected, if not ruined, before the conquest.

CHAPTER XIII

Another ruined City — Discovery of a Skeleton and Vase — The Seybo
Tree.

It was fortunate for the particular objects of our expedition that, go
where we would in this country, the monuments of its ancient inhabitants were
before our eyes. Near the village of Ticul, almost in the suburbs, are the ruins
of another ancient and unknown city. From the time of our arrival the memorials of it had been staring us in the face. The cura had some sculptured stones
of new and exceedingly pretty design; and heads, vases, and other relics, found
in excavating the ruins, were fixed in the fronts of houses as ornaments. My
first stroll with the cura was to these ruins.

At the end of a long street leading out beyond the campo santo we turned
to the right by a narrow path, overgrown with bushes covered with wild flowers,
and on which birds of beautiful plumage were sitting, but so infested with garrapatas that we had to keep brushing them off continually with the bough of
a tree.

This path led us to the hacienda of San Francisco, the property of a
gentleman of the village, who had reared the walls of a large building, but had
never finished it.

A short distance in the rear of the hacienda were the ruins of another city,
desolate and overgrown, having no name except that of the hacienda on which
they stand. At this time a great part of the city was completely hidden by the
thick foliage of the trees. Near by, however, several mounds were in full sight,
dilapidated, and having fragments of walls on the top. We ascended the highest,
which commanded a magnificent view of the great wooded plain, and at a
distance the towers of the church of Ticul rising darkly above.

From the great destruction of the buildings, I thought it unprofitable to attempt any exploration of these ruins, especially considering the insalubrity of
the place and our own crippled state. In the excavations constantly going on,
objects of interest were from time to time discovered, one of which, a vase,
was loaned to us to make a drawing of. Figure 12 represents two sides of the
vase; on one side is a border of hieroglyphics, with sunken lines running to
the bottom, and on the other the reader will observe that the face portrayed
bears a strong resemblance to those of the sculptured and stuccoed figures at
Palenque: the headdress, too, is a plume of feathers, and the hand is held out

FIG. 12

in the same stiff position. The vase is four and a half inches high, and five inches in diameter. It is of admirable workmanship, and realizes the account given by Herrera of the markets at the Mexican city of Tlascala. "There were gold-smiths, feather-men, barbers, baths, and *as good earthenware as in Spain.*"

It was not yet considered safe for me to return to Uxmal, and the sight of these vases induced me to devote a few days to excavating among the ruins. My great desire was to discover an ancient sepulchre, which we had sought in vain among the ruins of Uxmal. These were not to be looked for in the large mounds, or, at all events, it was a work of too much labour to attempt opening one of them. At length, after a careful examination, the cura selected one, upon which we began.

It was a square stone structure, with sides four feet high, and the top was rounded over with earth and stones bedded in it.

The Indians commenced picking out the stones and clearing away the earth with their hands. Fortunately, they had a crowbar, an instrument unknown in

FIG. 13

Central America, but indispensable here on account of the stony nature of the soil. We continued the work six hours, and the whole appearance of things was so rude that we began to despair of success, when, on prying up a large flat stone, we saw underneath a skull. The reader may imagine our satisfaction. We made the Indians throw away crowbar and machete, and work with their hands. I was exceedingly anxious to get the skeleton out, entire, but it was impossible to do so. It had no covering or envelope of any kind; the earth was thrown upon it as in a common grave, and as this was removed it all fell to pieces.

In collecting the bones, one of the Indians picked up a small white object, which would have escaped any but an Indian's eye. It was made of deer's horn, about two inches long, sharp at the point, with an eye at the other end. They all called it a needle, and the reason of their immediate and unhesitating opinion was the fact that the Indians of the present day use needles of the same material, two of which the cura procured for me on our return to the convent.

In digging round it and on the other side, at some little distance from the skeleton we found a large vase of rude pottery, resembling very much the cantaro used by the Indians now as a water-jar. It may have contained water or the heart of the skeleton.

They went on digging for two more days, but did not discover anything else.

However, among the ruins they did discover circular holes in the ground like those at Uxmal, and Stephens went down into one of them. The Indians here knew that they had been used to store rainwater and called them chultunes, *or wells.*

The last day we returned from the ruins earlier than usual, and stopped at the campo santo. In front stood a noble seybo tree. I had been anxious to learn something of the growth of this tree, but had never had an opportunity of doing it before. The cura told me that it was then twenty-three years old. Figure 13 represents this tree. We had found trees like it growing on the tops of the ruined structures at Copan and Palenque, and many had for that reason ascribed to the buildings a very great antiquity. This tree completely removed all doubts which I might have entertained, and confirmed me in the opinion I had before expressed, that no correct judgment could be formed of the antiquity of these buildings from the size of the trees growing upon them.

CHAPTER XIV

Departure from Ticul — Ruins of Nohpat — Return to Uxmal —
General Description of the Ruins.

The next day was Sunday, which I passed in making preparations for returning to Uxmal. I had, however, some distraction. In the morning the quiet of the village was a little disturbed by intelligence of a revolution in Tekax, a town nine leagues distant. Our sojourn in the country had been so quiet that it seemed unnatural, and a small revolution was necessary to make me feel at home. The insurgents had deposed the alcalde, appointed their own authorities, and laid contributions upon the inhabitants, and the news was that they intended marching three hundred men against Merida, to extort an acknowledgment of independence. Ticul lay in their line of march, but as it was considered very uncertain whether they would carry this doughty purpose into execution, I determined not to change my plan.

The next morning I bade farewell to the cura, with an understanding, that as soon as Doctor Cabot was able to return, the good padre would accompany him to finish his interrupted visit to us at Uxmal. My time at Ticul had not been lost. Besides exploring the ruins of San Francisco, I had received accounts of others from the cura, which promised to add greatly to the interest of our expedition.

That I might take a passing view of one of these places on my return to Uxmal, I determined to go back by a different road, across the sierra, which rises a short distance from the village of Ticul. In an hour I reached the top of the sierra, Looking back, my last view of the plain presented, high above everything else, the church and convent which I had left. I was an hour crossing the sierra, and on the other side my first view of the great plain took in the church of Nohcacab, standing like a colossus in the wilderness, the only token to indicate the presence of man. Descending to the plain, I saw nothing but trees, until, when close upon the village, the great church again rose before me, towering above the houses, and the only object visible.

The village was under the pastoral charge of the cura of Ticul, and in the suburbs I met his ministro on horseback, waiting, according to the directions of the former, to escort me to the ruins of Nohpat. At a league's distance we turned off from the main road, and, following a narrow path leading to some milpas, in fifteen minutes we saw towering before us lofty but shattered buildings, the relics of another ruined city. I saw at a glance that it would be indispensable for Mr. Catherwood to visit them. Nevertheless, I passed three hours on the ground, toiling in the hot sun, and at four o'clock, with strong apprehensions of another attack of fever, I mounted to continue my journey.

A little before dark I emerged from the woods, and saw Mr. Catherwood standing on the platform of the Casa del Gobernador, the sole tenant of the ruins of Uxmal. His Indians had finished their day's work, Bernaldo and Chiapa Chi had gone, and since Doctor Cabot left he had slept alone in our quarters.

During this time Catherwood had been busy making his drawings without any problems, and Stephens found him in good health.

On the twenty-fourth of December Doctor Cabot returned from Ticul, bringing back with him Albino, who was still in a rueful plight. Unfortunatley, the cura Carillo was unwell, and unable to accompany him, but had promised to follow in a few days. On Christmas eve we were all once more together, and Christmas Day, in spite of ourselves, was a holyday. No Indians came out to work.

Unable to do anything at the ruins, I walked down to the hacienda to see one of our horses which had a sore back. The hacienda was deserted, but the sound of violins led me to the place where the Indians were congregated. Preparations were making on a large scale for the evening feast. The place looked like a butcher's shambles, for they had cut up what had once composed eight turkeys, two hogs, and I do not know how many fowls.

The account of our residence at Uxmal is now drawing to a close, and it is time to bring before the reader the remainder of the ruins.

I have already mentioned the Casa del Gobernador and the Casa de las Tortugas, or House of the Turtles, the latter of which stands on the grand platform of the second terrace of the Casa del Gobernador, at the northwest corner.

Descending from this building, and on a line with the doorway of the Casa de las Monjas, going north, at the distance of two hundred and forty feet are two ruined edifices facing each other, and seventy feet apart, as laid down on the general plan of the ruins. Each is one hundred and twenty-eight feet long, and thirty feet deep, and, so far as they can be made out, they appear to have been exactly alike in plan and ornament. The sides facing each other were embellished with sculpture, and there remain on both the fragments of entwined colossal serpents, which ran the whole length of the walls.

In the centre of each façade, at points directly opposite each other, are the fragments of a great stone ring. Each of these rings was four feet in diameter, and secured in the wall by a stone tenon of corresponding dimensions. They appear to have been broken wilfully; of each, the part nearest the stem still projects from the wall, and the outer surface is covered with sculptured characters. We made excavations among the ruins along the base of the walls, in hope of discovering the missing parts of these rings, but without success.

These structures have no doorways or openings of any kind, either on the sides or at the ends. In the belief that they must have interior chambers, we made a breach in the wall of the one on the east to the depth of eight or ten feet, but we found only rough stones, hanging so loosely together as to make it dangerous for the Indians to work in the holes, and they were obliged to discontinue.

This excavation, however, carried us through nearly one third of the structure, and satisfied us that these great parallel edifices did not contain any interior apartments, but that each consisted merely of four great walls, filled up with a solid mass of stones. It was our opinion that they had been built expressly with reference to the two great rings facing each other in the façades, and that the space between was intended for the celebration of some public games, in which opinion we were afterward confirmed.

Stephens was on the right track since the building he refers to is the Ball Court. *This consists of two parallel structures and benches with sloping walls run along the bottom of each. These are joined to the main walls, which are plain on the inner sides. The stone rings through which the ball had to be shot are set in either wall and are decorated with glyphs that were later deciphered by Alberto Ruz as 649 AD.*

Passing between these buildings, and continuing in the same direction, we reach the front of the Casa de las Monjas, or House of the Nuns.

This building is quadrangular, with a courtyard in the centre. It stands on the highest of three terraces. The lowest is three feet high and twenty wide; the second, twelve feet high and forty-five feet wide; and the third, four feet high and five feet wide, extending the whole length of the front of the building.

The front is two hundred and seventy-nine feet long, and above the cornice, from one end to the other, it is ornamented with sculpture. In the centre is a gateway ten feet eight inches wide, spanned by the triangular arch, and leading to the courtyard. On each side of this gateway are four doorways with wooden lintels, opening to apartments averaging twenty-four feet long, ten feet wide, and seventeen feet high to the top of the arch, but having no communication with each other.

The building that forms the right or eastern side of the quadrangle is one hundred and fifty-eight feet long; that on the left is one hundred and seventy-three feet long, and the range opposite or at the end of the quadrangle measures two hundred and sixty-four feet.

These three ranges of buildings have no doorways outside, but the exterior

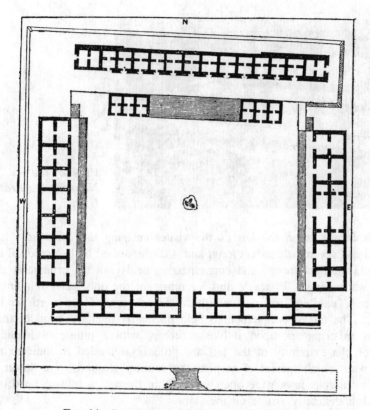

FIG. 14 PLAN OF THE COURTYARD. UXMAL

of each is a dead wall, and above the cornice all are ornamented with the same rich and elaborate sculpture. On the exterior of the range last mentioned, the designs are simple, and among them are two rude, naked figures.

Such is the exterior of this building. Passing through the arched gateway, we enter a noble courtyard, with four great façades looking down upon it, each ornamented from one end to the other with the richest and most intricate carving known in the art of the builders of Uxmal; presenting a scene of strange magnificence, surpassing any that is now to be seen among its ruins. This courtyard is two hundred and fourteen feet wide, and two hundred and fifty-eight feet deep.

Among my many causes of regret for the small scale on which I am obliged to present these drawings, none is stronger than the consequent inability to present, with all their detail of ornament, the four great façades fronting this courtyard. There is but one alleviating circumstance; which is, that the side most richly ornamented is so ruined that, under any circumstances, it could not be presented entire.

View of the Nunnery Quadrangle, Uxmal.

This façade is on the left of the visiter entering the courtyard. It is one hundred and seventy-three feet long, and is distinguished by two colossal serpents entwined, running through and encompassing nearly all the ornaments throughout its whole length. Plates V and VI represent the only parts remaining.

Plate V exhibits that portion of the façade toward the north end of the building. The tail of one serpent is held up nearly over the head of the other, and has an ornament upon it like a turban, with a plume of feathers. The marks on the extremity of the tail are probably intended to indicate a rattle-snake, with which species of serpent the country abounds. The lower serpent has its monstrous jaws wide open, and within them is a human head, the face of which is distinctly visible on the stone.

Plate VI represents the two entwined serpents enclosing and running through the ornaments over a doorway. The principal feature in the ornament enclosed is the figure of a human being, standing, but much mutilated. The bodies of the serpents, according to the representations of the same design in other parts of the sculpture, are covered with feathers.

At the end of the courtyard, and fronting the gate of entrance, is the façade of a lofty building, two hundred and sixty-four feet long, standing on a terrace twenty feet high. The ascent is by a grand but ruined staircase, ninety-five feet wide, flanked on each side by a building with sculptured front, and having three doorways, each leading to apartments within.

The height of this building to the upper cornice is twenty-five feet. It has thirteen doorways, over each of which rose a perpendicular wall ten feet wide and seventeen feet high above the cornice, making the whole height forty-two feet from the ground. These lofty structures were no doubt erected to give grandeur and effect to the building, and at a distance they appear to be turrets, but only four of them now remain. The whole great façade, including the turrets, is crowded with complicated and elaborate sculpture, among which are human figures rudely executed: two are represented as playing on musical

PLATE V

UXMAL

Portion of Western Building. Monjas.

PLATE VI

UXMAL

Portion of the Western Range of Building, Monjas.

instruments, one being not unlike a small harp, and the other in the nature of a guitar; a third is in a sitting posture, with his hands across his breast, and tied by cords, the ends of which pass over his shoulders.

This building has one curious feature. It is erected over, and completely encloses, a smaller one of older date. The doorways, walls, and wooden lintels of the latter are all seen, and where the outer building is fallen, the ornamented cornice of the inner one is visible.

From the platform of the steps of this building, looking across the courtyard, a grand view presents itself, embracing all the principal buildings that now tower above the plain, except the House of the Dwarf. Plate VII represents this view.

The last of the four sides of the courtyard, standing on the right of the entrance, is represented in Plate VIII. It is the most entire of any, and, in fact, wants but little more than its wooden lintels, and some stones which have been picked out of the façade beolw the cornice, to make it perfect.

The ornament over the centre doorway is the most important, the most complicated and elaborate, and of that marked and peculiar style which char-acterizes the highest efforts of these ancient builders. The ornaments over the other doorways are less striking, more simple, and more pleasing. In all of them there is in the centre a masked face with the tongue hanging out, sur-mounted by an elaborate headdress; between the horizontal bars is a range of diamond-shaped ornaments, in which the remains of red paint are still distinctly visible, and at each end of these bars is a serpent's head, with the mouth wide open.

Plate IX represents the southeast corner of this building.

I omit a description of the apartments opening upon this courtyard. We made plans of all of them, but they are generally much alike, except in the dimensions. The number in all is eighty-eight.

In the range last presented, however, there is one suite different from all the rest. The entrance to this suite is by the centre and principal doorway, and Plate X represents the interior. It consists of two parallel chambers, each thirty-three feet long and thirteen wide; and at each end of both chambers is a doorway communicating with other chambers nine feet long and thirteen wide. The door-ways of all these are ornamented with sculpture, and they are the only ornaments found in the interior of any buildings in Uxmal.

This complex had been named Casa de las Monjas, *or* The Nunnery, *by the first Spaniards to visit it, among them Diego López de Cogolludo, because they thought that the many rooms were where Maya priestesses had lived. It is one of the largest buildings in the Puuc zone, and was explored and restored in 1956 during the excavations led by Alberto*

PLATE VII

F. Catherwood

Jordan & Halpin

UXMAL

View from la Casa de las Monjas, Looking South.

PLATE VIII

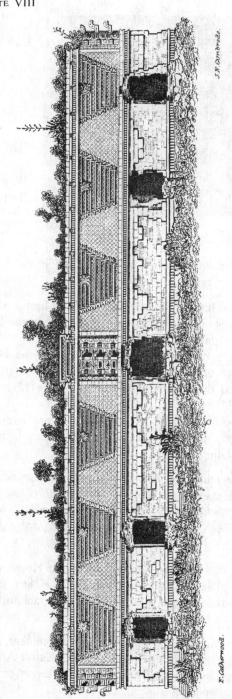

J.N. Ambrose.

UXMAL

Eastern Range of Building. Monjas.

F. Catherwood.

*West Building,
Nunnery Quadrangle,
Uxmal.*

*Ruz Lhuillier. This work also led to the conclusion that it had been built
in three different stages.*

At the back of the last-mentioned range of the Monjas is another, or rather
there are several ranges of buildings, standing lower than the House of the Nuns,
in irregular order, and much ruined.

To the first portion of these we gave the name of the House of the Birds,
from the circumstance of its being ornamented on the exterior with representations of feathers and birds rudely sculptured. Figure 15 represents a part of
these ornaments.

The remaining portion consists of some very large rooms, among which are
two fifty-three feet long, fourteen wide, and about twenty high, being the largest,
or at least the widest in Uxmal.

Very little now remains of the House of the Birds: *part of the south
façade can still be seen, and the north face, which is undecorated on the
lower half. The architrave is ornamented with plants and corn, while
the frieze looks like a thatched hut, above which are a few carvings of
birds.*

From this range of buildings we descend to the House of the Dwarf, also
known by the name of la Casa del Adivino, or the House of the Diviner, from
its overlooking the whole city, and enabling its occupant to be cognizant of all
that was passing around him.

*This is the explanation Stephens gives for the name here, yet in the book
about his first journey,* Incidents of Travel in Central America, Chiapas
and Yucatan, *he refers to the legend about the dwarf of Uxmal, told to
him by an Indian woman.*

Plate IX

UXMAL
South East Angle of Monjas.

Prudhomme S

PLATE X

FIG. 15

The courtyard of this building is one hundred and thirty-five beet by eighty-five. It is bounded by ranges of mounds from twenty-five to thirty feet thick, now covered with a rank growth of herbage, but which, perhaps, once formed ranges of buildings. In the centre is a large circular stone, like those seen in the other courtyards, called the Picote.

Plate XI represents the west front of this building, with the mound on which it stands. The base is so ruined and encumbered with fallen stones that it is difficult to ascertain its precise dimensions, but, according to our measurement, it is two hundred and thirty-five feet long, and one hundred and fifty-five wide. Its height is eighty-eight feet, and to the top of the building it is one hundred and five feet. Though diminishing as it rises, its shape is not exactly pyramidal,

Plate XI

UXMAL

West Front of the House of the Dwarf.

Pyramid of the Magician, Uxmal.

but its ends are rounded. It is encased with stone, and apparently solid from the plain.

A great part of the front presented in the engraving has fallen, and now lies a mass of ruins at the foot of the mound. Along the base, or rather about twenty feet up the mound, and probably once reached by a staircase, now ruined, is a range of curious apartments, nearly choked up with rubbish, and with the sapote beams still in their places over the door.

At the height of sixty feet is a solid projecting platform, on which stands a building loaded with ornaments more rich, elaborate, and carefully executed, than those of any other edifice in Uxmal. A great doorway opens upon the platform. The sapote beams are still in their places, and the interior is divided into two apartments. Both are entirely plain, without ornament of any kind, and have no communication with any part of the mound.

The steps or other means of communication with this building are all gone, and at the time of our visit we were at a loss to know how it had been reached; but, from what we saw afterward, we are induced to believe that a grand stair-case upon a different plan from any yet met with, and supported by a triangular arc, led from the ground to the door of the building, which, if still in existence, would give extraordinary grandeur to this great mound.

The front is much ruined, but even in its decay presents the most elegant and tasteful arrangement of ornaments to be seen in Uxmal, of which no idea could be given in any but a large engraving. The emblems of life and death appear on the wall in close juxta-position.

The interior is divided into three apartments, that in the centre being twenty-four feet by seven, and those on each side nineteen feet by seven. They have no communication with each other; two have their doors opening to the east and one to the west.

A narrow platform five feet wide projects from all the four sides of the building. The northern end is decayed, and part of the eastern front, and to this front ascends a grand staircase one hundred and two feet high, seventy feet wide, and containing ninety steps.

Plate XII represents this front. The steps are very narrow, and the staircase steep; and after we had cleared away the trees, and there were no branches to assist us in climbing, the ascent and descent were difficult and dangerous. The padre Cogolludo, the historian referred to, says that he once ascended these steps, and "that when he attempted to descend he repented; his sight failed him, and he was in some danger." He adds, that in the apartments of the building, which he calls "small chapels," were the "idols," and that there they made sacrifices of men, women, and children. Beyond doubt this lofty building was a great Teocalis, "El grande de los Kues," the great temple of idols worshipped by the people of Uxmal, consecrated by their most mysterious rites, the holiest of their holy places. "The High Priest had in his Hand a large broad, and sharp Knife made of Flint. Another Priest carried a wooden collar wrought like a snake. The persons to be sacrificed were conducted one by one up the Steps, stark naked, and as soon as laid on the Stone, had the Collar put upon their Necks, and the four priests took hold of the hands and feet. Then the high Priest with wonderful Dexterity ripped up the Breast, tore out the Heart, reeking, with his Hands, and showed it to the Sun, offering him the Heart and Steam that came from it."

This building, which stands on an oval shaped base, has been studied and restored on several occasions in work sponsored by the Mexican government. Between 1937 and 1940 this was led by the Mexican archeologist, Manuel Cirerol; during the fifties Alberto Ruz was in charge of explorations, and from 1968 to 1971 the archeologist César Sáenz. There are five distinct sub-structures, indicating that the pyramid was built in stages.

From the top of this mound we pass over the Casa del Gobernador to the grand structure marked on the general plan as the Casa de Palomos, or the House of the Pigeons, the front which is represented in Plate XIII. It is two hundred and forty feet long; the front is much ruined, the apartments are filled, and along the centre of the roof, running longitudinally, is a range of structures built in a pyramidal form, like the fronts of some of the old Dutch houses that still remain among us, but grander and more massive. These are nine in number, built of stone, about three fèet thick, and have small oblong openings through them. These openings give them somewhat the appearance of pigeon-houses, and from this the name of the building is derived. All had once been covered with figures and ornaments in stucco, portions of which still remain.

This complex, now known as the Dovecotes Group, *is formed of a large rectangular court with building on· all four sides. The name comes from*

Plate XII

Plate XIII

UXMAL
Casa de los Palomos.

*House of the
Doves, Uxmal.*

the north building, as the curious roof comb on the central part consists
of nine stepped triangles pierced with niches.

Besides these there was the Casa de la Vieja, or the House of the Old Woman,
standing in ruins. Once, when the wind was high, I saw the remains of the front
wall bending before its force. It is four or five hundred feet from the Casa del
Gobernador, and has its name from a mutilated statue of an old woman lying
before it.

*This ruined group contains two rooms where, according to oral tradition,
the 'mother' of the Dwarf of Uxmal lived.*

Near by are other monuments lying on the ground, overgrown and half
buried which were pointed out to us by the Indians on our first visit. North of
this there is a circular mound of ruins, probably of a circular building like that
of Mayapan. A wall which was said to encompass the city is laid down on the
plan so far as it can be traced; and beyond this, for a great distance in every
direction, the ground is strewed with ruins; but with this brief description I close.
I might extend it indefinitely, but I have compressed it within the smallest possible limits.

CHAPTER XV

Attacks from Fever and Ague — Final departure from Uxmal — Arrival
at Nohcacab — Ruins of Xcoch — A Mysterious Well — Ceremony
of El Velorio.

The reader, perhaps, is now anxious to hurry away from Uxmal, but he cannot be more anxious to do so than we were. We had finished our work, had resolved on the day for our departure, and had determined to devote the intermediate time to getting out of the wall and collecting together some ornaments for removal, and, having got the Indians fairly at work, we set about making some farewell Daguerreotype views. While working the camera under a blazing sun in the courtyard of the Monjas, I received a note from Mr. Catherwood advising me that his time had come, that he had a chill, and was then in bed. Presently a heavy rain came down, from which I took refuge in a damp apartment, where I was obliged to remain so long that I became perfectly chilled. On my return, I had a severe relapse, and in the evening Dr. Cabot, depressed by the state of things, and out of pure sympathy, joined us. Our servants went away, we were all three pinned to our beds together, and determined forthwith to leave Uxmal.

The next day it rained again, and we passed the hours in packing up, always a disagreeable operation, and then painfully so. The next day we departed, perhaps forever, from the Casa del Gobernador.

As we descended the steps, Mr. C. suggested that it was Newyear's Day. It was the first time this fact had presented itself; it called up scenes strikingly contrasted with our own miserable condition, and for the moment we would have been glad to be at home. Our cochés were in readiness at the foot of the terrace, and we crawled in; the Indians raised us upon their shoulders, and we were in motion from Uxmal.

Our housekeeping and household were again broken up. Albino and Bernaldo followed us, and as we passed along the edge of the milpa, half hidden among the cornstalks was the stately figure of Chiapa Chi. She seemed to be regarding us with a mournful gaze.

At the distance of two leagues they laid us down under a large seybo tree, opposite the hacienda of Chetulish, part of the domain of Uxmal. We remained a short time for our carriers to rest, and in two hours we reached the village of Nohcacab, and were laid down at the door of the casa real.

We had arrived at Nohcacab at an interesting and exciting moment. The village had just gone through the agony of a contested election. During the administration of the last alcalde, various important causes, among which were the improvements in the plaza, had roused the feelings of the whole community, and a strong notion prevailed, particularly among the aspirants to office, that the republic was in danger unless the alcaldes were changed.

The municipal elections of Nohcacab are, perhaps, more important than those of any other village in the state. The reader is aware of the great scarcity of water in Yucatan; that there are no rivers, streams, or fountains, and, except in the neighbourhood of aguadas, no water but what is obtained from wells. Nohcacab has three public wells, and it has a population of about six thousand entirely dependant upon them. Two of these wells are called norias, being larger and more considerable structures, in which the water is drawn by mules, and the third is simply a poso, or wen, having merely a cross-beam over the mouth, at which each comer draws with his own bucket and rope. For leagues around there is no water except that furnished by these wells. All the Indians have their huts or places of residence in the village, within reach of the wells; and when they go to work on their milpas, which are sometimes several miles distant, they are obliged to carry a supply with them. Every woman who goes to the noria for a cantaro of water carries a handful of corn, which she drops in place provided for that purpose: this tribute is intended for the maintenance of the mules, and we paid two cents for the drinking of each of our horses.

The custody and preservation of these wells are an important part of the administration of the village government. Thirty Indians are elected every year, who are called alcaldes of the wells, and whose business it is to keep them in good order, and the tanks constantly supplied with water. They receive no pay, but are exempted from certain obligations and services, which makes the office desirable; and no small object of the political struggle through which the village had passed, was to change the alcaldes of the wells. Buried among the ruins of Uxmal, the news of this important election had not reached us.

In Nohcacab they saw the ceremony of the transfer of authority and in the evening learned from the cura that their good friend the cura of Ticul was very sick (it was cholera, in fact). The rumour spread that his illness was a punishment for digging up the bones in San Francisco with Stephens.

Although the explorers were still suffering from fever themselves, Stephens and Dr. Cabot decided to go and see the priest, hoping that the doctor would be able to help. Arriving in Ticul next evening after a difficult journey, they heard that cura Carrillo was much better. Their visit next day seemed to give him so much pleasure that they stayed with him all day, riding back to Ticul the following morning. There they found Catherwood in much better health.

FIG. 16

A few days' rest had done wonders for us all, and we determined immediately too resume our occupations.

On leaving Uxmal we had directed our steps toward Nohcacab, (Figure 16) not from any attractions in the place itself, but on account of the ruins which we had heard of as existing in that neighbourhood; and, after ascertaining their position, we considered that they could be visited to the best advantage by making this place our head-quarters. We had the prospect of being detained there some time, and, as the casa real was low, damp, and noisy, and, moreover, our apartment was wanted for the schoolroom, by the advice of the padrecito we determined to abandon it, and take up our abode in the convent.

It is ascertained by historical accounts, that at the time of the conquest an Inidan town existed in this immediate neighbourhood, bearing the name of Nohcacab. This name is compounded of three Maya words, signifying literally the great place of good land; and from the numerous and extraordinary ruins scattered around, there is reason to believe that it was the heart of a rich, and what was once an immensely populous country. In the suburbs are numerous and large mounds, grand enough to excite astonishment, but even more fallen and overgrown than those of San Francisco, and, in fact, almost inaccessible.

The first place which we proposed visiting was the ruins of Xcoch, and in the very beginning of our researches in this neighbourhood we found that we were upon entirely new ground. The attention of the people had never been turned to the subject of the ruins in the neighbourhood. Xcoch was but a league distant, and, besides the ruins of buildings, it contained an ancient poso, or well, of mysterious and marvellous reputation, the fame of which was in everybody's mouth. This well was said to be a vast subterraneous structure, adorned with sculptured figures, an immense table of polished stone, and a plaza with columns supporting a vaulted roof, and it was said to have a subterraneous road, which led to the village of Mani, twenty-seven miles distant.

Notwithstanding this wondrous reputation and the publicity of the details, and although within three miles of Nohcacab, the intelligence we received was so vague and uncertain that we were at a loss how to make our arrangements for exploring the well. Not a white man in the place had ever entered it, though several had looked in at the mouth, who said that the wind had taken away their breath, and they had not ventured to go in. At eight o'clock the next morning we set out.

For a league we followed the camino real, at which distance we saw a little opening on the left, where one of our Indians was waiting for us. Following him by a narrow path just opened, we again found ourselves among ruins, and soon reached the foot of the high mound which towered above the plain, itself conspicuous from the House of the Dwarf at Uxmal, and which is represented in Figure 17. The ground in this neighbourhood was open, and there were the remains of several building, but all prostrate and in utter ruin.

Returning in the same direction, we entered a thick grove, in which we dismounted and tied our horses. It was the finest grove we had seen in the country, and within it was a great circular cavity or opening in the earth, twenty or thirty feet deep, with trees and bushes growing out of the bottom and sides, and rising above the level of the plain. It was a wild-looking place, and had a fanciful, mysterious, and almost fearful appearance; for while in the grove all was close and sultry, and without a breath of air, and every leaf was still, within this cavity the branches and leaves were violently agitated, as if shaken by an invisible hand.

This cavity was the entrance to the poso, or well, and its appearance was wild enough to bear out the wildest accounts we had heard of it.

Accompanied by several Indians carrying torches and ropes they entered through a low passage to explore the caverns and tunnels of the well. Finally they reached a deep basin of water, which had in fact suppied water to the inhabitants of the ancient ruined city.

On our return to the village we found that an unfortunate accident had occurred during our absence; a child had been run away with by a horse, thrown off, and killed. In the evening, in company with the alcalde, the brother of the

FIG. 17

padrecito, we went to the velorio, or watching. It was an extremely dark night, and we stumbled along a stony and broken street till we reached the house of mourning. Before the door were a crowd of people, and a large card-table, at which all who could find a place were seated playing cards. At the moment of our arrival, the whole company was convulsed with laughter at some good thing which one of them had uttered, and which was repeated for our benefit; a strange scene at the threshold of a house of mourning. We entered the house, which was crowded with women, and hammocks were vacated for our use, these being in all cases the seat of honour. The house, like most of those in the village, consisted of a single room rounded at each end. The floor was of earth, and the roof thatched with long leaves of the guano. From the cross-poles hung a few small hammocks, and in the middle of the room stood a table, on which lay the body of the child.

This ceremony of el velorio is always observed when there is death in a family. It is intended, as the padrecito told us, para divertirse, or to amuse and distract the family, and keep them from going to sleep. At twelve o'clck chocolate is served round, and again at daybreak; but in some respects the ceremony is different in the case of grown persons and that of children. In the latter, as they believe that a child is without sin, and that God takes it immediately to himself, the death is a subject of rejoicing, and the night is passed in card-playing, jesting, and story-telling. But in the case of grown persons, as they are not so sure what becomes of the spirit, they have no jesting or storytelling, and only play cards.

CHAPTER XVI

Ruins of Nohpat — Journey to Kabah — Return to the Village —
Festival of Corpus Alma — How to put a Saint under Patronage

The next day we set out for another ruined city. It lay on the road to Uxmal, and was the same which I had visited on my first return from Ticul, known by the name of Nohpat. At the distance of a league we turned off from the main road to the left, and, following a narrow milpa path, in fifteen minutes reached the field of ruins. One mound rose high above the rest, holding aloft a ruined building, as shown in Figure 18. At the foot of this we dismounted and tied our horses. It was one hundred and fifty feet high on the slope, and about two hundred and and fifty feet long at the base. At the top, the mound,

Fig. 18

with the building upon it, had separated and fallen apart, and while one side still supported part of the edifice, the other presented the appearance of a mountain slide. Cocome, our guide, told us that the separation had happened only with the floods of the last rainy season. We ascended on the fallen side, and, reaching the top, found, descending on the south side, a gigantic staircase, overgrown, but with the great stone steps still in their places, and almost entire. The ruined building on the top consisted of a single corridor, but three feet five inches wide, and, with the ruins of Nohpat at our feet, we looked out upon a great desolate plain studded with overgrown mounds, of which we took the bearings and names as known to the Indians; toward the west by north, startling by the grandeur of the buildings and their height above the plain, with no decay visible, and at this distance seeming perfect as a living city, were the ruins of Uxmal

Descending the mound, we passed around by the side of the staircase, and rose upon an elevated platform, in the centre of which was a huge and rude round stone, like that called the picote in the courtyards at Uxmal. At the base of the steps was a large flat stone, having sculptured upon it a colossal human figure in bas-relief, which is represented in Figure 19. The Indians said that it was the figure of a king of the antiguos and no doubt it was intended as a portrait of some lord or cacique.

FIG. 19

At a short distance to the southeast of the courtyard was another platform or terrace, about twenty feet high and two hundred feet square, on two sides of which were ranges of buildings standing at right angles to each other. One of them had two stories, and trees growing out of the walls and on the top, forming the most picturesque ruins we had seen in the country.

Leaving this neighbourhood, and passing by many ruined buildings and mounds, at the distance of six or seven hundred feet we reached an open place, forming the most curious and interesting part of this field of ruins. It was in the vicinity of three mounds, lines drawn from which to each other would form a right angle, and in the open space were some sculptured monuments, shattered, fallen, and some of them half buried. Strange heads and bodies lay broken and scattered, so that at first we did not discover their connexion; but, by examining carefully, we found two fragments, which, from the shape of the broken surfaces, seemed to be parts of one block, one of them representing a huge head, and the other a huger body. The latter we set up in its proper position, and with some difficulty, by means of poles, and ropes which the Indians took from their sandals, we got the other part on the top, and fitted in its place, as it had once stood. Figure 20 represents this monument.

FIG. 20

There were others of the same general character, of which the sculpture was more defaced and worn; and, besides these, there were monuments of a different character, half buried, and dispersed without apparent order, but which evidently had an adaptation to each other; after some examination, we made out what we considered the arrangement in which they had stood, and had them set up according to our combination. Figure 21 represents these stones. They vary from one foot four inches to one foot ten inches in length.

FIG. 21

Each stone is two feet three inches high. The subjects is the skull and cross-bones. The sculpture is in bas-relief, and the carving good, and still clear and distinct. Probably this was the holy place of the city, where the idols or deities were presented to the people with the emblems of death around them.

Stephens says that the only information he could collect about this ancient city was that the name Nohpat means 'great lord'. He also remarks that if they had discovered this city on their previous journey they would have stayed to explore it properly because the buildings, although in ruins, were almost as numerous as at Uxmal.

The next day, being the eighth of January, we set out for the ruins of Kabah. Our direction was south, on the camino real to Bolonchen. The descent from the great rocky table on which the convent stands was on this side rough, broken, and precipitous. We passed through a long street having on each side thatched huts, occupied exclusively by Indians. Some had a picturesque appearance, and Figure 22 represents one of them At the distance of two leagues we turned off by a milpa path on the left, and very soon found ourselves among trees, bushes, and a thick, overgrown foliage which, after the fine open field of Nohpat, we regarded as among the vicissitudes of our fortunes. Beyond we saw through an opening a lofty mound, overgrown, and having upon it the ruins of a building like the House of the Dwarf, towering above every other object, and proclaiming the site of another lost and deserted city. Moving on, again, through openings in the trees, we had a glimpse of a great stone edifice, with its front apparently

Fig. 22

entire. We had hardly expressed our admiration before we saw another, and at a few horses' length a third. Three great buildings at once, with façades which, at that distance, and by the imperfect glimpses we had of them, showed no imperfection, and seemed entire. We were taken by surprise.

Since we first set out in search of ruins we had not been taken so much by surprise. During the whole time of our residence at Uxmal, and until my forced visit to Ticul, and fortunate intimacy with the cura Carillo, I had not even heard of the existence of such a place. It was absolutely unknown; and the Indians who guided us having conducted us to these buildings, of all the rest seemed as ignorant as ourselves.

There was no rancho, and no habitation of any kind nearer than the village. The buildings themselves offered good shelter; with the necessary clearings they could be made extremely agreeable, and on many considerations it was advisible again to take up our abode among the ruins; but this arrangement was not without its dangers. The season of El Norte seemed to have no end; every day there was rain; the foliage was so thick that the hot sun could not dry the moisture before another rain came and the whole country was enveloped in a damp, unwholesome atmosphere. We determined, therefore, to continue our residence at the convent, and go out to the ruins every day.

Late in the afternoon we returned to the village, and in the evening had a levee of visiters. The sensation we had created in the village had gone on increasing, and the Indians were really indisposed to work for us at all. The arrival of a stranger even from Merida or Campeachy was an extraordinary event, and no Ingleses had ever been seen there before. The circumstance that we had come to work among the ruins was wonderful, incomprehensible. Within the memory of the oldest Indians these remains had never been disturbed.

It was late the next day when we reached the ruins. We could not set out before the Indians, for they might disappoint us altogether, and we could do nothing until they came, but, once on the ground, we soon had them at work. On both sides we watched each other closely, though from somewhat different motives: they from utter inability to comprehend our plans and purposes, and we from the fear that we should get no work out of them. If one of us spoke, they all stopped to listen; if we moved, they stopped to gaze upon us. Mr. Catherwood's drawing materials, tripod, sextant, and compass were very suspicious, and occasionally Doctor Cabot filled up the measure of their astonishment by bringing down a bird as it flew through the air. By the time they were fairly broken in to know what they had to do, it was necessary to return to he village.

The same labour was repeated the next day with a new set of men; but, by continual supervision and urging, we managed to get considerable work done. Albino was a valuable auxiliary; indeed, without him I could hardly have got on at all.

While we were working at the ruins, the people in the village were losing no time. On the eleventh began the fiesta of Corpus Alma, a festival of nine days' observance in honour of Santo Cristo del Amor. Its opening was announced by the ringing of church bells and firing of rockets, which, fortunately, as were away at the ruins, we avoided hearing; but in the evening came the procession and the baile, to which we were formally invited by a committee, consisting of the padrecito, the alcalde, and a much more important person than either, styled El Patron del Santo, or the Patron of the Saint.

The process of putting a saint under patronage is peculiar. Among the images distributed around the walls of the church, whenever one is observed to attract particular attention, as, for instance, if Indians are found frequently kneeling before it, and making offerings, the padre requires of the cacique twelve Indians to serve and take care of the saint, who are called mayoles. These are furnished according to the requisition, and they elect a head, but not from their own number, who is called the patron, and to them is intrusted the guardianship of the saint. The padre, in his robes of office, administers an oath, which is sanctified by sprinkling them with holy water. The patron is sworn to watch over the interests of the saint, to take care of all the candles and other offerings presented to him, and to see that his fête is properly observed; and the mayoles are sworn to obey the orders of the patron in all things touching the custody and service of the saint.

CHAPTER XVII

Ruins of Kabah — General Description — Closing Scene

In the mean time we continued our work at Kabah, and, during all our intercourse with the Indians, we were constantly inquiring for other places of ruins. All the ruins scattered about the country are known to the Indians under the general name of "Xlap-pahk," which means in Spanish "paredes viejas," and in English "old walls." The information we obtained was in general so confused that we were unable to form any idea of the extent or character of the ruins. A place they had never visited, though but a few leagues distant, they knew nothing about, and, from the extreme difficulty of ascertaining the juxtaposition of places, it was hard to arrange the plan of a route so as to embrace several. To some I made preliminary visits; those from which I expected most turned out not worth the trouble of going to, while others, from which I expected but little, proved extremely interesting.

As these pages will be sufficiently burdened, I shall omit all the preliminary visits, and present the long line of ruined cities in the order in which we visited them for the purposes of exploration. Chichen was the only place we heard of in Merida, and the only place we knew of with absolute certainty before we embarked for Yucatan; but we found that a vast field of research lay between us and it, and, not to delay the reader, I proceed at once to the ruins of Kabah.

Plate XIV represents the plan of the buildings of this city.

On this plan the reader will see a road marked "Camino Real to Bolonchen," and on the left a path marked "Path to Milpa." Following this path toward the field of ruins, the teocalis is the first object that meets his eye, grand, picturesque ruined, and covered with trees, like the House of the Dwarf at Uxmal, towering above every other object on the plain. It is about one hundred and eighty feet square at the base, and rises in a pyramidal form to the height of eighty feet. At the foot is a range of ruined apartments. The steps are all fallen, and the sides present a surface of loose stones, difficult to climb, except on one side, where the ascent is rendered practicable by the aid of trees. The top presents a grand view.

This building was the Great Pyramid, *which must have been an important temple. It is now in ruins, but the remains of a wide stairway can be seen on the south side and part of three roofless chambers on the top.*

PLATE XIV

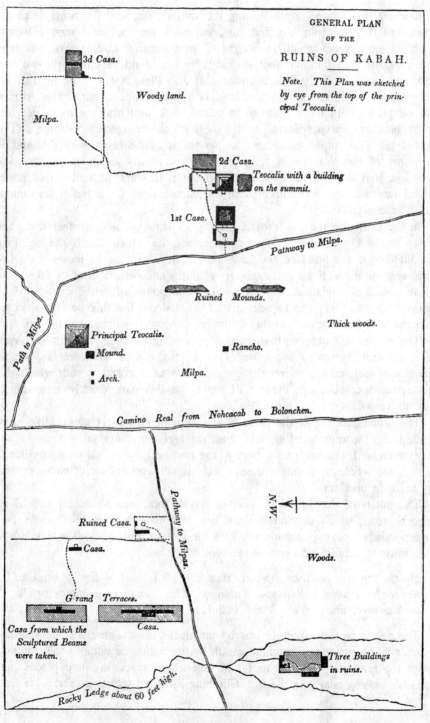

GENERAL PLAN

OF THE

RUINS OF KABAH.

Note. This Plan was sketched by eye from the top of the principal Teocalis.

3d Casa.

Woody land.

Milpa.

2d Casa.

Teocalis with a building on the summit.

1st Casa.

Pathway to Milpa.

Ruined Mounds.

Thick woods.

Path to Milpa.

Principal Teocalis.

Mound.

Rancho.

Arch.

Milpa.

Camino Real from Nohcacab to Bolonchen.

Pathway to Milpas.

Ruined Casa.

Casa.

N.W.

Woods.

Grand Terraces.

Casa.

Casa from which the Sculptured Beams were taken.

Three Buildings in ruins.

Rocky Ledge about 60 feet high.

Leaving this mound, again taking the milpa path, and following it to the distance of three or four hundred yars, we reach the foot of a terrace twenty feet high, the edge of which is overgrown with trees; ascending this, we stand on a platform two hundred feet in width by one hundred and forty-two feet deep, and facing us is the building represented in Plate XV. On the right of the platform, as we approach this building, is a high range of structures, ruined and overgrown with trees, with an immense back wall built on the outer line of the platform, perpendicular to the bottom of the terrace. On the left is another range of ruined buildings, not so grand as those on the right, and in the centre of the platform is a stone enclosure twenty-seven feet square and seven feet high like that surrounding the picote at Uxmal; but the layer of stones around the base was sculptured, and, on examination, we found a continuous line of hieroglyphics.

In the centre of the platform is a range of stone steps forty feet wide and twenty in number, leading to an upper terrace, on which stands the building. This building is one hundred and fifty-one feet in front, and the moment we saw it we were struck with the extraordinary richness and ornament of its façade. In all the buildings of Uxmal, without a single exception, up to the cornice which runs over the doorway the façades are of plain stone; but this was ornamented' from the very foundation, two layers under the lower cornice, to the top.

The reader will observe that a great part of this façade has fallen; toward the north end, however, a portion of about twenty-five feet remains, which, though not itself entire, shows the gorgeousness of decoration with which this façade was once adorned. Plate XVI represents this part, exactly as it stands, with the cornice over the top fallen.

The ornaments are of the same character with those at Uxmal, alike complicated and incomprehensible, and from the fact that every part of the façade was ornamented with sculpture, even to the portion now buried under the lower cornice, the whole must have presented a greater appearance of richness than any building at Uxmal.

The lintels of the doorways were of wood; these are all fallen, and of all the ornaments which decorated them not one now remains. No doubt they corresponded in beauty of sculpture with the rest of the façade. The whole now lies a mass of rubbish and ruin at the foot of the wall.

On the top was another structure that reminded them of similar ones on the roofs of some buildings at Palenque. This was more evidence of the architectural unity of the Maya culture.

The access to this structure was by no means easy. There was no staircase or other visible means of communicatioń, either within or without the building, but in the rear the wall and roof had fallen, and made in some places high mounds reaching nearly to the top. Climbing up these tottering fabrics was not

Plate XV

KABAH
Front of the 1st Casa.

*The Codz Poop,
Kabah.*

free from danger. Parts which appeared substantial had not the security of buildings constructed according to true principles of art; at times it was impossible to discover the supporting power, and the discorderly masses seemed held up by an invisible hand. While we were clearing off the trees upon the roof, a shower came up suddenly, and, as we were hurrying to descend and take refuge in one of the apartments below, a stone on the edge of the cornice gave way and carried me down with it. By great good fortune, underneath was a mound of ruins which reached nearly to the roof, and saved me from a fall that would have been most serious, if not fatal, in its consequences.

I have said that we were somewhat excited by the first view of the façade of this building. Ascending the steps and standing in the doorway of the centre apartment, we broke out into an exclamation of surprise and admiration. At Uxmal there was no variety; the interiors of all the apartments were the same. Here we were presented with a scene entirely new. Plate XVII represents the interior of this apartment. It consists of two parallel chambers, the one in front being twenty-seven feet long and ten feet six inches wide, and the other of the same length, but a few inches narrower, communicating by a door in the centre. The inner room is raised two feet eight inches higher than the front, and the ascent is by two stone steps carved out of a single block of stone, the lower one being in the form of a scroll. The sides of the steps are ornamented with sculpture, as is also the wall under the doorway. The whole design is graceful and pretty, and, as a mere matter of taste, the effect is extremely good.

In the engraving but one doorway appears on each side of the centre, the front wall at the two ends having fallen. On both sides of this centre doorway were two other doorways opening into apartments. Each apartment contains two chambers, with the back one raised, but there are no steps, and the only ornament is a row of small pilasters about two feet high under the door, and running the whole length of the room.

Such is a brief description of the façade and front apartments, and these

PLATE XVI

KABAH
Detail of Ornament 1st Casa.

*Decoration on
the Codz Poop
façade, Kabah.*

formed not more than one third of the building. At the rear and under the same roof were two ranges of apartments of the same dimensions with those just described, and having a rectangular area in front. The rest of the building, however, was in a much more ruinous condition than that presented. At both ends the wall had fallen, and the whole of the other front, with the roof, and the ruins filled up the apartments so that it was extremely difficult to make out the plan.

The whole of the terrace on this latter side is overgrown with trees, some of which have taken root among the fragments, and are growing out of the interior of the chambers.

Plate XVIII will give some idea of the manner in which the rankness of tropical vegetation is hurrying to destruction these interesting remains. The great branches overshadowing the whole cannot be exhibited in the plate, and no sketch can convey a true idea of the ruthless gripe in which these gnarled and twisted roots encircle sculptured stones.

Such is a brief description of the first building at Kabah.

This building is now known as Codz Poop, *meaning Rolled Mat. It stands on an artificial terrace, and the west front is decorated with masks of the rain god, Chaac.*

Descending the corner of the back terrace, at the distance of a few paces rises a broken and overgrown mound, on which stands a ruined building, called by the Indians the cocina, or kitchen, because, as they said, it had chimneys to let out smoke.

On the left of this mound is a staircase leading down to the area of Casa No. 2, and on the right is a grand and majestic pile of buildings, having no name assigned to it, and which, perhaps, when entire, was the most imposing structure at Kabah. It measured at the base one hundred and forty-seven feet on one side

PLATE XVII

KABAH
Interior of Centre Room 1st Casa.

PLATE XVIII

and one hundred and six on the other, and consisted of three distinct stories or ranges, one on the roof of the other, the second smaller than the first, and the third smaller than the second, having on each side a broad platform in front. Along the base on all four of the sides was a continuous range of apartments, with the doorways supported by pillars, and on the side fronting the rear of Casa No. 1 was another new and interesting feature.

This was a gigantic stone staircase, rising to the roof, on which stood the second range of apartments. This staircase was not a solid mass, resting against the wall of the mound, but was supported by the half of a triangular arch springing from the ground, and resting against the wall so as to leave a passage under the staircase. This staircase was interesting not only for its own grandeur and the novelty of its construction, but as explaining what had before been unintelligible in regard to the principal staircase in the House of the Dwarf at Uxmal.

The doorways of the ranges on the north side of this mound opened upon the area of Casa No. 2. The platform of this area is one hundred and seventy feet long, one hundred and ten broad, and is elevated ten feet from the ground. It had been planted with corn, and required little clearing. Plate XIX represents the front of this building, and the picote, or great stone found thrown down in all the courtyards and areas, is exhibited on one side in the engraving.

A ruined staircase rises from the centre of the platform to the roof of this range, which forms the platform in front of the principal building.

This staircase, like that last mentioned, is supported by the half of a triangular arch, precisely like the other already mentioned. The whole front was ornamented with sculpture, and the ornaments best preserved are over the doorway of the centre apartment, which, being underneath the staircase, cannot be exhibited in the engraving.

The principal building, it will be seen, has pillars in two of its doorways. At this place, for the first time, we met with pillars used legitimately, according to the rules of known architecture, as a support, and they added greatly to the interest which the other novelties here disclosed to us presented.

This is Stephens' description of the structure now called The Palace, *part of the* East Group, *which is one of the largest on this sie. The building actually has two stories, although Stephens counted three. The decoration of the upper part of the façade, three groups of small columns, is typical of the Puuc style of architecture in this region.*

Leaving this building, and crossing an overgrown and wooded plain, at the distance of about three hundred and fifty yards we reach the terrace of Casa No. 3. The platform of this terrace, too, had planted with corn, and was easily cleared. Plate XX represents the front of the edifice, which, when we first came upon it, was so beautifully shrouded by trees that it was painful to be obliged

PLATE XIX

KABAH
Front of Casa No. 2.

PLATE XX

KABAH
3ra Casa.

*The Palace,
Kabah.*

to disturb them, and we spared every branch that did not obstruct the view. While Mr. Catherwood was making his drawing, rain came on, and, as he might not be able to get his camera lucida in position again, he continued his work, with the protection of an India-rubber cloak and an Indian holding an umbrella

Fig. 23

*The Arch,
Kabah.*

over the stand. The rain was of that sudden and violent character often met with in tropical climates, and in a few minutes flooded the whole ground. The washing of the water from the upper terrace appears in the engraving.

Besides these, there are on this side of the camino real the remains of other buildings, but all in a ruinous condition, and there is one monument, perhaps more curious and interesting than any that has been presented. It is a lonely arch, of the same form with all the rest, having a span of fourteen feet (Figure 23). It stands on a ruined mound, disconnected from every other structure, in solitary grandeur. Darkness rests upon its history, but in that desolation and solitude, among the ruins around, it stood like the proud memorial of a Roman triumph. Perhaps, like the arch of Titus, which at this day spans the Sacred Way at Rome, it was erected to commemorate a victory over enemies.

Here Stephens is referring to the Triumphal Arch *that stands more or less in the center of the city. In Catherwood's drawing the central part has fallen, but this was reconstructed in the 1950's by the architect Ponciano Salazar. The arch seems to have marked the beginning of a 'white road'* (sacbé) *that connected this city with Uxmal.*

Beyond these buildings, none of the Indians knew of any ruins. Striking directly from them in a westerly direction through a thick piece of woods, without being able to see anything, but from observation taken from the top of the teocalis, and passing a small ruined building with a staircase leading to the roof, we reached a great terrace, perhaps eight hundred feet long and one hundred feet wide.

Two buildings stood upon this overgrown terrace. The first was two hundred and seventeen feet long, having seven doorways in front, all opening to single apartments except the centre one, which had two apartments, each thirty feet long. In the rear were other apartments, with doorways opening upon a court-yard, and from the centre a range of buildings ran at right angles, terminating in a large ruined mound. The wall of the whole of this great pile had been more ornamented than either of the buildings before presented except the first, but, unfortunately, it was more dilapidated. The doorways had wooden lintels, most of which have fallen.

To the north of this building is another, one hundred and forty-two feet in front and thirty-one feet deep, with double corridors communicating, and a gigantic staircase in the centre leading to the roof, on which are the ruins of another building. The doors of two centre apartments open under the arch of this great staircase. In that on the right we again found the prints of the red hand; not a single print, or two, or three, as in other places, but the whole wall was covered with them, bright and distinct as if but newly made.

This complex is the West Group, *which is in almost total ruin. On the walls of the most complete building can be seen red handprints which is why the natives called it* Dzalkabilkik, *meaning* 'Place of the Hands of Blood'.

All the lintels over the doorways are of wood, and all are still in their places, mostly sound and solid. The doorways were encumbered with rubbish and ruins. That nearest the staircase was filled up to within three feet of the lintel; and, in crawling under on his back, to measure the apartment, Mr. Catherwood's eye was arrested by a sculptured lintel, which, on examination, he considered the most interesting memorial we had found in Yucatan. On my return that day from a visit to three more ruined cities entirely unknown before, he claimed this lintel as equal in interest and value to all of them together. The next day I saw them, and determined immediately, at any trouble or cost, to carry them home with me; but this was no easy matter.

To get them out by our own efforts, however, was impossible; and after conferring with the padrecito, we procured a good set of men, and went down with crowbars for the purpose of working them out of the wall. Doctor Cabot, who had been confined to the village for several days by illness, turned out on this great occasion.

The lintel consisted of two beams, and the outer one was split in two lengthwise. They lapped over the doorway about a foot at each end, and were as firmly secured as any stones in the building, having been built in when the wall was constructed. Fortunately, we had the best set of assistants that ever came to us from Nohcacab, and their pride was enlisted in the cause. At length, almost against hope, having broken a rude arch almost to the roof, the inner beam was got out uninjured. Still the others were not safe, but, with great labour, anxiety, and good fortune, the whole three at length lay before us, with their sculptured faces uppermost.

The next day, knowing the difficulty and risk that must attend their transportation, we had the beams set up for Mr. Catherwood to draw.

Plate XXI represents this lintel, indicated in the engraving as three pieces of wood, but originally consisting of only two, that on which the figure is carved being split through the middle by some unequal pressure of the great superincumbent wall. The top of the outer part was worm-eaten and decayed, probably from the trickling of water, which, following some channel in the ornaments, touched only this part; all the rest was sound and solid.

The subject is a human figure standing upon a serpent. The faces was scratched, worn, and obliterated, the headdress was a plume of feathers, and the general character of the figure and ornaments was the same with that of the figures found on the walls at Palenque. It was the first subject we had discovered bearing such a striking resemblance in details, and connecting so closely together the builders of these distant cities.

But the great interest of this lintel was the carving. The beam covered with hieroglyphics at Uxmal was faded and worn. This was still in excellent preservation; the lines were clear and distinct; and the cutting, under any test, and without any reference to the people by whom it was executed, would be considered as indicating great skill and proficiency in the art of carving on wood. It was several days before I could get them away, but, to my great relief, they at length left the village on the shoulders of Indians, and I brought them with me safely to this city. The reader anticipates my conclusion, and if he have but a shade of sympathy with the writer, he mourns over the melancholy fate that overtook them but a short time after their arrival.

Once in New York, the lintel was exhibited in Catherwood's Panorama, where it was later destroyed in a fire in 1844.

There is no account of the existence of iron or steel among the aborigines on this continent. The general and well-grounded belief is, that the inhabitants had no knowledge whatever of these metals. How, then, could they carve wood, and that of the hardest kind?

In that large canoe which first made known to Columbus the existence of this great continent, among other fabrics of the country from which they came, the Spaniards remarked hatchets of copper, as it is expressed, for "hewing wood." Bernal Dias, in his account of the first voyage of the Spaniards along the coast of Guacaluco, in the Empire of Mexico, says, "It was a Custom of the Indians of this Province *invariably* to carry small Hatchets of Copper, very

PLATE XXI

KABAH
Carved Beam of Sapote Wood.

F. Catherwood.

bright, and the wooden Handles of which were highly painted, as intended both for Defence and Ornament." In my opinion, the carving of these beams was done with the copper instruments known to have existed among the aboriginal inhabitants, and it is not necessary to suppose, without and even against all evidence, that at some remote period of time the use of iron and steel was known on this continent, and that the knowledge had become lost among the latter inhabitants.

From the great terrace a large structure is seen at a distance indistinctly through the trees, and, pointing it out to an Indian, I set out with him to examine it. Descending among the trees, we soon lost sight of it entirely, but, pursuing the direction, the Indian cutting a way with his machete, we came upon a building, which, however, I discovered, was not the one we were in search of. It was about ninety feet in front, the walls were cracked, and all along the base the ground was strewed with sculptured stones, the carving of which was equal to any we had seen. Before reaching the door I crawled through a fissure in the wall into an apartment, at one end of which, in the arch, I saw an enormous hornet's nest; and in turning to take a hasty leave, saw at the opposite end a large ornament in stucco, having also a hornet's nest attached to it, painted, the colours being still bright and vivid, and surprising me as much as the sculptured beams. A great part had fallen, and it had the appearance of having been wantonly destroyed. Figure 24 represents this fragment.

FIG. 24

The ornament, when entire, appears to have been intended to represent two large eagles facing each othr; on each side are seen drooping plumes of feathers.

Beyond this was the great building which we had set out to find. The front was still standing, in some places, particularly on the corner, richly ornamented; but the back part was a heap of ruins.

In descending on the other side over a mass of ruins, I found at one corner a deep hole, which apparently led into a cave, but, crawling down, I found that it conducted to the buried door of a chamber on a new and curious plan. It had a raised platform about four feet high, and in each of the inner corners was a rounded vacant place, about large enough for a man to stand in; part of the back wall was covered with prints of the red hand. They seemed so fresh, and the seams and creases were so distinct, that I made several attempts with the machete to get one print off entire, but the plaster was so hard that every effort failed.

Beyond this was another building, so unpretending in its appearance compared with the first, that, but for the uncertainty in regard to what might be found in every part of these ruins, I should hardly have noticed it. This building had but one doorway, which was nearly choked up; but on passing into it I noticed sculptured on the jambs, nearly buried, a protruding corner of a plume of feathers. By closer inspection I found on the opposite jam a corresponding stone, but entirely buried. The top stone of both was missing, but I found them near by, and determined immediately to excavate the parts that were buried, and carry the whole away; but it was a more difficult business than that of getting out the beams. A solid mound of earth descended from the outside to the back wall of the apartment, choking the doorway to within a few feet of the top. To clear the whole doorway was out of the question, for the Indians had only their hands with which to scoop out the accumulated mass. The only way was to dig down beside each stone, then separate it from the wall with the crowbar, and pry it out. I was engaged in this work two entire days, and on the second the Indians wanted to abandon it.

Plates XXII and XXIII represent these two jambs as they stood facing each other in the doorway. Each consists of two separate stones, as indicated in the engravings. In each the upper stone is one foot five inches high, and the lower one four feet six inches, and both are two feet three inches wide. The subject consists of two figures, one standing, and the other kneeling before him. Both have unnatural and grotesque faces, probably containing some symbolical meaning. The headdress is a lofty plume of feathers, falling to the heels of the standing figure; and under his feet is a row of hieroglyphics.

These stone doorjambs were also taken to New York to be exhibited Catherwood's 'Panorama', but by the time they arrived this had burned down. Stephens gave the stones to a friend, John Church Cruger, who

PLATE XXII

F.Catherwood.   A.Jones.

KABAH
Figure on jamb of Doorway.

Plate XXIII

F.Catherwood.   A.Jones.

KABAH

Figure on jamb of Doorway.

shipped them to his estate on the Hudson River and built them into simulated ruins. They were found here in 1918 by Sylvanus G. Morley. He made arrangements for them to be bought by the American Museum of Natural History in New York, where they can be seen today.

In lifting these stones out of the holes and setting them up against the walls, I had been obliged to assist myself, and almost the moment it was finished I found that the fatigue and excitement had been too much for me. My bones ached; a chill crept over me; I looked around for a soft stone to lie down upon; but the place was cold and damp, and rain was threatening. I saddled my horse, and when I mounted I could barely keep my seat. At length I reached the village, and this was my last visit to Kabah; but I have already finished a description of its ruins.

At the time of my attack, Mr. Catherwood, Doctor Cabot, and Albino were all down with fever. I had a recurrence the next day, but on the third I was able to move about. The spectacle around was gloomy for sick men. From the long continuance of the rainy season our rooms in the convent (Figure 25)

FIG. 25

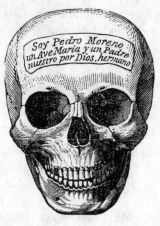

Fig. 26

were damp, and corn which we kept in one corner for the horses had swelled and sprouted.

Death was all around us. Anciently this country was so healthy that Torquemada says, "Men die of pure old age, for there are none of those infimities that exist in other lands; and if there are slight infirmities, the heat destroys them, and so there is no need of a physician there;" but the times are much better for physicians now, and Doctor Cabot, if he had been able to attend to it, might have entered into an extensive gratuitous practice. Adjoining the front of the church, and connecting with the convent, was a great charnel-house, along the wall of which was a row of skulls. At the top of a pillar forming the abutment of the wall of the staircase was a large vase piled full, and the cross was surmounted with them. Within the enclosure was a promiscuous assemblage of skulls and bones several feet deep. Along the wall, hanging by cords, were the bones and skulls of individuals in boxes and baskets, or tied up in cloths, with names written upon them. I took up one, and staring me in the face were the words, "Soy Pedro Moreno: un Ave Maria y un Padre nuestro por Dios, hermano." (Figure 26) "I am Peter Moreno: an Ave Maria and Paternoster for God's sake, brother."

Accustomed as we were to hold sacred the bones of the dead, the slightest memorial of a departed friend accidentally presented to view bringing with it a shade of sadness, such an exhibition grated harshly upon the feelings. I asked the padrecito why these skulls were not permitted to rest in peace, and he answered, what is perhaps but too true, that in the grave they are forgotten; but when dug up and placed in sight with labels on them, they remined the living of their former existence, of their uncertain state — that their souls may be in purgatory — and appeal to their friends, as with voices from the grave, to pray for them, and have masses said for their souls.

Volume II

CHAPTER I

Departure from Nohcacab — Ruins of Zayi

On the twenty-fourth of January we left Nohcacab. It was a great relief to bid farewell to this place, and the only regret attending our departure was the reflection that we should be obliged to return. The kindness and attentions of the padrecito and his brother, and, indeed, of all the villagers, had been unremitted, but the fatigue of riding twelve miles every day over the same ground, and the difficulty of procuring Indians to work, were a constant source of annoyance.

We were setting out on a tour which, according to the plan laid out, embraced a circuit of ruins, and required us to revisit Nohcacab, although our return would be only to make it a point of departure in another direction.

In consequence of this plan we left behind all our heavy luggage, and carried with us only the Daguerreotype apparatus, hammocks, one large box containing our tin table service, a candlestick, bread, chocolate, coffee, and sugar, and a few changes of clothing in pestaquillas.

We were all provided with good horses for the road. Mr. Catherwood had one on which he could make a sketch without dismounting; Dr. Cabot could shoot from the back of his. Mine could, on an emergency, be pushed into a hard day's journey for a preliminary visit. Albino rode a hard-mouthed, wilful beast, which shook him constantly like a fit of the fever and ague, and which we distinguished by the name of the trotter.

We were about entering a region little or not at all frequented by white men, and occupied entirely by Indians. Our road lay through the ruins of Kabah, a league beyond which we reached the rancho of Chack. This was a large habitation of Indians, under the jurisdiction of the village of Nohcacab. There was not a white man in the place, and as we rode through, the women snatched up their children, and ran from us like startled deer. In one part of the rancho was a casa real, being a long thatched hut with a large square before it, protected by an arbour of leaves, and on one side was a magnificent seybo tree, throwing its shade to a great distance round.

On leaving this rancho we saw at a distance on the left a high ruined building standing alone amid a great intervening growth of woods, and apparently inaccessible. Beyond, and at the distance of four leagues from Nohcacab, we reached the rancho of Schawill, which was our first stopping-place, on account of the ruins of Zayi in its immediate neighbourhood. This place also was inhabited exclusively by Indians, rancho being the name given to a settlement not of sufficient importance to constitute a village. The casa real, like that at Chack, was a large hut, with mud walls and a thatched roof. It had an open place in front about a hundred feet square, enclosed by a fence made of poles, and shaded by an arbour of palm leaves. Around the hut were large seybo trees. The hut, when swept out, and comparatively clear of fleas, made a large and comfortable apartment, and furnished ample swinging room for six hammocks, being the number requisite for our whole retinue.

Once settled in, they were visited by the mayor and his constables, together with many of the villagers. This place was in the parish of their old friend, the cura of Ticul, who had sent instructions that every assistance should be given to the travelers.

Although we had been some time in the country, we regarded this as really the beginning of our travels; and though the scenes we had met with already were not much like any we had ever encountered before, our first day's journey introduced us to some that were entirely new. The Indians assembled under the arbour, where they, with great formality, offered us seats, and the alcalde told us that the rancho was poor, but they would do all they could to serve us. Neither he nor any other in the place spoke a word of Spanish, and our communications were through Albino. We opened the interview by remonstrating against the charge of two reals for watering our horses, but the excuse was satisfactory enough. In the rainy season they had sources of supply in the neighbourhood, and these were perhaps as primitive as in any other section of the habitable world, being simply deposites of rain-water in the holes and hollows of rocks, which were called sartenejas. From the rocky nature of the country, these are very numerous.

Early in the morning we set out for the ruins of Zayi, or Salli. At a short distance from the rancho we saw in an overgrown milpa on our left the ruins of a mound and building, so far destroyed that they are not worth presenting.

After proceeding a mile and a half we saw at some distance before us a great tree-covered mound, which astonished us by its vast dimensions, and, but for our Indian assistants, would have frightened us by the size of the trees growing upon it. The woods commenced from the roadside. Our guides cut a path, and, clearing the branches overhead, we followed on horseback, dismounting at the foot of the Casa Grande. It was by this name that the Indians called the immense pile of white stone buildings, which, buried in the depths of a great forest, added new desolation to the waste by which they were surrounded. We tied our horses, and worked our way along the front. The trees were so close that we could take in but a small portion of it at once.

We were at no loss what to do, our great object now being to economize time. Without waiting to explore the rest of the ground, we set the Indians at work, and in a few minutes the stillness of ages was broken by the sharp ringing of the axe and the crash of falling trees. With a strong force of Indians, we were able, in the course of the day, to lay bare the whole of the front.

Dr. Cabot did not arrive on the ground till late in the day, and, coming upon it suddenly from the woods, when there were no trees to obstruct the view, and its three great ranges and immense proportions were visible at once, considered it the grandest spectacle he had seen in the country.

Plate I represents the front of this building. The view was taken from a mound, at the distance of about five hundred feet, overgrown and having upon it a ruined edifice. In clearing away the trees and undergrowth to this mound we discovered a pila, or stone, hollowed out, and filled with rain-water, which was a great acquisition to us while working at these ruins.

The plate represents so much of the building as now remains and can be presented in a drawing. It has three stories or ranges, and in the centre is a grand staircase thirty-two feet wide, rising to the platform of the highest terrace. This staircase, however, is in a ruinous condition, and, in fact, a mere mound, and all that part of the building on the right had fallen, and was so dilapidated that no intelligible drawing could be made of it; we did not even clear away the trees. The engraving represents all that part which remains, being the half of the building on the left of the staircase.

The lowest of the three ranges is two hundred and sixty-five feet in front and one hundred and twenty in depth. It had sixteen doorways, opening into apartments of two chambers each. The whole front wall has fallen; the interiors are filled with fragments and rubbish, and the ground in front was so encumbered with the branches of fallen trees, even after they had been chopped into pieces and beaten down with poles, that, at the distance necessary for making, a drawing, but a small portion of the interior could be seen. The two ends of this range have each six doorways, and the rear has ten, all opening into apartments, but in general they are in a ruinous condition.

The range of buildings on the second terrace was two hundred and twenty feet in length and sixty feet in depth, and had four doorways on each side of the grand staircase. Those on the left, which are all that remain, have two columns in each doorway, each column being six feet six inches high, roughly made, with square capitals, like Doric, but wanting the grandeur pertaining to all known remains of this ancient order. Filling up the spaces between the doorways are four small columns curiously ornamented, close together, and sunk in the wall. Between the first and second and third and fourth doorways a small staircase leads to the terrace of the third range. The platform of this terrace is thirty feet in front and twenty-five in the rear. The building is one hundred and fifty feet long by eighteen feet deep, and has seven doorways opening into as many apartments. The lintels over the doorways are of stone.

PLATE I

ZAYI

The Palace,
Sayil.

The exterior of the third and highest range was plain; that of the two other ranges had been elaborately ornamented; and, in order to give some idea of their character, I present in Plate II a portion of the façade of the second range. Among designs common in other places is the figure of a man supporting himself on his hands, with his legs expanded in a curious rather than delicate attitude.

Figure 1 represents the ground plan of the three ranges, and gives the dimensions of the terraces. The platforms are wider in front than in the rear; the apartments vary from twenty-three to ten feet, and the north side of the second range has a curious and unaccountable feature. It is called the Casa Cerrada, or closed house, having ten doorways, all of which are blocked up inside with stone and mortar. Like the well at Xcoch, it had a mysterious reputation in the village of Nohcacab, and all believed that it contained hidden treasure. Indeed, so strong was this belief, that the alcalde Segundo, who had never visited these ruins, resolved to take advantage of our presence; and, according to agreement in the village, came down with crowbars to assist us in breaking into the closed apartments and discovering the precious hoard. The first sight of these closed-up doorways gave us a strong desire to make the attempt; but on moving along we found that the Indians had been beforehand with us. In front of several were piles of stones, which they had worked out from the doorways, and under the lintels were holes, through which we were able to crawl inside; and here we found ourselves in apartments finished with walls and ceilings like all the others, but filled up (except so far as they had been emptied by the Indians) with solid masses of mortar and stone. There were ten of these apartments in all, 220 feet long and ten feet deep, which being thus filled up, made the whole building a solid mass; and the strangest feature was that the filling up of the apartments must have been simultaneous with the erection of the buildings, for, as the filling-in rose above the tops of the doorways, the men who performed it never could have entered

PLATE II

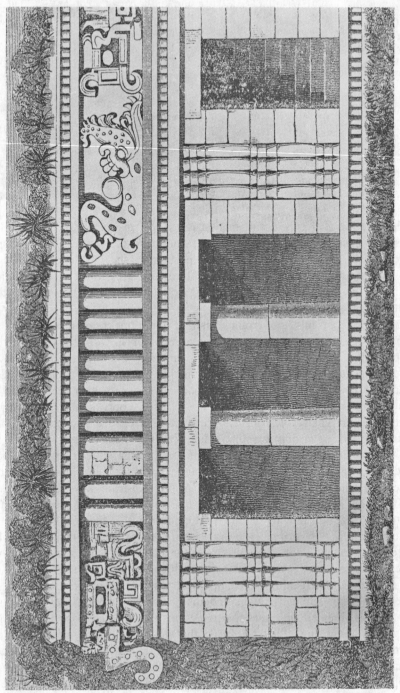

*Descending God and
Celestial Dragon.
Decoration on
the Palace, Sayil*

to their work through the doors. It must have been done as the walls were built, and the ceiling must have closed over a solid mass. Why this was so constructed it was impossible to say, unless the solid mass was required for the support of the upper terrace and building; and if this was the case, it would seem to have been much easier to erect a solid structure at once, without any division into apartments.

This building is now called the Grand Palace, *and is one of the most outstanding examples of Maya architecture. Here, round columns are used, showing a great advance in building technique. The decoration of the facade is particularly striking on the middle floor, where small columns alternate with masks of the rain god, the descending god and the celestial dragon.*

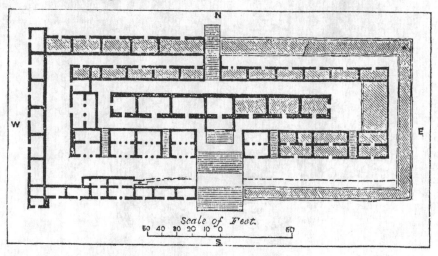

Scale of Feet.
50 40 30 20 10 0   50

FIG. 1

The top of this building commanded a grand view, no longer of a dead plain, but of undulating woodlands. Toward the northwest, crowning the highest hill, was a lofty mound, covered with trees, which, to our now practised eyes, it was manifest shrouded a building, either existing or in ruins. Climbing up this hill with great toil, we reached the wall of a terrace, and, climbing this, found ourselves at the foot of the building.

It was in a ruinous condition, and did not repay us for the labour; but over the door was a sculptured head with a face of good expression and workmanship. In one of the apartments was a high projection running along the wall; in another a raised platform about a foot high; and on the walls of this apartment was the print of the red hand.

In front of the Casa Grande, at the distance of five hundred yards, and also visible from the top, is another structure, strikingly different from any we had seen, more strange and inexplicable, and having at a distance the appearance of a New-England factory.

Figure 2 represents this building. It stands on a terrace, and may be considered as consisting of two separate structures, one above the other. The lower

FIG. 2

one, in its general features, resembled all the rest. It was forty feet in front, low, and having a flat roof, and in the centre was an archway running through the building. The front is fallen, and the whole so ruined that nothing but the archway appears in the engraving. Along the middle of the roof, unsupported, and entirely independent of everything else, rises a perpendicular wall to the height of perhaps thirty feet. It is of stone, about two feet thick, and has oblong openings through it about four feet long and six inches wide, like small windows. It had been covered with stucco, which had fallen off, and left the face of rough stone and mortar; and on the other side were fragments of stuccoed figures and ornaments. An Indian appears before it in the act of killing a snake, with which all the woods of Yucatan abound. Since we began our exploration of American ruins we had not met with anything more inexplicable than this great perpendicular wall. It seemed built merely to puzzle posterity.

This seems to be the building now know as the Observatory, *which is a temple with a roof crest, standing on a pyramidal base.*

These were the only buildings in this immediate neighbourhood which had survived the wasting of the elements; but, inquiring among the Indians, one of them undertook to guide me to another, which he said was still in good preservation. Our direction was south-southwest from the Casa Grande; and at the distance of about a mile, the whole intermediate region being desolate and overgrown, we reached a terrace, the area of which far exceeded anything we had seen in the country. We crossed it from north to south, and in this direction it must have been fifteen hundred feet in length, and probably was quite as much in the other direction; but it was so rough, broken, and over-grown, that we did not attempt to measure it.

On this great platform was the building of which the Indian had told us; I had it cleared, and Mr. Catherwood drew it the next day, as it appears in Plate III.

In several places the great platform is strewed with ruins, and probably other buildings lie buried in the woods, but without guides or any clew whatever, we did not attempt to look for them.

It was strange and almost incredible that, with these extraordinary monu-ments before their eyes, the Indians never bestowed upon them one passing thought. They had the same superstitious feelings as the Indians of Uxmal; they believed that the ancient buildings were haunted, and, as in the remote region of Santa Cruz del Quiché, they said that on Good Friday of every year music was heard sounding among the ruins.

PLATE III

ZAYI

CHAPTER II

Well of Chack — Ruins of Sabachshé

The next morning, while Mr. Catherwood was engaged in drawing the building represented in the last engraving, Dr. Cabot and myself set out to visit the one which we had passed in coming from the rancho of Chack.

In the suburbs of the rancho we turned off to the right by a path, which we followed for some distance on horseback, when it changed its direction, and we dismounted. From this place our guides cut a path through the woods, and we came out upon a large field of táje, being long stems growing close together, eight or ten feet high, straight, and about half an inch thick, having a yellow flower on the top, which is a favourite food for horses. On one side of this field we saw the high building before referred to, and on the other side was a second not visible before. A bird which the doctor wished to procure lighted on a tree growing upon the latter, and we went to it, but found nothing of particular interest, and struck across the field of táje for the former.

The building stood on the top of a stony hill, on a terrace still firm and substantial. It consisted of two stories, the roof of the lower one forming the platform in front of the upper, and had a staircase, which was broken and ruined. The upper building had a large apartment in the centre, and a smaller one on each side, much encumbered with rubbish, from one of which we were driven by a hornet's nest, and in another a young vulture, with a hissing noise, flapped its plumeless wings and hopped out of the door.

Leaving this, we toiled back to our horses, and, returning to the road, passed through the rancho, about a mile beyond which we reached the pozo, or well, the accounts of which we had heard on our first arrival.

Near the mouth were some noble seybo trees, throwing their great branches far and wide, under which groups of Indians were arranging their calabashes and torches, preparing to descend; others, just out, were wiping their sweating bodies. At one moment an Indian disappeared, and at the next another rose up out of the earth. We noticed that there were no women, who, throughout Yucatan, are the drawers of water, and always seen around a well, but we were told that no woman ever enters the well of Chack; all the water for the rancho was procured by the men, which alone indicated that the well was of an extraordinary character.

Our first movement was down a hole by a perpendicular ladder, at the foot of which we were fairly entered into a great cavern. Our guides preceded us with bundles of táje lighted for torches, and we came to a second descent almost perpendicular, which we achieved by a ladder laid flat against the rock. Beyond this we moved on a short distance, still following our guides, and still descending, when we saw their torches disappearing, and reached a wild hole, which also we descended by a long rough ladder. At the foot of this the rock was damp and slippery, and there was barely room enough to pass around it, and get upon another ladder down the same hole, now more contracted, and so small that, with the arms akimbo, the elbows almost touched on each side. At this time our Indians were out of sight; and in total darkness, feeling our way by the rounds of the ladder, we cried out to them, and were answered by distant voices directly underneath. Looking down, we saw their torches like moving balls of fire, apparently at an interminable distance below us.

At the foot of this ladder there was a rude platform as a resting-place, made to enable those ascending and descending to pass each other. Descending the next ladder, both above and below us were torches gleaming in the darkness. We had still another ladder to descend, and the whole perpendicular depth of this hole was perhaps two hundred feet.

From the foot of this ladder there was an opening to the right, and from it we soon entered a low, narrow passage, through which we crawled on our hands and knees. With the toil and the smoke of the torches the heat was almost beyond endurance. The passage enlarged and again contracted, descending steeply, and so low that the shoulders almost touched the roof. This opened upon a great chasm at one side, and beyond we came to another perpendicular hole, which we descended by steps cut in the rock. From this there was another low, crawling passage, and, almost stifled with heat and smoke, we came out into a small opening, in which was a basin of water, being the well. The place was crowded with Indians filling their calabashes, and they started at the sight of our smoky white faces as if El Demonio had descended among them. It was, doubtless, the first time that the feet of a white man had ever reached this well.

And this well was not, as at Xcoch, the occasional resort of a straggling Indian, nor the mere traditionary watering-place of an ancient city. It was the regular and only supply of a living population. The whole rancho of Chack was entirely dependant upon it, and in the dry season the rancho of Schawill, three miles distant.

After exploring the well they set off again toward the rancho of Chaví.

We arrived at the rancho in good season. Mr. Catherwood had finished his drawing, and Bernaldo was ready with his dinner. We had nothing to detain us, ordered carriers forthwith for our luggage, and at half past two we were in the saddle again in search of ruined cities.

At the distance of two leagues we reached the rancho of Sannacté, the Indians of which were the wildest people in appearance we had yet seen.

Beyond the outskirts of the rancho was a large clearing for a milpa, within which, naked and exposed to full view, were two ancient buildings. The milpa was enclosed by a fence, and was overgrown with táje. We tied our horses to the stems of the táje, and, leaving them eating the flowers, followed a path which led between the two buildings. Figure 3 represents the one on the left.

FIG. 3

It stands on a terrace, still strong and substantial, and, fortunately, clear of trees, though many were growing on the top. It has five apartments; the façade above the cornice is fallen, and between the doorways are fragments of small columns set in the wall. On the other side of the milpa was another edifice, holding aloft a high wall, like that we had seen at Zayi, extraordinary in its appearance and incomprehensible in its uses and purposes. From the tact and facility we had now acquired, a short time sufficed for our examination of this place, and, with one more added to our list of ruined cities, we mounted, and resumed our journey.

At half past five we reached the rancho of Sabachshé, lying on the camino real from Ticul to Bolonchen, and inhabited entirely by Indians. The casa real stood on an elevation in an open place. This rancho was distinguished by a well, the sight of which was more grateful to us than that of the best hotel to the traveller in a civilized country. We were scratched with thorns, and smarting with garrapata bites, and looked forward to the refreshment of a bath. The well was built by the present owner, and formerly the inhabitants were dependant entirely upon the well at Tabi, six miles distant! Besides its real value, it presented a curious and lively spectacle. A group of Indian women was around it. It had no rope or fixtures of any kind for raising water, but across the mouth was a round beam laid upon two posts, over which the women were letting down and hoisting up little bark buckets. Every woman brought with her and carried away her own bucket and rope, the latter coiled up and laid on the top of her head, with the end hanging down behind, and the coil forming a sort of headdress.

Near the well was the hut of the alcalde, enclosed by a rude fence, and within were dogs, hogs, turkeys, and fowls, which all barked, grunted, gobbled, and cackled together as we entered. The yard was shaded by orange-trees loaded with ripe and unusually large fruit. Under one of them was a row of twenty or thirty wild boars' jaws and tusks, trophies of the chase, and memorials attesting the usefulness of the barking dogs. The noise brought the alcalde to the door, a heavy and infirm old man, apparently rich, and suffering from the high living indicated by his hogs and poultry; but he received us with meekness and humility. We negotiated forthwith for the purchase of some oranges, and bought thirty for a medio, stipulating that they should all be the largest and best on the trees; after which, supporting himself by his cane, he hobbled on to the casa real, had it swept out, and assigned Indians to attend upon us.

Early in the morning we found a large gathering round the house to escort us to the ruins.

Crossing the fence of the last hut, we entered a thick growth of trees. As if instinctively, every Indian drew his machete, and in a few minutes they cut a path to the foot of a small building, not rich in ornament, but tasteful. We gave directions, all the Indians fell to work, and in a few minutes the small terrace in front was cleared. In half an hour space enough was cleared for Mr. Catherwood to set up his camera lucida. The same alertness was shown in preparing a place for him to stand in, and half a dozen stood ready to hold an umbrella for his protection against the sun.

Plate IV represents the front of the building. Its design is tasteful and even elegant, and when perfect it must have presented a fine appearance. It has a single doorway, opening into a chamber twenty-five feet long by ten wide. Above the door is a portion of plain masonry, and over this a cornice

PLATE IV

SABACHTSCHE

supporting twelve small pilasters, having between them the diamond ornament, then a massive cornice, with pilasters and diamond work, surmounted by another cornice, making in all four cornices; an arrangement we had not previously met with.

While Mr. Catherwood was making his drawing, the Indians stood around under the shade of the trees, looking at him quietly and respectfully, and making observations to each other. All at once an enormous iguana, or lizard, doubled the corner of the building, ran along the front, and plunged into a crevice over the door, burying his whole body, but leaving the long tail out. Among these unsophisticated people this reptile is a table delicacy, and here was a supper provided for some of them. All the Indians, one after the other, had a pull at the tail, but could not make him budge. At length two of them contrived to get hold together, and, while pulling with all their strength, the tail came off by the roots, a foot and half long in their hands. The Indians picked away the mortar with their machetes, and enlarged the hole until they got his hind legs clear, when, griping the body above the legs, they again hauled; but, though he had only the fore legs to hold on with, they could not tear him out. They then untied the ropes of their sandals, and, fastening them above the hind legs, and pulling till the long body seemed parting like the tail, they at length dragged him out.

This over, we moved on in a body, carrying the iguana, to the next building, which was situated in a different direction, about a quarter of a mile distant, and completely buried in woods. It was seventy-five feet long, and had three doorways, leading to the same number of apartments. A great part of the front had fallen; Plate V represents that which remains. With some slight difference in the detail of ornament, the character is the same as in all the other buildings, and the general effect pleasing. Growing on the roof are two maguey plants, Agave Americana, in our latitude called the century plant, but under the hot sun of the tropics blooming every four or five years. There are four species of this plant in Yucatan: the maguey, from which is produced the pulqué, a beverage common in all the Mexican provinces, which, taken in excess, produces intoxication; the henneken, which produces the article known in our markets as Sisal hemp; the sabila, with which the Indian women wean children, covering the breast with the leaf, which is very bitter to the taste; and the peta, having leaves twice as large as the last, from which a very fine white hemp is made.

While Mr. C. was engaged in drawing this structure, the Indians told us of two others half a league distant. I selected two of them for guides, and, with the same alacrity which they had shown in everything else, nine volunteered to accompany me. We had a good path nearly all the way, until the Indians pointed out a white object seen indistinctly through the trees, again uttering, with strong gutturals, the familiar sound of "Xlappahk," or old walls.

PLATE V

F. Catherwood.   S.H.Gimber.

SABACHTSCHE

In a few minutes they cut a path to it. The building was larger than the last, having the front ornamented in the same way, much fallen, though still present- ing an interesting spectacle. As it was not much overgrown, we set to work and cleared it, and left it for another, in regard to which I formed some curious expectations, for the Indians described it as *very new*. It lay on the same path, to the left in returning to the rancho, and separated from us by a great field of táje, through which we were obliged to cut a path for several hundred yards to the foot of the terrace. The walls were entire and very massive; but climbing up it, I found only a small building, consisting of but two apartments, the front much fallen, and the doors filled up, but no sign or token distinguishing it as *newer* or more modern; and I now learned, what I might have done before by a little asking, that all they meant by their description of it was, that it was the *newest* known to them, having been discovered but twelve years before, accidentally, on clearing the ground for a milpa.

On the walls of this desolate edifice were prints of the "mano colorado," or red hand. These prints were larger than any I had seen. In several places I measured them with my own, opening the fingers to correspond with those on the wall. The Indians said it was the hand of the master of the building.

The mysterious interest which, in my eyes, always attached to this red hand, has assumed a more definite shape. I have been advised that in Mr. Catlin's collection of Indian curiosities, made during a long residence among our North American tribes, was a tent presented to him by the chief of the powerful but now extinct race of Mandans, which exhibits, among other marks, two prints of the red hand; and I have been farther advised that the red hand is seen constantly upon the buffalo robes and skins of wild animals brought in by the hunters on the Rocky Mountains, and, in fact, that it is a symbol recognised and in common use by the North American Indians of the pres- ent day.

Some researchers into the Maya zone have the theory that these red handprints could be symols of Kebul, 'the divine creative hand', one of the forms of the god Itzamná, lord of the heavens.

CHAPTER III

The Ruins of Labná

The next morning we set out for the ruins of Labnà. Our road lay southeast, among hills, and was more picturesque than any we had seen in the country. At the distance of a mile and a half we reached a field of ruins, which, after all we had seen, created in us new feelings of astonishment. It was one of the circumstances attending our exploration of ruins in this country, that until we arrived on the ground we had no idea of what we were to meet with. The accounts of the Indians were never reliable. When they gave us reason to expect much we found but little, and, on the other hand, when we expected but little a great field presented itself. Of this place even our friend the cura Carillo had never heard. Our first intelligence of ruins in this region was from the brother of the padrecito at Nohcacab, who, however, had never seen them himself. Since our arrival in the country we had not met with anything that excited us more strongly, and now we had mingled feelings of pain and pleasure; of pain, that they had not been discovered before the sentence of irretrievable ruin had gone forth against them; at the same time it was matter of deep congratulation that, before the doom was accomplished, we were permitted to see these decaying, but still proud memorials of a mysterious people.

Plate VI represents a pyramidal mound, holding aloft the most curious and extraordinary structure we had seen in the country. It put us on the alert the moment we saw it. We passed an entire day before it, and, in looking back upon our journey among ruined cities, no subject of greater interest presents itself to my mind. The mound is forty-five feet high. The steps had fallen; trees were growing out of the place where they stood, and we reached the top by clinging to the branches; when these were cleared away, it was extremely difficult to ascend and descend. The maguey plants cut down in making the clearing appear fallen on the steps.

A narrow platform forms the top of the mound. The building faces the south, and when entire measured forty-three feet in front and twenty feet in depth. It had three doorways, of which one, with eight feet of the whole structure, has fallen, and is now in ruins. The centre doorway opens into two chambers, each twenty feet long and six feet wide.

Above the cornice of the building rises a gigantic perpendicular wall to the height of thirty feet, once ornamented from top to bottom, and from

PLATE VI

LABNA

one side to the other, with colossal figures and other designs in stucco, now broken and in fragments, but still presenting a curious and extraordinary appearance, such as the art of no other people ever produced. Along the top, standing out on the wall, was a row of death's heads; underneath were two lines of human figures in alto relievo (of which scattered arms and legs alone remain), the grouping of which, so far as it could be made out, showed considerable proficiency in that most difficult department of the art of design. Over the centre doorway, constituting the principal ornament of the wall, was a colossal figure seated, of which only a large tippet and girdle, and some other detached portions, have been preserved. Conspicuous over the head of this principal figure is a large ball, with a human figure standing up beside it, touching it with his hands, and another below it with one knee on the ground, and one hand thrown up as if in the effort to support the ball, or in the apprehension of its falling upon him.

Mr. Catherwood made two drawings at different hours and under a different position of the sun, and Dr. Cabot and myself worked upon it the whole day with the Daguerreotype.

Our best view was obtained in the afternoon, when the edifice was in shade, but so broken and confused were the ornaments that a distinct representation could not be made even with the Daguerreotype, and the only way to make out all the details was near approach by means of a ladder; we had all the woods to make one of, but it was difficult for the Indians to make one of the length required; and when made it would have been too heavy and cumbersome to manage on the narrow platform in front. Besides, the wall was tottering and ready to fall. One portion was already gone in a perpendicular line from top to bottom, and the reader will see in the engraving that on a line with the right of the centre doorway the wall is cracked, and above is gaping, and stands apart more than a foot all the way to the top. In a few years it must fall. Its doom is sealed.

Fortunately this did not happen; the building now known as the Great Pyramid *or* Mirador *still stands and has been restored by the Mexican government. It is a rectangular pyramid with terraces, although the walls are in ruins. The most important feature of it is the roof crest, placed on the front wall, that has perforations and protuberances to secure the stucco decoration. On the wall at the west corner can be seen the remains of the figure of a goddess, and in the upper part two ballgame players, those referred to by Stephens in his description of this construction.*

At the distance of a few hundred feet from this structure, in sight at the same time as we approached it, is an arched gateway, remarkable for its beauty of proportions and grace of ornament. Plate VII represents this gateway. On

PLATE VII

LABNA
Gateway

The Arch of Labná.

the right, running off at an angle of thirty degrees, is a long building much fallen, which could not be comprehended in the view. On the left it forms an angle with another building, and on the return of the wall there is a doorway, not shown in the engraving, of good proportions, and more richly ornamented than any other portion of the structure. The effect of the whole combination was curious and striking, and, familiar as we were with ruins, the first view, with the great wall towering in front, created an impression that is not easily described.

The gateway is ten feet wide, passing through which we entered a thick forest, growing so close upon the building that we were unable to make out even its shape; but, on clearing away the trees, we discovered that this had been the principal front, and that these trees were growing in what had once been the area, or courtyard. The doors of the apartments on both sides of the gateway, each twelve feet by eight, opened upon this area. Over each doorway was a square recess, in which were the remains of a rich ornament in stucco, with marks of paint still visible, apparently intended to represent the face of the sun surrounded by its rays, probably once objects of adoration and worship, but now wilfully destroyed. Plate VIII represents this front.

The Arch of Labná is one of the splendors of Maya architecture, with its fine decoration. The north face has a frieze with panels of latticework and stylized huts, while the other is decorated with Greek frets and small columns. The central arch is trapezoid shaped and the sides are ornamented with frets, small columns and circles. At the eastern side of the arch are the remains of another building.

Northeast from the mound on which the great wall stands, and about one hundred and fifty yards distant, is a large building, erected on a terrace, and hidden among the trees growing thereupon, with its front much ruined, and having but few remains of sculptured ornaments. Still farther in the same

PLATE VIII

LABNA
Interior of Gateway

*Arch of Labná,
rear view.*

direction, going through the woods, we reach the grand, and, without extravagance, a really magnificent building.

The whole long façade was ornamented with sculptured stone, of which, large as the engraving is, the details cannot appear; but, to give some idea of their character, a detached portion is represented in Plate IX, and, I ought at the same time to remark, is perhaps the most curious and interesting of any. It is at the left end of the principal building, and in the angle of the corner are the huge open jaws of an alligator, or some other hideous animal, enclosing a human head.

The reader will form some idea of the overgrown and shrouded condition of this building from the fact that I had been at work nearly the whole day upon the terrace, without knowing that there was another building on the top. In order to take in the whole front at one view, it was necessary to carry the clearing back some distance into the plain, and in doing this I discovered the upper structure. The growth of trees before it was almost equal to that on the terrace, or in any part of the forest. The whole had to be cleared, the trees thrown down upon the terrace, and thence dragged away to the plain. This building consists of single narrow corridors, and the façade is of plain stone, without any ornaments.

The platform in front is the roof of the building underneath, and in this platform was a circular hole, like those we had seen at Uxmal and other places, leading to subterraneous chambers. This hole was well known to the Indians, and had a marvellous reputation; and yet they never mentioned it until I climbed up to examine the upper building. They said it was the abode of el dueño de la casa, or the owner of the building. I immediately proposed to descend, but the old Indian begged me not to do so, and said apprehensively to the others, "Who knows but that he will meet with the owner?" I immediately sent for rope, lantern, and matches; and, absurd as it may seem, as I looked upon the wild figures of the Indians standing round the hole, and their earnest

PLATE IX

LABNA

*Corner of the
Palace, Labná.*

faces, it was really exciting to hear them talk of the owner. As there was a difficulty in procuring rope, I had a sapling cut and let down the hole, by means of which I descended with a lantern.

The chamber was entirely different in shape from those I had seen before. The latter were circular, and had dome-shaped ceilings. This had parallel walls and the triangular-arched ceiling; in fact, it was in shape exactly like the apartments above ground.

When I came out they looked at me with admiration. They told me that there were other places of the same kind, but they would not show them to me, lest some accident should happen; and as my attempt drew them all from work, and I could not promise myself any satisfactory result, I refrained from insisting.

This description corresponds to the complex called the Great Palace, *that was built at several different periods. There are the remains of three stairways, and another can be made out running to the upper story. The walls are built of large smooth stones. In the lower part there 42 rooms and three groups of chambers above. The decorations of the façade are similar to those of Sayil, with small columns, masks of Chaac, and on the center corner is a human head in the jaws of a serpent. On the terrace of the Palace is the entrance to the cistern or* chultún *described by Stephens that was used for storing rainwater.*

They were able to work quickly on this site thanks to the help of many of the Indians from the hacienda.

From the number of Indians at our command, and their alacrity in working, we had been enabled to accomplish much in a very short time. In three days they finished all that I required of them. When I dismissed them, I gave a half dollar extra to be divided among seventeen, and as I was going away Bernabé exclaimed, "Ave Maria, que gracias dan a vd." "Ave Maria, what thanks they give you."

The natives of Labná, unlike those in other places, were not afraid to go to the ruins at night, or even to sleep there. There were other buildings on this site, but all very ruined, so Stephens used the last day of his stay to visit the hacienda of Tabí with Bernardo, while Catherwood put the finishing touches to his drawings.

As the ancient structures near the hacienda were completely ruined, Stephens went to explore a nearby cave where, he had heard, there were sculpted figures and a sort of chapel. Once inside he saw that these were simply stalagtites and strange rock formations.

Bolonchen: Cenote   *F. Catherwood*

Panoramic of Uxmal   F. Catherwood

Uxmal: Archway   F. Catherwood

Gateway at Labna

F. Catherwood

Chichen Itza: Ku-Kul-Kan Pyramid   F. Catherwood

Temple at Tulum

F. Catherwood

Castle at Tulum.   F. Catherwood

Izamal: Face of Itzamna   F. Catherwood

CHAPTER IV

Journey to the Rancho of Kewick — Visit to the Ruins —
Journey to Xul

The next morning we resumed our journey in search of ruined cities. Our next point of destination was the rancho of Kewick, three leagues distant. Mr. Catherwood set out with the servants and luggage, Dr. Cabot and myself following in about an hour. The Indians told us there was no difficulty in finding the road, and we set out alone. About a mile from the rancho we passed a ruined building on the left, surmounted by a high wall, with oblong apertures, like that mentioned at Zayi as resembling a New-England factory. We passed through two Indian ranchos, and a league beyond came to a dividing point, where we found ourselves at a loss. Both were mere Indian footpaths, seldom or never traversed by horsemen, and, having but one chance against us, we selected that most directly in line with the one by which we had come. In about an hour the direction changed so much that we turned back, and, after a toilsome ride, reached again the dividing point, and turned into the other path. The whole distance to Kewick was but three leagues; we had been riding hard six hours, and began to fear that we had made a mistake in turning back, and at every step were going more astray. In the midst of our perplexities we came upon an Indian leading a wild colt, who, without asking any questions, or waiting for any from us, waved us back, and, tying his colt to a bush, led us across the plain into another path, following which some distance, he again struck across, and put us into still another, where he left us, and started to return to his colt. We were loth to lose him, and urged him to continue as our guide; but he was impenetrable until we held up a medio, when he again moved on before us. In our desolate and wandering path we had seen in different places, at a distance, and inaccessible, five high mounds, holding aloft the ruins of ancient buildings; and doubtless there were more buried in the woods. At three o'clock we entered a dense forest, and came suddenly upon the casa real of Kewick, standing alone, almost buried among trees, the only habitation of any kind in sight; and, to increase the wondering interest which attended every step of our journey in that country, it stood on the platform of an ancient terrace, strewed with the relics of a ruined edifice. The steps of the terrace had fallen and been newly laid, but the walls were entire, with all the stones in place. We tied our horses at the foot of the terrace, and ascended

Fig. 4

the steps. The casa real had mud walls and a thatched roof, and in front was an arbour. Sitting down under the arbour, with our hotel on this ancient platform, we had seldom experienced higher satisfaction on reaching a new and unknown field of ruins. We had still two hours of daylight; and, anxious to have a glimpse of the ruins before night, we had some fried eggs and tortillas got ready.

They were visited by the owner of the rancho, who was an Indian, the first they had met in this position and something they found surprising.

Our hasty dinner over, we asked for Indians to guide us to the ruins, and were somewhat startled by the objections they all made on account of the garrapatas. Since we left Uxmal the greatest of our small hardships had been the annoyance of these insects; in fact, it was by no means a small hardship. During the dry season the little pests are killed off by the heat of the sun, and devoured by birds, but for which I verily believe they would make the country uninhabitable. Nevertheless, we were somewhat startled at the warning conveyed by the reluctance of the Indians; and when we insisted upon going, they gave us another alarming intimation by cutting twigs, with which, from the moment of starting, they whipped the bushes on each side, and swept the path before them.

Beyond the woods we came out into a comparatively open field, in which we saw on all sides through the trees the Xlappahk, or old walls, now grown so familiar, a collection of vast remains and of many buildings. We worked our way to all within sight. The façades were not so much ornamented as some we had seen, but the stones were more massive, and the style of architecture was simple, severe, and grand. Nearly every house had fallen, and one long ornamented front lay on the ground cracked and doubled up as if shaken off by the vibrations of an earthquake, and still struggling to retain its upright position, the whole presenting a most picturesque and imposing scene of ruins, and conveying to the mind a strong image of the besom of destruction sweeping over a city. Night came upon us while gazing at a mysterious painting, and we returned to the casa real to sleep.

Early the next morning we were again on the ground, with our Indian proprietor and a large party of his criados; and as the reader is now somewhat familiar with the general character of these ruins, I select from that great mass around only such as have some peculiarity.

The first is that represented in Plate X. It had been the principal doorway, and was all that now remained of a long line of front, which lay in ruins on the ground. It is remarkable for its simplicity, and, in that style of architecture, for its grandeur of proportions.

The painting itself was curious; the colours were bright, red and green predominating; the lines clear and distinct, and the whole was more perfect than any painting we had seen.

Figure 5 represents this painting. It exhibits a rude human figure, surrounded by hieroglyphics, which doubtless contain the whole of its story. It is 30 inches long by 18 inches wide, and the prevailing colour is red.

Stephens decided that he would take out the stone for it to be drawn properly and then transport it to the U.S.A. The owner was perfectly willing, so the Indians set to work. It was very difficult to remove, and once it was on the ground it was found to be much too heavy to be moved any distance. Stephens therefore asked the owner to keep it somewhere protected from the rain.

I shall present but one more view from the ruins of Kewick. It is part of the front of a long building, forming a right angle with the one last referred to. The terraces almost join, and though all was so overgrown that it was difficult to make out the plan and juxtaposition, the probability is that they formed two

PLATE X

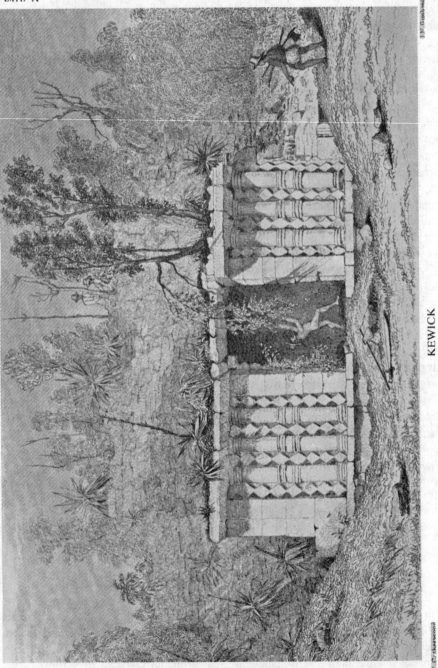

F. Catherwood

J. N. Gimbrede

KEWICK

FIG. 5

sides of a grand rectangular area. The whole building measures two hundred and thirty feet in length. In the centre is a wide ruined staircase leading to the top. Plate XI represents half of the building to the line of the staircase, the other half being exactly similar.

The remaining ruins of Kewick we left as we found them. Fallen buildings and fragments of sculptured stone strew the ground in every direction; but it is impossible to give the reader an idea of the impression produced by wandering among them. For a brief space only we broke the stillness of the desolate city, and left it again to solitude and silence.

Until now only the central part of this site has been explored in fact, and the exact extent of it is not known. The building drawn by Catherwood (Plate X) is the Edifice of the Lozenges, *so called because of the decoration. Work has recently been done to strengthen this building.*

Northeast of this construction is the Edifice of the Tied Columns, *composed of rather strange columns with a sort of 'binding' in the*

PLATE XI

Catherwood.

Jukinson.

KEWICK

middle. On the ceiling of the north room are the remains of paintings done in red, black and blue.

Trying to find the ancient city's source of water, Stephens and his companions were taken to a cave called Actún *and later to an aguada. They were told that in the dry season, stone embankments could be seen here that must have been built by the ancient inhabitants.*

At two o'clock we returned to the casa real. We had "done up" another ruined city, and were ready to set out again; but we had one serious impediment in the way. I have mentioned that on our arrival at this place we gave Albino a dollar, but I omitted to say that it was our last. On setting out on this journey, we had reduced our personal luggage to hammocks and petaquillas, the latter being oblong straw baskets without fastenings, unsafe to carry money in, and silver, the only available coin, was too heavy to carry about the person. At Sabachshé we discovered that our expenses had overrun our estimates, and sent Albino back to Nohcacab with the keys of our money trunk, and directions to follow us in all haste to this place. On counting the scattering medios of private stock, we found that we had enough to pay for transporting our luggage to the village of Xul, but if we tarried over the night and Albino did not come, both ourselves and our horses must go without rations in the morning, and then we should have no means of getting away our luggage.

Leaving special charge for Albino to follow, at three o'clock we set out. The proprietor accompanied us, and at half past five we made a dashing entry into the village of Xul, with horses, and servants, and carriers, and just one solitary medio left.

The casa real of this village was the poorest they had seen on their travels, and they decided that in any case they could not stay there, since supplies would have to be payed for immediately. The convent was nearby, but they had heard that the cura of Xul was rich, money-conscious and eccentric. However, as he was also 'lord' of a ruined city they wanted to visit, they reluctantly decided to go and see him.

But, although rich, he was a padre. Without dismounting, I rode over to the convent. The padre came out to meet me, and told me that he had been expecting us every day. I dismounted, and he took my horse by the bridle, led him across the corridor, through the sala, and out to the yard. He asked why my companions did not come over, and, at a signal, in a few minutes their horses followed mine through the sala.

The cura, don José Gerónimo Rodriguez, had made several improvements to Xul, digging a well that had cost 1500 Mexican dollars and building cisterns in the courtyard of his house. Thanks to this, the village now had seven thousand inhabitants. A mixture of the old and the new could be seen here, as the village stood on the site of an ancient Indian city.

During the evening we had a levée of all the principal white inhabitants, to the number of about six or eight. Among them was the proprietor of the *rancho* and ruins of Nohcacab, to whom we were introduced by the cura, with a tribute to our antiquarian, scientific, and medical attainments, which showed an appreciation of merit it was seldom our good fortune to meet with. The proprietor could give us very little information about the ruins, but undertook to make all the necessary arrangements for our exploration of them, and to accompany us himself.

The evening was wearing away without any opportunity of entering upon this interesting subject, when, to our great satisfaction, we heard the clattering of horses' hoofs, and Albino made his appearance. The production of a bag of dollars fixed us in our high position, and we were able to order Indians for the rancho of Nohcacab the next day. We finished the evening with a warm bath in a hand-basin, under the personal direction of the cura, which relieved somewhat the burning of garrapata bites, and then retired to our hammocks.

CHAPTER V

Journey to the Rancho of Nohcacab — Visit to the Ruins — Visit
to another ruined City — Journey to Ticul — Arrival at Ticul —
A Village Festival

Early the next morning we set out for the rancho of Nohcacab, three
leagues distant. The proprietor had gone before daylight, to receive us on the
ground. We had not gone far when Mr. C. complained of a slight headache,
and wishing to ride moderately, Dr. Cabot and myself went on, leaving him
to follow with the luggage. The morning air was fresh and invigorating, and
the country rolling, hilly, and picturesque.

At nine o'clock we reached the rancho, which showed the truth of the
Spanish proverb, "La vista del amo engorda el caballo;" "The sight of the master fattens the horse." The first huts were enclosed by a well-built stone wall,
along which appeared, in various places, sculptured fragments from the ruins.
Beyond was another wall, enclosing the hut occupied by the master on his
visits to the rancho, the entrance to which was by a gateway formed of two
sculptured monuments of curious design and excellent workmanship, raising
high our expectations in regard to the ruins on this rancho, and sustaining the
accounts we had heard of them.

The proprietor was waiting to receive us, and, having taken possession of
an empty hut, and disposed of our horses, we accompanied him to look over
the rancho.

While we were thus engaged, our baggage carriers arrived with intelligence
that Mr. Catherwood was taken ill, and they had left him lying in the road.
I immediately applied to the propietor for a coché and Indians, and he, with
great alacrity undertook to get them ready; in the mean time I saddled my
horse and hastened back to Mr. Catherwood, whom I found lying on the ground,
with Albino by his side, under the shade of the tree by the fountain, with an
ague upon him, wrapped up in all the coverings he could muster, even to the
saddlecloths of the horses. While he was in this state, two men came along,
bestriding the same horse, and bringing sheets and ponchas to make a covering
for the coché. The path was narrow, and lined on each side with thorn bushes,
the spikes of which stuck in the naked flesh of the Indians as they carried the
coché, and they were obliged to stop frequently and disentangle themselves.
On reaching the rancho I found Doctor Cabot down with a fever. From the

excitement and anxiety of following Mr. Catherwood under the hot sun, and now finding Doctor Cabot down, a cold shivering crept over me, and in a few minutes we were all three in our hammocks. A few hours had made a great change in our condition; and we came near bringing our host down with us. He had been employed in preparing breakfast upon a large scale, and seemed mortified that there was no one to do it justice. Out of pure good feeling toward him, I had it brought to the side of my hammock. My effort made him happy, and I began to think my prostration was merely the reaction from over-excitement; and by degrees what I began to please our host I continued for my own satisfaction. The troubles of my companions no longer disturbed me. My equanimity was perfectly restored, and, breakfast over, I set out to look at the ruins.

Passing through one of the huts, we soon came to a hill covered with trees and very steep, up which the proprietor had cut, not a mere Indian path, but a road two or three yards wide, leading to a building standing upon a terrace on the brow of the hill. The façace above the cornice had fallen, and below it was of plain stone. The interior was entire, but without any distinguishing features. Following the brow of this hill, we came to three other buildings, all standing on the same range, and without any important variations in the details, except that in one the arch had no overlapping stone, but the two sides of the ceiling ran up to a point, and formed a complete angle. These, the Indians told us, were the only buildings that remained. That from which the pillars in the church at Xul were taken was a mere mass of ruins. I was extremely disappointed. From the accounts which had induced us to visit this place, we had made larger calculations. It was the first time I had been thoroughly disappointed. There were no subjects for the pencil, and, except the deep and abiding impression of moving among the deserted structures of another ruined and desolate city, there was nothing to carry away. The proprietor seemed mortified that he had not better ruins to show us, but I gave him to understand that it was not his fault, and that he was in nowise to blame. The Indians sympathized in the mortification of their master, and, to indemnify me, told me of two other ruined cities, one of which was but two leagues from the village of Xul.

I returned and made my report, and Mr. Catherwood immediately proposed a return to the village. Albino had given him an alarming account of the unhealthiness of the rancho, and he considered it advisable to avoid sleeping there a single night. Doctor Cabot was sitting up in his hammock, dissecting a bird. A recurrence of fever might detain us some time, and we determined on returning immediately to Xul. Our decision was carried into execution as promptly as it was made, and, leaving our luggage to the care of Albino, in half an hour, to the astonishment of the Indians and the mortification of the proprietor, we were on our way to the village.

Its was late in the evening when we arrived, but the cura received us as kindly as before.

Stephens wanted to visit the ruins mentioned by the Indians, and the cura found him a guide as far as a rancho in the same direction.

At six o'clock the next morning we started, neither Mr. Catherwood nor Doctor Cabot being able to accompany me. At the distance of about two leagues we reached an Indian rancho, where we learned from an old woman that we had passed the path leading to the ruins. We could not prevail on her to go back and show us the way, but she gave us a direction to another rancho, where she said we could procure a guide.

We were fortunate in finding at this place an Indian, who, for reasons known to himself and the wife of the master, was making a visit during the absence of the latter at his milpa. Retracing our steps, and crossing the camino real, we entered the woods on the other side, and tying our horses, the Indian cut a path up the side of a hill, on the top of which were the ruins of a building. The outer wall had fallen, leaving exposed to view the inner half of the arch, by which, as we approached it, my attention was strongly attracted. This arch was plastered and covered with painted figures in profile, much mutilated, but in one place a row of legs remained, which seemed to have belonged to a procession, and at the first glance brought to my mind the funeral processions on the walls of the tombs at Thebes. In the triangular wall forming the end of the room were three compartments, in which were figures, some having their heads adorned with plumes, others with a sort of steeple cap, and carrying on their heads something like a basket; and two were standing on their hands with their heels in the air. These figures were about a foot high, and painted red. The drawing was good, the attitudes were spirited and life-like, and altogether, even in their mutilated state, they were by far the most interesting paintings we had seen in the country.

There was one other building, and these two, my guide said, were all, but probably others lie buried in the woods. Returning to our horses, he led me to another extraordinary subterraneous well, which probably furnished water to the ancient inhabitants.

In a few minutes we mounted to return to the village. Ruins were increasing upon us, to explore which thoroughly would be the work of years; we had but months, and were again arrested by illness. For some days, at least, Mr. Catherwood would not be able to resume work. I was really distressed by the magnitude of what was before us, but, for the present, we could do nothing, and I determined at once to change the scene. The festival of Ticul was at hand, and that night it was to open with el báyle de las Mestizas, or the Mestiza ball. Ticul lay in our return route, nine leagues from the village of Xul, but I determined to reach it that evening.

They reached Xul at eleven o'clock in the morning, had breakfast and, in spite of the scorching heat, Stephens and Albino continued on their way. After a long, difficult ride through the mountains, they reached the top of the last range as night was falling. From there they had a fine view of the hermitage of Nuestra Señora del Pilar and the village of Oxcutzcab. Stopping in the village only for a drink of water, they continued towards Ticul.

We roused the barking dogs of two villages, of which, however, I could distinguish nothing but the outline of their gigantic churches, and at nine o'clock rode into the plaza of Ticul. It was crowded with Indians, blazing with lights, and occupied by a great circular scaffold for a bull-ring, and a long, enclosed arbour, from the latter of which strains of music gave notice that the báyle de las Mestizas had already begun.

Once more I received a cordial welcome from the cura Carillo; but the music from the arbour reminded me that the moments of pleasure were fleeting. Our trunks had been ordered over from Nohcacab, and, making a hurried toilet, I hastened to the ball-room, accompanied by the padre Brizeña; the crowd outside opened a way, Don Philippe Peon beckoned to me as I entered, and in a moment more I was seated in one of the best places at the báyle de las Mestizas. After a month in Indian ranchos, that day toiling among ruins, almost driven to distraction by garrapatas, clambering over frightful sierra, and making a journey worse than any sixty miles in our country, all at once I settled down at a fancy ball, amid music, lights, and pretty women, in the full enjoyment of an armchair and a cigar.

El báyle de las Mestizas was what might be called a fancy ball, in which the señoritas of the village appeared as las Mestizas, or in the costume of Mestiza women: loose white frock, with red worked border round the neck and skirt, a man's black hat, a blue scarf over the shoulder, gold necklace and bracelets. The young men figured as vaqueros, or major domos, in shirt and pantaloons of pink striped muslin, yellow buckskin shoes, and low, round-crowned, hard-platted straw hat, with narrow brim rolled up at the sides, and trimmed with gold cord and tassels.

At daylight the next morning the ringing of bells and firing of rockets announced the continuance of the fiesta; high mass was performed in the church, and at eight o'clock there was a grand exhibition of lassoing cattle in the plaza by amateur vaqueros.

This over, all dispersed to prepare for the báyle de dia, or ball by daylight. I sat for an hour in the corridor of the convent, looking out upon the plaza. The sun was beaming with intense heat, and the village was as still as if some great calamity had suddenly overtaken it. At length a group was seen crossing the plaza: a vaquero escorting a Mestiza to the ball, holding over her head a red silk umbrella to protect her from the scorching rays of the sun; then an old lady and gentleman, children, and servants, a complete family group, the females all in white, with bright-coloured scarfs and shawls. Other groups appeared crossing in other directions, forming picturesque and pleasing spectacles in the plaza. I walked over to the arbour. Although in broad daylight, under the glare of a midday sun, and shaded only on one side by hemp bagging, as the Mestizas look their seats they seemed prettier than the night before.

The báyle de dia was intended to give a picture of life at a hacienda, and there were two prominent personages, who did not appear the evening before, called fiscales, being the officers attendant upon the ancient caciques, and representing them in their authority over the Indians.

As each Mestiza arrived they quietly put aside the gentleman escorting her, and conducted the lady to her seat. If the gentleman did not give way readily, they took him by the shoulders, and walked him to the other end of the floor.

All the Mestizas were again called out in order, presenting the same pretty spectacle I had seen the evening before.

At twelve o'clock preparations were made for a déjeûner à la fourchette, dispensing, however, with knives and forks. The centre of the floor was cleared, and an enormous earthen jar, equal in capacity to a barrel, was brought in, containing frigoles, or black beans fried. Another vessel of the same size had a preparation of eggs and meat, and near them was a small mountain of tortillas, with all which it was the business of the Mestizas to serve the company. At two o'clock, to my great regret, the ball of las Mestizas broke up. It was something entirely new, and remains engraven on my mind as the best of village balls.

CHAPTER VI

Bullfights — Horse-race — A Ball of Etiquette — Calendar of the
Ancient Indians

In the afternoon commenced the first bull-fight. The bull-fights of
Ticul had a great reputation throughout the country. At the last, a toreador
was killed, which gave a promise of something exciting. The young men of the
village still appeared in character as vaqueros, and before the fight they had
a horse-race, which consisted in riding across the ring, one at a time, in at one
door and out at the other, and then racing in the same way through the other
two doors. It was a fine opportunity of exhibiting horses and horsemanship, and
was a sort of pony scamper.

After these came the toreadores, or bull-fighters, who, to do them justice,
were by far the worst-looking men I saw in the country, or anywhere else.
They were of a mixed blood, which makes, perhaps, the worst race known,
viz, the cross of the Indian and African, and called Pardos. Their complexion
is a black tinge laid upon copper, and, not satisfied with the bountiful share
of ugliness which nature had given them, these worthies had done something
for themselves in the way of costume, which was a vile caricature of the common
European dress, with some touches of their own elegant fancy. Their horses,
being borrowed by the committee of arrangements, with the understanding that
if killed they were to be paid for, were spavined, foundered, one-eyed, wretched
beasts.

*He describes how the bull was attacked with spears, killed messily and
dragged from the arena.*

From the bull-fight we again went to the ball, which, in the evening, was
the báyle del etiquettte, no gentleman being admitted without pantaloons.

*In other words, men wearing regional costume, which includes loose
cotton pants, were not allowed to attend.*

The whole aspect of things was changed; the vaqueros were in dress suits,
or such undress as was not unbecoming at a village ball. The señoritas had
thrown aside their simple Mestiza dresses, and appeared in tunicas, or frocks,
made to fit the figure, or, rather, to cut the figure in two. The Indian dances
had disappeared, and quadrilles and contradances, waltzes and gallopades, supplied their place.

At ten the next day there was another bull-fight; then a horse-race from the plaza down the principal street to the house of Don Philippe Peon; and in the afternoon yet another bull-fight.

The next day Mr. Catherwood and Doctor Cabot arrived. Both had had a recurrence of fever, and were still very weak. In the evening was the carnival ball, but before the company had all arrived. We were again scattered by the rain. All the next day it was more abundant than we had seen it in the country, and completely destroyed all the proposed gayeties of the carnival.

We had one clear day, which we devoted to taking Daguerreotype like-nesses of the cura and two of the Mestizas; and, beside the great business of balls, bull-fights, Daguerreotyping, and superintending the morals of the padres, I had some light reading in a manuscript entitled, "Antigua Chronologia Yuca-teca," "Ancient Chronology of Yucatan; or, a simple Exposition of the Method used by the Indians to compute Time." This essay was presented to me by the author, Don Pio Perez, whom I had the satisfaction of meeting at this place.

The essay explains at large the principles imbodied in the calendar of the ancient Indians. It has been submitted for examination (with other interesting papers furnished me by Don Pio, which will be referred to hereafter) to a distinguished gentleman, known by his researches into Indian languages and antiquities, and I am authorized to say that it furnishes a basis for some inter-esting comparisons and deductions, and is regarded as a valuable contribution to the cause of science.

From the examination and analysis made by the distinguished gentleman before referred to, I am enabled to state the interesting fact, that the calendar of Yucatan, though differing in some particulars, was substantially the same with that of the Mexicans. It had a similar solar year of three hundred and sixty-five days, divided in the same manner, first, into eighteen months of twenty days each, with five supplementary days; and, secondly, into twenty-eight weeks of thirteen days each, with an additional day. It had the same method of distinguishing the days of the year by a combination of those two series, and the same cycle of fifty-two years, in which the years, as in Mexico, are distinguished by a combination of the same series of thirteen, with another of four names or hieroglyphics; but Don Pio acknowledges that in Yucatan there is no certain evidence of the intercalation (similar to our leap year, or to the Mexican secular addition of thirteen days) necessary to correct the error resulting from counting the year as equal to three hundred and sixty-five days only.

It will be seen, by reference to the essay, that, besides the cycle of fifty-two years common to the Yucatecans and Mexicans, and, as Don Pio Perez asserts (on the authority of Veytia), to the Indians of Chiapas, Oaxaca, and Soco-nusco, those of Yucatan had another age of two hundred and sixty, or of three hundred and twelve years, equal to five or six cycles of fifty-two years, each of which ages consisted of thirteen periods (called Ajau or Ajau Katun) of twenty years each, according to many authorities, but, in Don Pio's opinion, twenty-four years.

A calendar is a work of science, founded upon calculations, arbitrary signs, and symbols, and the similarity shows that both nations acknowledged the same starting points, attached the same meaning to the same phenomena and objects, which meaning was sometimes arbitrary, and not such as would suggest itself to the untutored. It shows common sources of knowledge and processes of reasoning, similarity of worship and religious institutions, and, in short, it is a link in a chain of evidence tending to show a common origin in the aboriginal inhabitants of Yucatan and Mexico.

Don Pío Pérez had come from Peto especially to talk with Stephens and give him a copy of 'Ancient Chronology of Yucatán', *compiled from information he had copied from the archives of Peto and Maní. The ancient Mayas had perfected their mathematics and calendar, and the documents that Pérez gave to the American explorer later helped toward a better understanding of Maya culture. This knowledge was increased when the manuscript of Bishop Diego de Landa,* 'Relación de las Cosas de Yucatán' *(Account of Things in Yucatán) was published, in a French translation, in 1864.*

CHAPTER VII

Ruins of Sacbey — Paved road — Ruins of Xampon — "Old Walls."
called by Indians Xlapphak — Rancho of Cunhuhu — Visit to the
Ruins

On the fourteenth of February we returned to Nohcacab. We had sent Albino before to make all our necessary arrangements, and on the fifteenth we took our final leave of this village. Our luggage was again reduced to the smallest possible compass: hammocks, a few changes of clothes, and Daguerreotype apparatus, all the rest being forwarded to meet us at Peto. The chief of our Indian carriers was a sexton, who had served out his time, an old neighbour in the convent, whom we had never seen sober, and who was this morning particularly the reverse.

On setting out our direction was again south, and again our road was over the sepulchres of cities. At the distance of two miles we saw "old walls" on an eminence at the right; a little farther three ruined buildings on the same side of the road; and beyond these we came to the ruins of Sacbey. These consist of three buildings, irregularly disposed, one of which is represented in Plate XII. It faces the south, measures fifty-three feet front by twelve feet six inches deep, and has three small doorways. Another, a little farther south, is about the size of the former, and has three apartments, with two columns in the centre doorway. The third is so ruined that its plan could not be made out.

A short distance beyond is one of the most interesting monuments of antiquity in Yucatan. It is a broken platform or roadway of stone, about eight feet wide and eight or ten inches high, crossing the road, and running off into the woods on both sides. I have before referred to it as called by the Indians Sacbey, which means, in the Maya language, a paved way of pure white stone. The Indians say it traversed the country from Kabah to Uxmal; and that on it couriers travelled, bearing letters to and from the lords of those cities, written on leaves or the bark of trees.

It had been my intention to explore thoroughly the route of this ancient road, and, if possible, trace it through the woods to the desolate cities which it once connected, and it was among the vexations of our residence at Nohcacab that we had not been able to do so. The difficulty of procuring Indians to work, and a general recurrence of sickness, rendered it impossible.

PLATE XII

SACBEY

Stephens had heard of the roads running between various Maya cities, but it was not until this moment that he saw that they really existed. The 'white roads' or sacbeob *were later studied by other investigators, confirming the reports of priests and chroniclers and showing that they were built of stone and gravel held together with a sort or white cement called* sacab *and were of both social and commercial importance.*

Again passing "old walls" on each side of the road, at the distance of two leagues we reached Xampon, where stand the remains of an edifice which, when entire, must have been grand and imposing, and now, but for the world of ruins around, might excite a stranger's wonder. Its form was rectangular, its four sides enclosing a hollow square. It measured from north to south eighty feet, and from east to west one hundred and five. Two angles only remain, one of which is represented in Plate XIII. It stood alone, and an Indian had planted a milpa around it. From this "old walls" were again visible, which the Indians called Kalupok.

Beyond we saw at a distance two other places, called Hiokowitz and Kuepak, ruined and difficult of access, and we did not attempt to reach them.

The heat was intense; we exhausted our waccals of water, and as there was no stream or fountain, our only chance of a supply was from a deposite of rain-water in the hollow of some friendly rock.

It was late in the afternoon when we reached the savanna of Chunhuhu, and rode up to the hut at which I had tied my horse on my former visit.

The hut was buit of upright poles, had a steep projecting roof thatched with palm leaves, and the sides protected by the same material; as we stopped in front, we saw a woman within mashing maize for tortillas, which promised a speedy supper. She said her husband was away; but this made no difference to us, and, after a few more words, we all entered, the woman at the moment bolting for the door, and leaving us in exclusive possession. Very soon, how-ever, a little boy, about eight years old, came down and demanded the maize, which we were loth to give up, but did not consider ourselves authorized to retain.

Being provided for ourselves, we next looked to our horses. There was no difficulty about their food, for a supply of corn had fallen into our hands, and the grass on the savanna was the best pasture we had seen in the country; but we learned, to our dismay, from the little boy, who was the only person we saw, that there was no water. Our horses had not touched water since morning, and, after a long, hot, and toilsome journey, we could not think of their going without all night.

The little boy was hovering about the rancho in charge of a naked sister some two years old, and commissioned, as he told us himself, to watch that we did not take anything from the hut. For a medio he undertook to show me the place where they procured water, and, mounting his little sister upon

Plate XIII

Catherwood

Johnsen

XAMPON

his back, he led the way up a steep and stony hill. I followed with the bridle of my horse in my hand, and, without any little girl on my back, found it difficult to keep up with him. On the top of the hill were worn and naked rocks, with deep hollows in them, some holding perhaps as much as one or two pails of water. I led my horse to one of the largest. He was always an extraordinary water drinker, and that evening was equal to a whole temperance society. The little Indian looked on as if he had sold his birthright, and I felt strong compunctions; but, letting the morrow take care of itself, I sent up the other horses, which consumed at a single drinking what might, perhaps, have sufficed the family a month.

The next morning at daylight we sent Albino with the Indians to begin clearing around the ruins, and after breakfast we followed. The path lay through a savanna covered with long grass, and at the distance of a mile we reached two buildings, which I had seen before, and were the inducement to this visit.

The first is that represented in Plate XIV. It stands on a substantial terrace, but lower than most of the others. The front is one hundred and twelve feet long, and when entire must have presented a grand appearance. The end on the left in the engraving has fallen, carrying with it one doorway, so that now only four appear. The doorway was the largest and most imposing we had seen in the country, but, unfortunately, the ornaments over it were broken and fallen. In the centre apartment the back corridor is raised, and the ascent to it is by three steps.

All the doorways were plain except the centre one (the second to the left in the engraving), which is represented in Plate XV. It is in a dilapidated condition, but still presents bold and striking ornaments. Even on this scale, however, the details of the sitting figures above the cornice do not appear.

While we were engaged in making a clearing in front of this building, two young men came down upon the terrace from the corner that was fallen, and apparently from the top of the building, with long guns, the locks covered with deer-skin, and all the accoutrements of caçadores, or hunters.

We were so pleased with their appearance that we proposed to one of them to accompany us in our search after ruins.

The one whom we engaged was named Dimas, and he continued with us until we left the country.

On the same line, and but a short distance removed, though on a lower terrace, is another building, measuring eighty-five feet in front, which is represented in Plate XVI. It had a freshness about it that suggested the idea of something more modern than the others. The whole was covered with a coat of plaster but little broken, and it confirmed us in the opinion we had entertained before, that the fronts of all the buildings had been thus covered.

Our meeting with these young men was a fortunate circumstance for us in exploring these ruins. From boyhood their father had had his rancho on

PLATE XIV

F. Catherwood.

Jordan & Halpin.

CHUNHUHU

PLATE XV

F. Catherwood.

Jordan & Halpin.

CHUNHUHU

PLATE XVI

CHUNHUHU

F. Catherwood.

J. N. Gimbred.

the savanna, and with their guns they had ranged over the whole country for leagues around.

From the terrace of the first building we saw at a distance a high hill, almost a mountain, on the top of which rose a wooded elevation surrounding an ancient building. There was something extraordinary in its position, but the young men told us it was entirely ruined, and, although it was then but eleven o'clock, if we attempted to go it, we could not return till after dark. They told us, also, of others at the distance of half a league, more extensive, and some of which, they said, were, in finish and preservation, equal to these.

At one o'clock Doctor Cabot and myself, under the guidance of Dimas, set out to look for them. It was desperately hot. We passed several huts, and at one of them asked for some water; but it was so full of insects that we could barely taste it. Dimas led us to the hut of his mother, and gave us some from a vessel in which the insects had settled to the bottom.

Beyond this we ascended the spur of a high hill, and coming down into a thickly-wooded valley, after the longest half league we ever walked, we saw through the trees a large stone structure. On reaching it, and climbing over a broken terrace, we came to a large mound faced on all sides with stone, which we ascended, and crossing over the top, looked down upon an overgrown area, having on each side a range of ruined buildings, with their white façades peering through the trees; and beyond, at a distance, and seemingly inaccessible, was the high hill with the ruins on the top, which we had seen from the terrace of the first building. Hills rose around us on every side, and, for that country, the scene was picturesque, but all waste and silent. The stillness of the grave rested upon the ruins, and the notes of a little flycatcher were the only sounds we heard.

The ruins in sight were much more extensive than those we had first visited, but in a more ruinous condition. We descended the mound to the area in front, and, bearing down the bushes, passed in the centre an uncouth, upright, circular stone, like that frequently referred to before, called the picote, or whipping-post, and farther on we reached an edifice, which Mr. Catherwood afterward drew, and which is represented in Plate XVII. It is thirty-three feet in front, and has two apartments, each thirteen feet long by eight feet six inches deep, and conspicuous in the façade are representations of three uncouth human figures, in curious dresses, with their hands held up by the side of the head, supporting the cornice.

These ruins, Dimas told us, were called Schoolhoke, but, like the others, they stand on what is called the savanna of Chunhuhu; and the ruined building on the top of the hill, visible from both places, seems towering as a link to connect them together. What the extent of this place has been it is impossible to say.

We returned to the rancho worn down with fatigue, just in time to escape

PLATE XVII

S.H. Garbet

F. Catherwood

CHUNHUHU

a violent rain. This brought within, as an accompaniment to the fleas of the night before, our carriers and servants, and we had eleven hammocks, in close juxtaposition, and through the night a concert of nasal trombones, with Indian variations. The rain continued all the next day, and as no work could be done, Mr. Catherwood took advantage of the opportunity to have another attack of fever. We were glad of it on another account, for we had kept a man constantly employed in the woods searching for water; our horses had exhausted all the rocky cavities around, and we could not have held out another day. The rain replenished them, and relieved us from some compunctions.

In the afternoon the little boy came down with a message from his mother, desiring to know when we were going away. Soon afterward the poor woman herself was seen hovering about the house. She considered that it was really time to come. With great difficulty, we prevailed upon her to enter the hut, and told her she might return whenever she pleased. She laughed goodnaturedly, an, after looking round carefully to see that nothing was missing, went away comforted by our promise to depart the next day.

CHAPTER VIII

Ruins of Ytsimpte — Arrival at the Village of Bolonchen — Wells —
Visit to an extraordinary Cave

Our party this morning divided into three parcels. The carriers set out direct for Bolonchen; Mr. Catherwood went, under the guidance of Dimas, to make a drawing of the last building, and Doctor Cabot, myself, and Albino to visit another ruined city, all to meet again at Bolonchen in the evening.

At one o'clock we came to a rancho of Indians, where we bought some tortillas and procured a guide. Leaving the camino real, we turned again into a milpa path, and in about an hour came in sight of another ruined, city, known by the name of Ytsimpte. From the plain on which we approached we saw on the left, on the brow of a hill, a range of buildings, six or eight hundred feet in length, all laid bare to view, the trees having just been felled; and as we drew near we saw Indians engaged in continuing the clearing. On arriving at the foot of the buildings, Albino found that clearing was made by order of the alcalde of Bolonchen, at the instance and under the direction of the padre, in expectation of our visit and our benefit!

We had another subject of congratulation on account of our horses. There was an aguada in the neighbourhood, to which we immediately sent them, and, carrying our traps up to the terrace of the nearest building, we sat down before it to meditate and lunch.

This over, we commenced a survey of the ruins. The clearings made by our unknown friends enabled us to form at once a general idea of their character and extent, and to move from place to place with comparative facility. These ruins lie in the village of Bolonchen, and the first apartment we entered showed the effects of this vicinity. All the smooth stones of the inner wall had been picked out and carried away for building purposes, and the sides presented the cavities in the bed of mortar from which they had been taken.

From the extent of these remains, the masses of sculptured stones, and the execution of the carving, this must have been one of the first class of the aboriginal cities. In morai influence there was none more powerful. Ruin had been so complete that we could not profit by the kindness of our friends, and it was melancholy that when so much had been done for us, there was so little for us to do.

A short ride brought us to the suburbs of the village of Bolonchen, and we entered a long street, with a line of straggling houses or huts on each side.

After settling into the casa real they were visited by the 'vecinos' (white inhabitants), who invited them to take chocolate with them, and said that the cura was still taking his siesta.

We had time to look at the only objects of interest in the village, and these were the wells, which, after our straits at Chunhuhu, were a refreshing spectacle, and of which our horses had already enjoyed the benefit by a bath.

Bolonchen derives its name from two Maya words: *Bolon*, which signifies nine, and *chen*, wells, and it means the nine wells. From time immemorial, nine wells formed at this place the centre of a population, and these nine wells are now in the plaza of the village. Their origin is as obscure and unknown as that of the ruined cities which strew the land, and as little thought of.

The custody and preservation of these wells form a principal part of the business of the village authorities, but, with all their care, the supply lasts but seven or eight months in the year. This year, on account of the long continuance of the rainy season, it had lasted longer than usual, and was still abundant. The time was approaching, however, when these wells would fail, and the inhabitants be driven to an extraordinary cueva at half a league from the village.

At about dark Mr. Catherwood arrived, and we returned to the casa real. In a room fifty feet long, free from fleas, servants, and Indian carriers, and with a full swing for our hammocks, we had a happy change from the hut at Chunhuhu.

During the evening the cura came over to see us, but, finding we had retired, did not disturb us; early in the morning he was rapping at our door, and would not leave us till we promised to come over and take chocolate with him.

There was one great difficulty in the way of our visiting the cueva at this time. Since the commencement of the rainy season it had not been used; and every year, before having recourse to it, there was a work of several days to be done in repairing the ladders. As this, however, was our only opportunity, we determined to make the attempt.

The cura undertook to make the arrangements, and after breakfast we set out, a large party, including both Indians and vecinos.

At the distance of half a league from the village, on the Campeachy road, we turned off by a well-beaten path, following which we fell into a winding lane, and, descending gradually, reached the foot of a rude, lofty, and abrupt opening, under a bold ledge of overhanging rock, seeming a magnificent entrance to a great temple for the worship of the God of Nature. Figure 6 represents this aperture, an Indian with a lighted torch being seen just entering.

We disencumbered ourselves of superfluous apparel, and, following the Indian, each with a torch in hand, entered a wild cavern, which, as we advanced,

Fig. 6

became darker. At the distance of sixty paces the descent was precipitous, and we went down by a ladder about twenty feet. Here all light from the mouth of the cavern was lost, but we soon reached the brink of a great perpendicular descent, to the very bottom of which a strong body of light was thrown from a hole in the surface, a perpendicular depth, as we afterward learned by measurement, of two hundred and ten feet.

From the brink on which we stood an enormous ladder, of the rudest possible construction, led to the bottom of the hole. It was between seventy and eighty feet long, and about twelve feet wide, made of the rough trunks of saplings lashed together lengthwise, and supported all the way down by horizontal trunks braced against the face the precipitous rock. The ladder was double, having two sets or flights of rounds, divided by a middle partition, and the whole fabric was lashed together by withes. It was very steep, seemed precarious and insecure, and confirmed the worst accounts we had heard of the descent into this remarkable well.

Our Indians began the descent, but the foremost had scarcely got his head below the surface before one of the rounds slipped, and he only saved himself by clinging to another. The ladder having been made when the withes were green, these were now dry, cracked, and some of them broken. We attempted a descent with some little misgivings, but, by keeping each hand and foot on a different round, with an occasional crash and slide, we all reached the foot of the ladder; that is, our own party, our Indians, and some three or four of our escort, the rest having disappeared.

Plate XVIII represents the scene at the foot of this ladder. Looking up, the view of its broken sides, with the light thrown down from the orifice above, was the wildest that can be conceived. As yet the reader is only at the mouth of this well; but, to explain to him briefly its extraordinary character, I give its name, which is Xtacumbi Xunan. The Indians understand by this La Señora escondida, or the lady hidden away; and it is derived from a fanciful Indian story that a lady stolen from her mother was concealed by her lover in this cave.

Every year, when the wells in the plaza are about to fail, the ladders are put into a thorough state of repair. A day is appointed by the municipality for closing the wells in the plaza, and repairing to the cueva; and on that day a great village fête held in the cavern at the foot of this ladder.

Figure 7 will give some imperfect idea of a section of this cave.

On one side of the cavern is an opening in the rock, as shown in the engraving, entering by which, we soon came to an abrupt descent, down which was another long and trying ladder. It was laid against the broken face of the rock, not so steep as the first, but in a much more rickety condition; the rounds were loose, and the upper ones gave way on the first attempt to descend. The cave was damp, and the rock and the ladder were wet and slippery. At this place the rest of our attendants left us, the ministro being the last deserter. It was evident that the labour of exploring his cave was to be greatly increased by the state of the ladders, and there might be some danger attending it, but, even after all that we had seen of caves, there was something so wild and grand in this that we could not bring ourselves to give up the attempt. Fortunately, the cura had taken care to provide us with rope, and, fastening one end round a large stone, an Indian carried the other down to the foot of the ladder. We followed, one at a time; holding the rope with one hand, and with the other grasping the side of the ladder, it was impossible to carry a torch, and we were obliged to feel our way in the dark, or with only such light as could reach us from the torches above and below. At the foot of this ladder was a large cavernous chamber, from which irregular passages led off in different

PLATE XVIII

F. Catherwood   S.H. Gimber

BOLONCHEN
Cueva or well

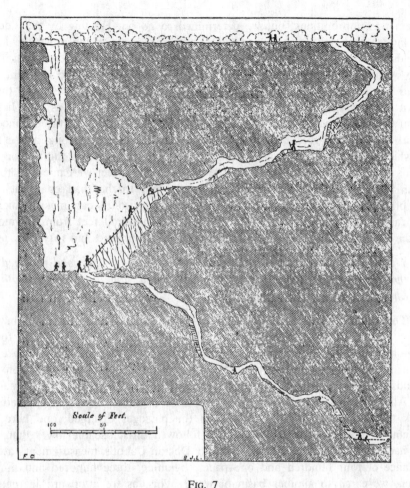

FIG. 7

directions to deposites or sources of water. Doctor Cabot and myself, attended by Albino, took one of the passages indicated by the Indians, of which some imperfect idea is given in the section.

Moving on by a slight ascent over the rocks, at the distance of about seventy-five feet we came to the foot of a third ladder nine feet long, two or three steps beyond another five feet high, both which we had to go up, and six paces farther a fifth, descending, and eighteen feet in length. A little beyond we descended another ladder eleven feet long, and yet a little farther on we came to one — the seventh — the length and general appearance of which induced us to pause and consider. By this time. Albino was the only attendant left. This long ladder was laid on a narrow, sloping face of rock, protected on one side by a perpendicular wall, but at the other open and precipitous. Its aspect was unpropitious, but we determined to go on. Holding by the side of the ladder next the rock, we descended, crashing and carrying down the loose rounds, so that when we got to the bottom we had cut off all communication with Albino; he could not descend, and, what was quite as inconvenient, we could not get back. It was now too late to reflect. We told Albino to throw down our torches, and go back for Indians and rope to haul us out. In the mean time we moved on by a broken, winding passage, and, at the distance of about two hundred feet, came to the top of a ladder eight feet long, at the foot of which we entered a low and stifling passage; and crawling along this on our hands and feet, at the distance of about three hundred feet we came to a rocky basin full of water. Before reaching it one of our torches had gone out, and the other was then expiring. From the best calculation I can make, which is not far out of the way, we were then fourteen hundred feet from the mouth of the cave, and at a perpendicular depth of four hundred and fifty feet.

The two explorers were glad of the chance to take a bath, and reflected that perhaps no white man before them had done so at this depth underground.

The Indians call this basin Chacka, which means agua colorada, or red water; but this we did not know at the time, and we did not discover it, for to economize our torch we avoided flaring it, and it lay on the rock like an expiring brand, admonishing us that it was better not to rely wholly upon our friends in the world above, and that it would be safer to look out for ourselves.

Albino returned with Indians and ropes. We hauled ourselves up, and got back to the open chamber from which the passages diverged; and here the Indians pointed out another, which we followed till it became lower than any we had yet explored; and, according to Doctor Cabot's measurement, at the distance of four hundred and one paces, by mine, three hundred and ninety-seven, we came to another basin of water. This, as we afterward learned, is called Pucuelha, meaning that it ebbs and flows like the sea. In returning we turned off twice by branching passages, and reached two other basins of water; and when we got back to the foot of the great staircase, exhausted and almost worn out, we had the satisfaction of learning, from friends who were waiting to hear our report, that there were seven in all, and we had missed three. All have names given them by the Indians, two of which I have already mentioned.

The third is called Sallab, which means a spring; the fourth Akahba, on account of its darkness; the fifth Chocohá, from the circumstance of its being always warm; the sixth Occiha, from being of a milky colour; and the seventh Chimaisha, because, it has insects called ais.

The great point was the fact, that from the moment when the wells in the plaza fail, the whole village turns to this cave, and four or five months in the year derives from this source its only supply.

We returned to the casa real, made a lavation, which we much needed, and went over to the cura's to dine. The cura had unsettled our plans. He had made inquiries, and been informed that there were no ruins at San Antonio, but only a cueva, and we had had enough of these to last us for some time; moreover, he advised us of other ruins, of which we had not heard before. These were on the rancho of Santa Ana, belonging to his friend Don Antonio Cerbera, the alcalde.

CHAPTER IX

Rancho of Santa Rosa — Visit to the Ruins of Labphak

Early the next morning we resumed our journey. On leaving the village we were soon again in the wilderness. We had escaped the region of eternal stones, and the soil was rich and loamy. A league beyond this we reached the rancho of Santa Rosa. It was a very rare thing in this country to notice any place for its beauty of situation, but we were struck with this, though perhaps its beauty consisted merely in standing upon a slight elevation, and commanding a view of an open country.

The major domo was somewhat surprised at the object of our visit. The ruins were about two leagues distant, but he had never seen them, and had no great opinion of ruins generally. He immediately sent out, however, to notify the Indians to be on the ground in the morning, and during the evening he brought in one who was to be our guide.

The night at this rancho was a memorable one. We were so scourged by fleas that sleep was impossible. Mr. Catherwood and Dr. Cabot resorted to the Central American practice of sewing up the sheets into a bag, and all night we were in a fever.

The next morning we started for the ruins of Labphak, taking care to carry our luggage with us, and not intending, under any circumstances, to return. The major domo accompanied us. It was luxurious to ride on a road free from stones. In an hour we entered a forest of fine trees, and a league beyond found a party of Indians, who pointed us to a narrow path just opened, wilder than anything we had yet travelled. After following this some distance, the Indians stopped, and made signs to us to dismount. Securing the horses, and again following the Indians, in a few minutes we saw peering throught the trees the white front of a lofty building, which, in the imperfect view we had of it, seemed the grandest we had seen in the country. The whole building, with all its terraces, was overgrown with gigantic trees. The Indians cutting a path along the front, we moved on from door to door, and wandered through its desolate chambers. For the first time in the country we found interior staircases, one of which was entire, every step being in its place. The stones were worn, and we almost expected to see the foot-prints of the former occupants. The sky was overcast, and portended the coming of another Norte. The wind swept over the ruined building, so that in places we were obliged to cling to the branches of the trees to save ourselves from falling.

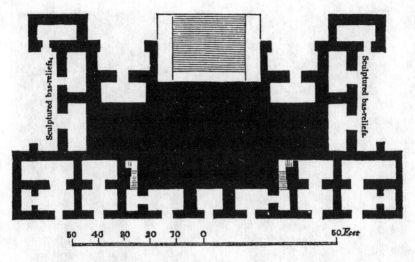

FIG. 8

It seemed almost sacrilege to disturb the repose in which this building lay, and to remove its burial shroud, but soon, amid the ringing of the axe and machete, and the crash of falling trees, this feeling wore away.

In the mean time Mr. Catherwood, still an invalid, and deprived of sleep the night before, had his hammock slung in an apartment at the top of the building. By afternoon the clearing was finished, and he made his drawing, which appears in Plate XIX.

The lowest range or story is one hundred and forty-five feet in length. The roof and a portion of the façade have fallen, and almost buried the centre doorways. The apartments containing the staircases are indicated hereinafter in Figure 8. Each staircase consists of two flights, with a platform at the head of the first, which forms the foot of the second, and they lead out upon the roof, under the projection which stands like a watchtower in the wall of the second range, and from this range two interior staircases lead out in the same way to the platform of the third.

In front was a grand courtyard, with ranges of ruined buildings, forming a hollow square, and in the centre a gigantic staircase rose from the courtyard to the platform of the third story. On the platform of the second terrace, at each end, stood a high square building like a tower, with the remains of rich ornaments in stucco; and on the platform of the third, at the head of the grand staircase, one on each side of it, stood two oblong buildings, their façades adorned with colossal figures and ornaments in stucco, seemingly intended as a portal to the structure on the top. In ascending the grand staircase, cacique, priest, or stranger had before him this gorgeously ornamented portal, and passed through it to enter the centre apartment of the upper story.

Plate XIX

LABPHAK

T. Catherwood.

Figure 8 represents the ground-plan of the lower range. It consists of ranges of narrow apartments on all four of the sides, opening outward, and the reader will see that it has fitness, and uniformity of design and proportion. The grand staircase, forty feet wide, is indicated in the engraving. The interior, represented in black, forms the foundation for the support of the two upper ranges. It is cut off and enclosed on all sides by the inner wall, has no communication with any of the apartments, and is apparently a solid mass. Whether it really is solid or contains apartments, remains, as in other structures of the same kind, a question for the investigation of future explorers. Under the circumstances attending our visit, we were utterly unable to attempt anything of the kind.

The reader will notice in the plan two places marked "sculptured bas-reliefs." In these places are carved tablets set in the wall, as at Palenque, and, except at Palenque, this was the only place in all our wanderings in which we found bas-reliefs thus disposed.

Plate XX represents the bas-reliefs referred to.

Night was almost upon us when Albino inquired in what apartment he should hang up our hammocks. In the interest of our immediate occupations we had not thought of this; a buzzing in the woods gave ominous warning of moschetoes, and we inclined to the highest range; but it was unsafe to carry our things up, or to move about the broken terraces in the dark. We selected, as the most easy of access, the rooms indicated in the engraving by the second doorway on the left.

Except a small ruined structure which we passed on the way to this building, as yet we had seen only this one with the ranges around the courtyard. It was clear that it did not stand alone; but we were so completely buried in the woods that it was utterly impossible to know which way to turn in search of others. In making our clearing we had stumbled upon two circular holes, like those found at Uxmal, which the Indians called chultunes, or cisterns, and which they said existed in all parts, and Doctor Cabot, in pursuit of a bird, had found a range of buildings at but a short distance, disconnected from each other, and having their façades ornamented with stucco.

In the afternoon the wind increased to a regular Norther, and at night all the Indians were driven in by the rain.

The next day the rain continued, and the major domo left us, taking with him nearly all the Indians. This put an end to the clearing, Mr. Catherwood had a recurrence of fever, and in the intervals of sunshine Dr. Cabot and myself worked with the Daguerreotype.

In the mean time, from the difficulty of procuring water and necessaries, we found our residence at these ruins uncomfortable. Mr. Catherwood, too, was unable to work, the woods were wet with the rain, and we considered it advisable to change the scene. There is no place which we visited that we were

PLATE XX

A. Jones

F. Catherwood

LABPHAK
Bas relief on Stone

so reluctant to leave unfinished, and none that better deserved a month's exploration.

In the ruins that Stephens calls Labphak, now known as Xlabpak, Xtampak *or* X'lapak, *one building stands out; a three-storied structure with vaulted rooms, masks of the god Chaac on the outside corners and more stylized ones at the center of the façade. There are other buildings which have not been explored.*

CHAPTER X

On Thursday, the twenty-fourth of February, we broke up and left the ruins. A narrow path brought us out into the camino real, along which we passed several small ranchos of sugar-cane. At eleven o'clock we reached the hacienda of Jalasac, the appearance of which, after a few days' burial in the woods, was most attractive and inviting; and here we ventured to ask for water for our horses. The master made us dismount, sent our horses to an aguada, and had some oranges picked from the tree, sliced, and sprinkled with sugar, for ourselves. He told us that his establishment was nothing compared with Señor Trego's, a league distant, whom, he said, we, of course, knew, and would doubtless stop with a few days.

Resuming our journey, at the distance of a league we reached another rancho, which would have been creditable in any country for its neatness and arrangement. Our road ran through a plaza, or square, with large seybo trees in the centre and neat white houses on all the sides; and before the door of one of them we saw a horse and cart! an evidence of civilization which we had nor seen till that time in the country. This could be no other than Señor Trego's. We stopped in the shade, Señor Trego came out of the principal house, told the servants to take our horses, and said he had been expecting us several days. We were a little surprised, but, as we were very uncertain about our chances for a dinner, we said nothing. Entering the house, we fell into fine large hammocks; and Señor Trego told us that we were welcome on our own account, even without the recommendation of the Padre Rodríguez of Xul. This gave us a key to the mystery.

The mystery was that they had never heard of Señor Trego, but on hearing what he said they remembered that Padre Rodríguez had given them a letter for a friend of his. They had left this behind accidentally, and obviously it had been for this man.

Señor Trego made us feel at once that there was to be no reserve in his hospitality; and when he ordered some lemonade to be brought in immediately, we did not hesitate to suggest the addition of two fowls boiled, with a little rice thrown in.

Señor Trego (or more correctly Trejo) took them over his property, where sugar cane was grown and processed; there was also a distillery and a large number of pigs, but the explorers were most interested in the well in the courtyard and the ceiba trees that Trejo himself had planted. The oldest was of only twelve years' growth and they were amazed by its size.

At four o'clock we resumed our journey, and toward dark, passing some miserable huts in the suburbs, we reached the new village of Iturbide, standing on the outposts of civilization, the great point to which the tide of emigration was rolling, the Chicago of Yucatan.

The reader may not consider the country through which we have been travelling as over-burdened with population, but in certain parts, particularly in the district of Nohcacab, the people did so consider it. Crowded and oppressed by the large landed proprietors, many of the enterprising yeomanry of this district determined to seek a new home in the wilderness. Bidding farewell to friends and relatives, after a journey of two days and a half they reached the fertile plains of Zibilnocac, from time immemorial an Indian rancho. Here the soil belonged to the government; every man could take up what land he pleased, full scope was offered to enterprise, and an opportunity for development not afforded by the over-peopled region of Nohcacab.

The approach was by a long street, at the head of which, and in the entrance to the plaza, we saw a gathering, which in that country seemed a crowd, giving an indication of life and activity not usual in the older villages; but drawing nearer, we noticed that the crowd was stationary, and, on reaching it, we found that, according to an afternoon custom, all the principal inhabitants were gathered around a card-table, playing monte; rather a bad symptom, but these hardy pioneers exhibited one good trait of character in their close attention to the matter in hand. They gave us a passing glance and continued the game.

In Iturbide they were approached by a man of around fifty who said he had met them in Nohcacab. He explained that since Iturbide was a new village there was little accommodation, but that he would find them somewhere to stay. Albino made some inquiries and later told them that their new-found friend was Don Juan, one of the oldest settlers of the village and one of the most influential inhabitants.

The next morning a short time enabled us to see all the objects of interest in the new village of Iturbide. Five years before the plough had run over the ground now occupied by the plaza, or, more literally, as the plough is not known in Yucatan, the plaza is on the ground formerly occupied by an old milperia, or cornfield. Within the plaza were memorials of older and better times, indications of a more ingenious people than the civilized whites by whom it is now occupied. At one end was a mound of ruins, which had once supported an ancient building; and in the centre was an ancient well, unchanged from the time of its construction, and then, as for an unknown length of time before, supplying water to the inhabitants.

Besides these memorials, from a street communicating with the plaza we saw a range of great mounds, the ruins of the ancient city of Zibilnocac, which had brought us to Iturbide.

On the way to the ruins we passed another ancient well, of the same construction with that in the plaza, but filled up with rubbish, and useless. The Indians called it Stu-kum, from a subject familiar to them, and presenting not a bad idea of a useless well; the word meaning a calabash with the seeds dried up. A short walk brought us into an open country, and among the towering ruins of another ancient city. The field was in many places clear of trees, and covered only with plantations of tobacco, and studding it all over were lofty ranges and mounds, enshrouded in woods, through which white masses of stone were glimmering, and rising in such quick succession, and so many at once, that Mr. Catherwood, in no good condition for work, said, almost despondingly, that the labours of Uxmal were to begin again.

They had attracted a crowd of curious villagers as they set out for the ruins, but nobody had a machete. A few men were sent back to fetch them and Catherwood, already unwell, became so ill that he returned too. Clearing the site took most of the day.

Don Juan had invited them to eat with him and, perhaps in return, afteward asked Dr. Cabot to help his wife. He gave advice about the treatment of a sick child, who improved so much overnight that the doctor soon had too many patients for comfort.

The next morning Mr. Catherwood made an effort to visit the ruins. Our numerous escort of the former occasion were all missing, and, except an Indian who had a tobacco patch in the neighbourhood, we were entirely alone. This Indian held an umbrella over Mr. Catherwood's head to protect him from the sun, and, while making the drawing, several times he was obliged by weakness to lie down and rest. I was disheartened by the spectacle. Although, considering the extent of illness in our party, we had in reality not lost much time, we had been so much embarrassed, and it was so disagreeable to be moving along with this constant liability to fever and ague, that here I felt very much disposed to break up the expedition and go home, but Mr. Catherwood persisted.

Plate XXI represents the front of this building. It is one hundred and fifty-four feet in front and twenty feet seven inches in depth. It differed in form from any we had seen, and had square structures rising in the centre and at each end, as seen in ruins in the engraving; these were called towers, and at a distance had that appearance. The façades of the towers were all ornament with sculptured stone. Several of the apartments had tobacco leaves

PLATE XXI

ITURBIDE

spread out in them to dry. In the centre, one apartment was encumbered with rubbish, cutting off the light from the door, but in the obscurity we saw on one of the stones, along the layer in the arch, the dim outline of a painting like that at Kewick; in the adjoining apartment were the remains of paintings, the most interesting, except those near the village of Xul, that we had met with in the country, and, like those, in position and general effect reminding me of processions in Egyptian tombs. Unfortunately, they were too much mutilated to be drawn, and seemed surviving the general wreck only to show that these aboriginal builders had possessed more skill in the least enduring branch of the graphic art.

Back of this building, or, rather, on the other front, was a thriving tobacco patch, the only thriving thing we saw at Iturbide; and on the border another ancient well, now, as in ages past, furnishing water, and from which the Indian attending the tobacco patch gave us to drink. Beyond were towering mounds and vestiges, indicating the existence of a greater city than any we had yet encountered. In wandering among them Dr. Cabot and myself counted thirty-three, all of which had once held buildings aloft. The field was so open that they were all comparatively easy of access, but the mounds themselves were overgrown. I clambered up them till the work became tiresome and unprofitable; they were all, as the Indians said, puras piedras, pure stones; no buildings were left; all had fallen; and though, perhaps, more than at any other place, happy that it was our fortune to wander among these crumbling memorials of a once powerful and mysterious people.

CHAPTER XI

Lake of Peten — Expedition of Don Martin Ursua — Rancho
of Noyaxche

Our journey in this direction is now ended. We were on the frontier
of the inhabited part of Yucatan, and within a few leagues of the last village.
Beyond was a wilderness, stretching off to the Lake of Peten, and that region
of Lacandones, or unbaptized Indians, in which, according to the suggestion
made in my previous volumes, lay that mysterious city never reached by a
white man, but still occupied by Indians precisely in the same state as before
the discovery of America. A venerable ecclesiastic in Merida had furnished
me with an itinerary of the journey through the wilderness to the Lake of
Peten, and I had some hope of being led on from place to place until we should
reach a point which might unravel all mystery, and establish a connecting link
between the past and present; but this hope was accompanied by a fear, and,
perhaps fortunately for us, we did not hear of ruins beyond.

As yet, however, our face is still set toward the Lake of Peten. In this lake
are numerous islands, one of which is called Peten Grande, Peten itself being
a Maya word, signifying and island; and before turning back I wish to present
this island for one moment to the reader. It now belongs to the government
of Guatimala, and is under the ecclesiastical jurisdiction of the Bishop of Yucatan. Formerly it was the principal place of the province of Itza, which
province, for one hundred and fifty years after the subjugation of Yucatan,
maintained its fierce and native independence. In the year 1608, sixty-six years
after the conquest, two Franciscan monks, alone, without arms, and in the
spirit of peace, set out to conquer this province by converting the natives to
Christianity. The limits of these pages will not permit me to accompany them
in their toilsome and dangerous journey, but, according to the account of one
of them as given by Cogolludo, at ten o'clock at night they landed on the island,
were provided with a house by the king, and the next day preached to the
Indians; but the latter told them that the time had not yet come for them to
become Christians, and advised the monks to go away and return at some other
day. Nevertheless, they carried them round to see the town, and in the middle of
one the temples they saw a great idol of the figure of a horse, made of lime
and stone, seated on the ground on his haunches, with his hind legs bent, and
raised on his fore feet, being intended as an image of the horse which Cortez

left at that place on his great journey from Mexico to Honduras. On that occasion the Indians had seen the Spaniards fire their muskets from the backs of the horses, and supposing that the fire and noise were caused by the animals, they called this image Tzimin Chac, and adored it as the god of thunder and lightning. As the monks saw it, one of them, says the author of the account, seemed as if the Spirit of the Lord had descended upon him; and, carried away by zealous fervour, seized the foot of the horse with his hand, mounted upon the statue, and broke in in pieces. The Indians immediately cried out to kill them; but the king saved them, though they were obliged to leave the island.

In the year 1695, Don Martin Ursua obtained the government of Yucatan, and, in pursuance of a proposal previously submitted by him to the king, and approved by the council of the Indies, undertook the great work of opening a road across the whole continent from Campeachy to Guatimala.

The work of opening the road was begun in 1695. In prosecuting it, the Spaniards encountered vestiges of ancient buildings raised on terraces, deserted and overgrown, and apparently very ancient.

On the twenty-first of January, 1697, Don Martin de Ursua set out from Campeachy to take command of the expedition in person, with a vicar-general and assistant, already nominated by the bishop, for the province of Itza. On the last day of February he had timber cut on the borders of Peten for the construction of vessels which should convey them to the island. The thirteenth of March was appointed for the day of embarcation. Some of the Spaniards, knowing the immense number of Indians on the island, and the difficulty of conquering it, represented to the general the rashness of this undertaking; but, says the historian, carried away by his zeal, faith, and courage, he answered that, having in view the service of God and the king, and the drawing of miserable souls from the darkness of heathenism, under the favour and protection of the Virgin Mary, whose image he carried on the royal standard, and engraven on his heart, he alone was sufficient for this conquest, even if it were much more difficult.

He embarked with one hundred and eight soldiers, leaving one hundred and twenty, with auxiliary Indians, and two pieces of artillery, as a garrison for the camp. Half way across he encountered fleets of canoes filled with warlike Indians; but taking no notice of them, and moving on toward the island the Spaniards saw assembled immense numbers, prepared for war; Indians crowded the tops of the small islands around; the canoes followed them on the lake, and enclosed them in a half moon between themselves and the shore. As soon as within reach, the Indians, by land and water, poured upon them a shower of arrows. The arrows from the shore were like thick rain. The Spaniards could scarcely be restrained, and one soldier, wounded in the arm, and enraged by the pain, fired his musket; the rest followed; the general could no longer control them, and, without waiting till they reached the shore, as soon as the oars stopped all threw themselves into the water, Don Martin de Ursua among them. The Indians were thick as if collected at the mouth of a cannon; but at the horrible noise and destruction of the fire-arms they broke and fled in terror. The Spaniards entered the deserted town, and hoisted the royal standard on the highest point of Peten. With a loud voice they returned thanks to God for his mercies, and Don Martin Ursua took formal possesion of the island and the territory of Itza in the name of the king. This took place on the thirteenth of March, 1697, one hundred and fifty-five years after the foundation of Merida.

We have, then, accounts of visits by the padres sixty years after the subjugation of Yucatan, and a detailed account of the conquest of Itza, one hundred and fifty-five years afterward; and what did they find on the island? The monks say that, when taken to look over the city, they went to the middle and highest part of the island to see the kues and adoratorios of the heathen idols, and that "there were twelve or more of the size of the largest churches in the villages of the Indians in the province of Yucatan, each one of which was capable of containing more than one thousand persons."

According to both Cogolludo and Villagutierres, who drew their conclusions from occurrences of such late date as to leave but little room for error, the Itzites, or people of Itza, were originally from the land of Maya, now Yucatan, and once formed part of that nation. At the time of the insurrection of the caciques of Maya, and the destruction of Mayapan, Canek, one of the rebellious caciques, got possession of the city of Chichen Itza. As it is sometimes said, on account of the foretelling of the arrival of the Spaniards by one of their prophets, but more probably on account of the insecurity of this possessions, he withdrew with his people from the province of Chichen Itza to the most hidden and impenetrable part of the mountains, and took possession of the Lake of Peten, establishing his residence on the large island which now bears that name. This emigration, according to the history, took place but about one hundred years before the arrival of the Spaniards.

And where are these kues, adoratorios, and temples now? In both my journeys into that country, it was always my intention to visit the island of Peten, and it has been a matter of deep regret that I was never able to do so; but as the result of my inquiries, particularly from the venerable cura who furnished me with the itinerary, and who lived many years on the island, I am induced to believe that there are no buildings left, but that there are feeble vestiges, not enough in themselves to attract the attention of mere curiosity.

The reader will perhaps think that I have gone quite far enough, and that is is time to come back.

The next on our list were the ruins of Macoba, lying on the rancho of our friend the cura of Xul, and then in the actual occupation of Indians. We had our Indian carriers in attendance at the village; but, unluckily, while preparing to set out, Mr. Catherwood was taken with fever, and we were obliged to postpone our departure.

The next day it rained. On Sunday the rain still continued. Early in the morning the ministro came over from the village of Hpochen to say mass, and, while lounging about to note the prospect in regard to the weather, I stopped under the shed where the gaming-table remained ready for use, to which, when mass was over, all the better classes came from the church in clean dresses, prepared for business.

While waiting for Catherwood to recover, Stephens noticed that the main occupation of many of the men in Iturbide was gambling. They played for money, of course, and when they had none, for corn, tobacco and even pigs.

In the afternoon the rain ceased, and we bade farewell to the new village of Iturbide. As we passed, Don Juan left his place at the table to bid us goodby, and a little before dark we reached the rancho Noyaxche of Señor Trego, where we again received a cordial welcome, and in his intelligent society found a relief from the dulness of Iturbide.

CHAPTER XII

An Aguada — Arrival at Macobá — The Ruins

The next morning after beakfast we again set out. Señor Trego escorted us, and, following a broad wagon road made by him for the passage of the horse and cart, at the distance of a mile and a half we came to a large aguada, which is represented in Plate XXII. It was apparently a mere pond, picturesque, and shaded by trees, and having the surface covered with green water plants, called by the Indians Xicin-chah, which, instead of being regarded as a blot upon the picturesque, were prized as tending to preserve the water from evaporation. Indians were then filling their water-jars, and this aguada was the only watering-place of the rancho. These aguadas had become to us interesting objects of consideration. Ever since our arrival in the country, we had been told that they were artificial, and, like the ruined cities we were visiting, the works of the ancient inhabitants.

Failing in his attempt to procure water from the well, before referred to, in the plaza, in 1836 Señor Trego turned his attention to this aguada. He believed that it had been used by the ancients as a reservoir, and took advantage of the dry season to make an examination, which satisfied him that his supposition was correct. For many years it had been abandoned, and it was then covered three or four feet deep with mud. At first he was afraid to undertake with much vigour the work of clearing it out, for the prejudices of the people were against it, and they feared that, by disturbing the aguada, the scanty supply then furnished might be cut off. On clearing out the mud, he found an artificial bottom of large flat stones. These were laid upon each other in this form, ⌐‾‾‾‾‾‾‾⌐ and the interstices were filled in with clay of red and brown colour, of a different character from any in the neighbourhood.

Near the centre, in places which he indicated as we rode along the bank, he discovered four ancient wells. These were five feet in diameter, faced with smooth stone not covered with cement, eight yards deep, and at the time of time of the discovery were also filled with mud. And, besides these, he found along the margin upward of four hundred casimbas, or pits, being holes into which the water filtered, and which, with the wells, were intended to furnish a supply when the aguada should be dry.

The whole bottom of the aguada, the wells, and pits, were cleared out. It so happened that the next year was one of unusual scarcity, and the whole

PLATE XXII

country around was perfectly destitute of water. That year, Señor Trego said, more than a thousand horses and mules came to this aguada, some even from the rancho of Santa Rosa, eighteen miles distant, with barrels on their backs, and carried away water.

Leaving the aguada, our road lay over a level and wooded plain, then wet and muddy from the recent rains, and at the distance of a league we reached the sugar rancho of a gentleman from Oxcutzcab, who had been a co-worker with Señor Trego in clearing out the aguada, and confirmed all that the latter had told us.

In the afternoon we passed the campo santo of Macoba, and very soon, ascending a hill, we saw through the trees the "old walls" of the ancient inhabitants. It was one of the wildest places we had seen; the trees were grander, and we were somewhat excited on approaching it, for we had heard that the old city was repeopled, and that Indians were again living in the buildings. It was almost evening; the Indians had returned from their work; smoke was issuing from the ruins, and, as seen through the trees, the very tops seemed alive with people; but as we approached we almost turned away with sorrow. It was like the wretched Arabs of the Nile swarming around the ruined temples of Thebes, a mournful contrast of present misery and past magnificence.

Among these ruins a rancho had been erected for the major domo, and as everything we had heretofore seen belonging to the cura of Xul was in fine order, we had no fears about our accommodations; but we found that nothing in this world must be taken for granted. The rancho was thatched, and had a dirty earthen floor, occupied by heaps of corn, beans, eggs, boxes, baskets, fowls, dogs, and pigs.

Although they had the place swept, it was still infested with fleas.

Fortunately, we suffered excessively from cold, which prevented us from being thrown into a fever, but it was one of the worst nights we had passed in the country.

Next morning Bernardo and the carriers arrived. They had lost their way and wandered around until ten o'clock the night before, when they had found a rancho. With an Indian to guide them they had set out again very early that morning.

The ruins at this place were not so extensive as we expected to find them. There were but two buildings occupied by the Indians, both in the immediate neighbourhood of our hut, and much ruined, one which is represented in Plate XXIII. A noble alamo tree was growing by its side, and holding it up, which, while I was in another direction, the Indians had begun to cut down, but which, fortunately, I returned in time to save. The building is about 120 feet front, and had two stories, with a grand staircase on the other side, now ruined. The upper story was in a ruinous condition, but parts of it were occupied by Indians.

PLATE XXIII

MACOBA

That afternoon Stephens and Cabot rode through a fine forest to the aguada, hoping to see some of the rare birds they had been told about. They returned in time to help Catherwood make a plan of the buildings, and with that their work was finished. As their presence had caused a commotion among the Indians, the major domo was very relieved to hear that they would be leaving.

I have nothing to say concerning the history of these ruins. They are the only memorials of a city which, but for them, would be utterly unknown, and I do not find among my notes any memoranda showing how or from whom we first received the intelligence of their existence.

Our road lay through the same great forest in which the ruins stood. At the distance of a league we descended from the high ground, and reached a small aguada. From this place the road for some distance was hilly until we came out upon a great savanna covered with a growth of bushes, which rose above our heads so thick that they met across the path, excluding every breath of air, without shielding us from the sun, and exceedingly difficult and disagreeable to ride through. At one o'clock we reached the suburbs of the rancho of Puut. The settlement was a long line of straggling huts, which, as we rode through them under the blaze of a vertical sun, seemed to have no end. I inquired of a woman peeping out of a door for the casa real, and was directed to a ruined hut on the same side, at the door, or, rather, at the doorway of which I dismounted, but had hardly crossed the threshold when I saw my white pantaloons speckled with little jumping black insects. I made a hasty retreat, and saw a man at the moment moving across the plaza, who asked me to his house, which was clean and comfortable, and when Mr. Catherwood came up the women of the house were engaged in preparing our dinner.

From this place we intended to visit the ruins of Mankeesh, but we learned that it would require a large circuit to reach them, and, at the same time, we received intelligence of other ruins of which we had not heard before, at the rancho of Yakatzib, on the road we had intended taking. We determined for the present to continue on the route we had marked out.

CHAPTER XIII

Rancho of Jalal — Ruins of Yakatzib — Village of Becanchen —
Hacienda of Zaccacal — Visit to the Ruins

At seven o'clock the next morning we started, and at the distance of
a league reached the rancho of Jalal, from which we turned off to the aguada
to water our horses. Plate XXIV represents this aguada. When we first came
down upon its banks it presented one of the most beautifully picturesque scenes
we met with in the country. It was completely enclosed by a forest, and had
large trees growing around the banks and overhanging the water. The surface
was covered with water weeds like a carpet of vivid green, and the aguada
had a much higher interest than any derived from mere beauty. According
to the accounts we had received at the rancho, ten years before it was dry, and
the bottom covered with mud several feet deep. The Indians were in the habit
of digging pits in it for the purpose of collecting the water which filtered
through, and in some of these excavations they struck upon an ancient well,
which, on clearing it away, was found to be of singular form and construction.
It had a square platform at the top, and beneath was a round well, faced
with smooth stones, from twenty to twenty-five feet deep. Below this was another
square platform, and under the latter another well of less diameter, and about
the same depth. The discovery of this well induced farther excavations, which,
as the whole country was interested in the matter, were prosecuted until upward
of forty wells were discovered, differing in their character and construction,
and some idea of which may be formed from Figure 9. These were all cleared
out, and the whole aguada repaired, since which it furnishes a supply during
the greater part of the dry season, and when this fails the wells appear, and
continue the supply until the rains come on again.

*They continued toward the rancho of Akabcib, where there were also
ruins, but coming to a settlement where there were many paths they did
not know which one to follow. They asked some women, but did not
understand the long answer in Maya, so went on, trusting to luck. After
riding for some distance they began to wonder whether the rancho they
had passed through was Akabcib. Albino arrived, and then a boy who
guided them onto the way. They soon reached a small ruined building,
but there was so little to see that they did not even get off their horses
but turned and continued their journey.*

PLATE XXIV

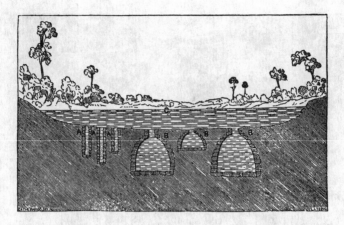

FIG. 9

At two o'clock we reached the foot of a stony sierra, or mountain range, toilsome and laborious for the horses, but Mr. Catherwood remarked that his pricked up his ears and trod lightly, as if just beginning a journey. From the top of the same sierra we saw at its foot, on the other side, the village of Be-canchen, where, on arriving, we rode through the plaza, and up to a large house, the front of which was adorned with a large red painting of a major domo on horseback, leading a bull into the ring. We inquired for the casa real, and were directed to a miserable thatched house, where a gentleman stepped out and recognized Mr. Catherwood's horse, which had belonged to Don Simon Peon, and through the horse he recognised me, having seen me with Don Simon at the fair at Jalacho, on the strength of which he immediately offered his house for a posada, or inn, which offer, on looking at the casa real, we did not hesitate to accept.

We were still on the great burial-ground of ruined cities. In the corridor of the house were sculptured stones, which our host told us were taken from the ancient buildings in the neighbourhood; they had also furnished materials for the foundation of every house on the plaza; and besides these there were other memorials. In the plaza were eight wells, then furnishing an abundant supply of water, and bearing that stamp which could not be mistaken, of the hand of the ancient builders.

The history of this village has all the wildness of romance, and, indeed, throughout this land of sepulchred cities the genius of romance sits enthroned. Its name is derived from this stream of water, being compounded of the Maya words *Becan*, running, and *chen*, a well. Twenty years ago the country round about was a wilderness of forest. A solitary Indian came into it, and made a clearing for his milpa. In doing so he struck upon the running stream, followed it until he found the water gushing from the rock, and the whole surface now occupied by the plaza is pierced with ancient wells. The Indians gathered round the wells, and a village grew up, which now contains six thousand inhabitants.

At this place we determined to separate; Mr. Catherwood to go on direct to Peto, a day and a half's journey distant, and lie by a few days to recruit, while Doctor Cabot and I made a retrograde and circuitous movement to the village of Mani. While speaking of our intention, a by-stander, Don Joaquin Sais, a gentleman of the village, told us of ruins on his hacienda of Zaccacal, eight leagues distant by a milpa road, and said that if we would wait a day, he would accompany us to visit them; but as we could not, he gave us a letter to the major domo.

Early the next morning Doctor Cabot and I set out with Albino and a single Indian, the latter carrying a petaquilla and hammocks.

Toward evening, escorted by the major domo and a vaquero to show the way, I set out for the ruins. At the distance of half a mile on the road to Tekax, we turned off into the woods to the left, and very soon reached the foot of a stone terrace. The vaquero led the way up it on horseback, and we followed, dismounting at the top. On this terrace was a circular hole like those before referred to at Uxmal and other places, but much larger.

Beyond this, on a higher terrace, among many remains, were two buildings, one of which was in a good state of preservation, and the exterior was ornamented all around with pillars set in the wall, somewhat different from those in the façades of other buildings, and more fanciful. The interior consisted of but a single apartment, fifteen feet long and nine feet wide. The ceiling was high, and in the layer of flat stones along the centre of the arch was a single stone, like that seen for the first time at Kewick, ornamented with painting.

This building stood in front of another more overgrown and ruined, which had been an imposing and important edifice.

Short as my visit was, there were few considerations that could have tempted me to remain longer. The garrapatas would soon be over, but they continued with the rainy season, and, in fact, increased and multiplied. I discovered them the moment I dismounted, and at first attempted to whip them off, but wishing to get through before night, I hurried round this building, creeping under branches and tearing aside bushes, and, actually covered with the abominable insects, started for the road.

In hurrying forward I unwittingly crossed the track of a procession of large black ants. These processions are among the extraordinary spectacles of that country, darkening the ground for an hour at a time; and the insect has a sting equal to that of hornets, as I quickly learned on this occasion.

I returned to the house, where the major domo kindly provided me with warm water for a bath, which cooled the fever of my blood. At night, for the first time in the country, we had at one end of the room the hammocks of the women, but this was not so bad as ants or garrapatas.

CHAPTER XIV

Village of San José — Hacienda of Santa María — Arrival at the
City of Tekax — Akil — Arrival at Mani

M arch 5. Early the next morning we set out for the ruins of San José. At seven o'clock we reached the pueblocito, or little village, of that name, pleasantly situated between a range of hills and a sierra, containing about two hundred inhabitants, among whom, as we rode into the plaza, we saw several white men. At the casa real we found a cacique of respectable appearance, who told us that there were no "old walls" in that village, which report of his, other Indians standing round confirmed. We were not much disappointed, nor at all anxious to find anything that would make it necessary to change our plans; to lose no time, we determined to push on to Mani, eight leagues distant, and applied for an Indian to carry our hammocks, which the cacique undertook to provide.

> They talked with the priest, who said that there were ruins at Ticum, the head of the curacy, and Stephens was tempted to go. However, he found out that the constructions had been destroyed to supply building material for the church, convent and all the stone houses of the village.

The wife and a little daughter of our carrier accompanied him to the top a hill beyond the village, where they bade him farewell as if he was setting out on a long and dangerous journey. The attachment of the Indian to his home is a striking feature of his character. The affection which grows up between the sexes was supposed by the early writers upon the character of the Indians not to exist among them, and probaby the sentiment and refinement of it do not; but circumstances and habit bind together the Indian man and woman as strongly as any known ties. When the Indian grows up to manhood he requires a woman to make him tortillas, and to provide him warm water for his bath at night. He procures one, sometimes by the providence of the master, without much regard to similarity of tastes or parity of age; and though a young man is mated to an old woman, they live comfortably together. If he finds her guilty of any great offence, he brings her up before the master or the alcalde, gets her a whipping, and then takes her under his arm and goes quietly home with her. The Indian husband is rarely harsh to his wife, and the devotion of wife to her husband is always a subject of remark. They share their pleasures as well as their labours; go up together with all their children to some village fiesta, and one of the most afflicting incidents in their lot is a necessity that takes the husband from his home.

In the suburbs of the village we commenced ascending the sierra, from the top of which we saw at the foot the hacienda of Santa Maria. Behind it rose a high mound, surrounded by trees, indicating that here too were the ruins of an ancient city.

The proprietor came out to receive us, and, pointing to the mound, we made some inquiry about the building, but he did not comprehend us, and, supposing that we meant some old ranchos in that direction, said that they were for the servants. We succeeded, however, in coming to an understanding about the mound, and the master told us that he had never been to it; that there was no path; that if we attempted to go to it we should be eaten up by garra-patas, and he called some Indians, who said that it was entirely in ruins. This was satisfactory, for the idea of being loaded with garrapatas to carry about till night had almost made me recoil.

Leaving the hacienda, we entered, with a satisfaction that can hardly be described, upon a broad road for carretas and calesas. We had emerged from the narrow and tangled path of milpas and ranchos, and were once more on a camino real. Very soon we reached Tekax, one of the four places in Yucatan bearing the name of a city, and I must confess that I felt some degree of excitement. Throughout Yucatan our journey had been so quiet, so free from danger or interruption of any kind, that, after my Central American experience, it seemed unnatural. Yucatan was in state of open rebellion against Mexico; we had heard of negotiations, but there had been no tumult, confusion, or blood-shed. Tekax alone had broken the general stillness, and while the rest of the country was perfectly quiet, this interior city had got up a small revolution on its own account, and for the benefit of whom it might concern.

A contingent of soldiers had been sent from Merida, the capital, and quickly reached Tecax. By next morning the rebellion had already ended without arms being used, and the leaders of both sides were on the friendliest terms. The travelers found Tecax a charming town full of life.

As we rode along all eyes were turned upon us. We stopped in the plaza, which, with its great church and the buildings around it, was the finest we had seen in the country, and all the people ran out to the corridors to gaze at us. It was an unprecedented thing for strangers to pass through this place. European saddles, holsters, and arms were strange, and, including Albino, we made the cabalistic number of three which got up the late revolution.

Our road lay for some distance along the sierra. It was broad, open, and the sun beat fiercely upon us. At half past ten we reached Akil, and rode up to the casa real. At the door was a stone hollowed out like those often before referred to, called pilas. In the steps and foundation were sculptured stones from ruined mounds in the immediate neigbourhood, and the road along the yard of the church ran through a mound, leaving part on each side, and the excavated mass forming on one side the wall of the convent yard.

At a quarter before three we resumed our journey. The sun was still very hot; the road was straight, stony, and uninteresting, a great part of the way through overgrown milpas. At half past five we reached Mani, again finding over the door and along the sides of the casa real sculptured stones, some of them of new and curious designs; in one compartment was a seated figure, with what might seem a crown and sceptre, and the figures of the sun and moon on either side of his head, curious and interesting in themselves, independent of the admonition that we were again on the site of an aboriginal city.

In all our journey through this country there were no associations. Day after day we rode into places unknown beyond the boundaries of Yucatan, with no history attached to them, and touching no chord of feeling. Mani, however, rises above the rest, and, compared with the profound obscurity or the dim twilight in which other places are enveloped, its history is plainly written.

When the haughty caciques of Maya rebelled against the supreme lord, and destroyed the city of Mayapan, the reigning monarch was left with only the territory of Mani, the people of which had not joined in the rebellion.

It has been mentioned that on their arrival at Tihoo the Spaniards encamped on a cerro, or mound, which stood on the site now occupied by the plaza of Merida. While in this position, surrounded by hostile Indians, their supplies cut off and straitened for provisions, one day the scouts brought intelligence to Don Francisco Montejo of a great body of Indians, apparently warlike, advancing toward them. From the top of the cerro they discovered the multitude, and among them one borne on the shoulders of men, as if extended on a bier. As the Indians drew near to the cerro, they lowered to the ground the person whom they carried on their shoulders, who approached alone, threw down his bow and arrow, and, raising both hands, made a signal that he came in peace. Immediately all the Indians laid their bows and arrows on the ground, and, touching their fingers to the earth, kissed them, also in token of good-will.

The chief advanced to the foot of the mound, and began to ascend it. Don Francisco stepped forward to meet him, and the Indian made him a profound reverence; Don Francisco received him with cordiality, and, taking him by the hand, conducted him to his quarters.

This Indian was Tutul Xiu, the greatest lord in all that country, the lineal descendant of the royal house which once ruled over the whole land of Maya, and then cacique of Mani. He said that, moved by the valour and perseverance of the Spaniards, he had come voluntarily to render obedience, and to offer his aid and that of his subjects for the pacification of the rest; and he brought a large present of turkeys, fruits, and other provisions. He had come to be their friend; he desired, also, to be a Christian, and asked the adelantado to go through some Christian ceremonies.

Tutul Xiu was accompanied by other caciques, whose names, as found in an Indian manuscript, have been handed down. They remained with the Spaniards seventy days, and on taking leave, Tutul Xiu promised to send ambassadors to solicit the other chiefs, though they were not his vassals, to render obedience to the Spaniards.

Afterward he despatched the caciques who went with him to render submission to the Spaniards, as ambassadors to the Lords of Zotuta, called the Cocomes, and the other nations to the east as far as the region where now stands the city of Valladolid, making known to them his resolution, and the friendship he had contracted with the Spaniards, and beseeching them to do the same; representing that the Spaniards were determined to remain in the land, had established themselves in Campeachy, and were preparing to do so in Tihoo.

The ambassadors proceeded to the district of Zotuta, and made known their embassy to Nachi Cocom, the principal lord of that territory. The latter requested them to wait four or five days for their answer, and in the mean time convoked all his dependant caciques, who, in concert with this chief, determined to make a great wild-boar hunt, ostensibly to fête the ambassadors. Under this pretext, they enticed them from the inhabited parts of the country into a dense forest, and feasted them three days. On the fourth they assembled to eat beneath a large sapote tree, and the last act of the feast was to cut the throats of the ambassadors, sparing but one, whom they charged to inform Tutul Xiu of their reception of his embassy, and to reproach him with his cowardice; but though they spared the life of this one, they put out his eyes with an arrow, and sent him, under the charge of four captains, to the territory of Tutul Xiu, where they left him and returned to their own country.

Among the wonders unfolded by the discovery of these ruined cities, what made the strongest impression on our minds was that fact that their immense population existed in a region so scantily supplied with water. Throughout the whole country there is no stream, or spring, or living fountain, and, but for the extraordinary caves and hollows in the rocks from which the inhabitants at his day drink, they must have been entirely dependant upon artificial fountains, and literally upon the rain that came down from heaven.

It was late on Saturday afternoon when we reached Mani. The guarda of Indians had served their term of a week in attendance at the casa real, and were now retiring from office, as usual all intoxicated, but we got a large room swept out, had it furnished with chairs and tables, and our hammocks hung up; and here, amid the wrecks of cities, we were almost in ruins ourselves.

CHAPTER XV

Visit to the Ruins — Books and ancient Characters of the Indians
burned by the Spaniards — Archives of Mani — Ancient Map

I had an uncommon degree of satisfaction at waking up in Mani. I had heard of this place on my first visit to Uxmal, of relics and heirlooms in the hands of the cacique, and of ruins, which, however, we were advised were not worth visiting.

At the end of a street leading to the well we saw a long building, pierced in the middle by the street, and part still standing on each side. We saw at a glance that it was not the work of the antiguos, but had been erected by the Spaniards since the conquest, and yet we were conducted to it as one of the same class with those we had found all over the country; though we did meet with one intelligent person, who smiled at the ignorance of the people, and said that it was a palace of *El Rey,* or the *king,* Montejo

Near this building, and at the corner of the street, is the well referred to in the conclusion of my legend of the House of the Dwarf at Uxmal. "The old woman (the mother of the Dwarf) then died, but at the Indian village of Mani there is a deep well, from which opens a cave that leads under ground an immense distance to Merida. In this cave, on the bank of a stream, under the shade of a large tree, sits an old woman, with a serpent by her side, who sells water in small quantities, not for money, but only for a criatura, or baby, to give the serpent to eat; and this old woman is the mother of the Dwarf." The entrance to the well was under a great shelf of overhanging rock, forming the mouth of a magnificent cavern, wild enough to sustain the legend.

Albino had inquired of the cacique for the ancient relics of which we had heard accounts, and the Indians brought a copy of Cogolludo, wrapped up and treasured with great care in the casa real. This did not astonish us much, and they opened the book and pointed out a picture, the only one in it, being a representation of the murder of the ambassadors of Tutul Xiu; and while we were looking at it they brought out and unrolled on the floor an old painting on cotton cloth, being the original from which Cogolludo had the engraving made. The design was a coat of arms bordered with the heads of the murdered ambassadors, one of which has an arrow fixed in the temple, intended to represent the ambassador who had his eyes put out with this weapon. In the centre is a tree growing out of a box, representing the sapote tree at Zotuta, under which the murder was committed, and which, the Indians say, is still standing. This tree I shall have occasion to mention again hereafter. The painting had evidently been executed by an Indian, and probably very near the time of the occurrence which it was intended to commemorate. It is an object of great reverence among the Indians of Mani. In fact, throughout our whole journeyings, either in Central America or Yucatan, it was the first and only instance in which we met with any memorial in the hands of the Indians, tending to keep alive the memory of any event in their history.

In 1571, twenty-nine years after the foundation of Merida, some Indians of Mani relapsed and became idolaters, practising in secret their ancient rites.

Intelligence of their backsliding reached the ears of the provincial in Merida, who came to Mani in person, and forthwith established himself as inquisitor. Some who had died obstinately in the secret practice of idolatrous rites had been buried in sacred ground; he ordered their bodies to be dug up, and their bones thrown into the fields; and, in order to strike terror into the minds of the Indians, and root out the memory of their ancient rites, on a day appointed for that purpose, attended by the principal of the Spanish nobility, and in the presence of a great multitude of Indians, he made them bring together all thier books and ancient characters, and publicly burned them, thus destroying at once the history of their antiquities.

The painting prompted Stephens to look for more documents. He was given permission to examine the archives and among them found an ancient book written in Maya. The only person who could make any attempt at reading it was the schoolmaster, but even he was not familiar with the written language, particulary this, which was three hundred years old. In the back of the book was a curious map, dated 1557, with Maní at its center.

The schoolmaster offered to make copies of the documents and of passages where the name Uxmal appeared. These interested Stephens most because he though that with them he would be able to prove that the city was still inhabited at the time of the Conquest.

He took the copies to Don Pío Pérez, who found some errors, and Padre Carrillo later went to Maní to make exact copies of the map and documents, and also made a translation. This showed that the papers recorded an agreement among the governors of different towns on their lands and boundaries.

Toward evening we strolled over to the church and convent, which are among the grandest of these early structures erected in Yucatan, proud monuments of the zeal and labour of the Franciscan friars. They were built under the direction of Friar Juan of Merida, distinguished as a warrior and conqueror, but who threw aside the sword and put on the habit of a monk. According to

PLATE XXV

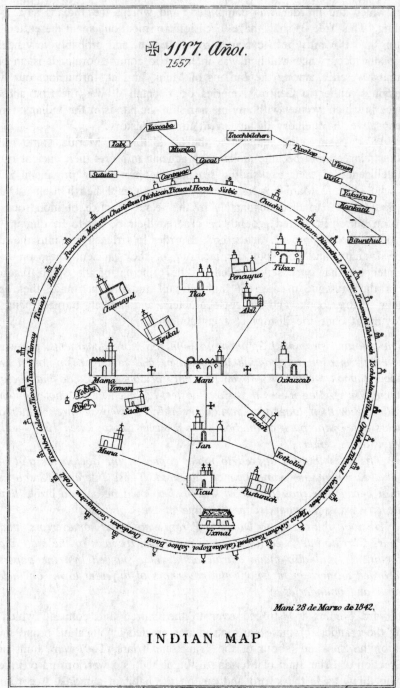

✠ 1557. Añoi.
1557

Mani 28 de Marzo de 1842.

INDIAN MAP

Charles Copley, Sc. N.Y.

Cogolludo, they were both finished in the short space of seven months, the cacique who had been lord of that country furnishing six thousand Indians. Built upon the ruins of another race, they are now themselves tottering and going to decay.

CHAPTER XVI

Departure from Mani — Ornithology of Yucatan — Indian Almanac
— Arrival at Chichen — Magnificent Appearance of the Ruins

Monday, March 7. Before daylight the next morning we left Mani.

Our present mode of travelling favoured Doctor Cabot's particular objects. His best chance for procuring birds was always on the road, the time passed at ruins, on account of the density of the woods and underbrush, being in a great measure lost to him.

*Little or nothing was known about the ornithology of Yucatán, so Dr.
Cabot's research was completely original.*

Doctor Cabot has published, in the Boston Journal of Natural History, an account of his observations upon one rare and splendid bird, the ocellated turkey, of which one stuffed specimen at the Jardin des Plantes, and another in the collection of the Earl of Derby, are the only two known to exist, and of which, besides obtaining a stuffed specimen, we succeeded in transporting two living birds from the interior, and embarking them for home, but lost them overboard on the voyage. I have hopes that he may be induced to publish a full account of his observations upon the ornithology of Yucatan.

We stopped that night at Tixmeach, eight leagues distant, a neat village with a well one hundred and forty-four feet deep, at which every woman drawing from it left a handful of maize for a cantaro of water, and we paid a medio for watering our horses; and setting out before daylight the next morning, at half past nine we reached Peto, where we found Mr. Catherwood and our luggage on the hands of our friend Don Pio Perez.

Peto is the head of a department, of which Don Pio Perez was gefe politico. It was a well-built, town, with streets indicated, as at Merida, by figures on the tops of the houses.

At this place we found letters and packets of newspapers from home, forwarded to us from Merida, and, except attending to them, our time was devoted almost exclusively to long and interesting conversations with Don Pio on matters connected with the antiquities of the country.

Besides preparing a series of verbal forms and other illustrations of the grammar of the Maya language, according to memoranda made by the same distinguished gentleman before referred to, he gave me a vocabulary in manuscript, containing more than four thousand Maya words, and an almanac, prepared by himself, according to the Indian system of computation, for the year from the 16th of July, 1841, to the 15th of July, 1842.

Besides these, he furnished me with the copy of one other document, which, if genuine and authentic, throws more light upon aborginal history than any other known to be in existence. It is a fragment of a Maya manuscript, written from memory by an Indian, at some time not designated, and entitled "Principal epochs of the ancient history of Yucatan."

It purports to give the series of "katunes," or epochs, from the time of the departure of the Toltecs from the country of Tulapan until their arrival at this, as it is called, island of Chacno-uitan, occupying, according to Don Pio's computation of katunes, the lapse of time corresponding with that between the years 144 and 217 of the Christian era.

It assigns dates to the discovery of Bacalar and then of Chichen Itza, both within the three epochs corresponding with the time between. A.D. 360 and A.D. 432; the colonization of Champoton, and its destruction; the times of wandering through the uninhabited forests, and establishing themselves a second time at Chichen Itza, within epochs corresponding with the lapse between A.D. 888 and A.D. 936.

The epoch of the colonization of Uxmal, corresponding with the years between A.D. 936 and 1176 A.D.; the epochs of wars between the governors of Chichen Itza and Mayapan; the destruction of the latter city by the Uitzes of the Sierras, or highlanders; and the arrival of the Spaniards, adding that "Holy men from the East came with them;" and the manuscript terminates with the epoch of the first baptism and the arrival of the first bishop.

On the afternoon of the 11th of March we bade farewell to Don Pio Perez, and set out for Chichen. Ever since we left home we had had our eyes upon this place. We had become eager to reach it, and the increasing bulk of these volumes warns me that I must not now linger on the road. I shall therefore barely say that the first night we stopped at the village of Taihxiu, the second at Yaxcaba, and at noon of the third day we reached Pisté, about two miles distant from Chichen.

At four o'clock we left Pisté, and very soon we saw rising high above the plain the Castillo of Chichen. In half an hour we were among the ruins of this ancient city, with all the great buildings in full view, casting prodigious shadows over the plain, and presenting a spectacle which, even after all that we had seen, once more excited in us emotions of wonder. The camino real ran through the midst of them, and the field was so open that, without dismounting, we rode close in to some of the principal edifices. Involuntarily we lingered, but night was approaching, and, fairly dragging ourselves away, we rode on, and in a few minutes reached the hacienda. Vaqueros were shouting, and a large drove of cattle was pouring in at the gate. We were about following, but a crowd of men and women on the steps of the hacienda shouted to us not to come in, and a man ran toward us, throwing up both hands, and shut the gate directly in our faces. This ominous demonstration did not mean anything churlish; on the contrary, all was done out of kindness. We had been expected for three months. Through the agency of friends the proprietor had advised the major domo of our intended visit, directing him to do all in his power to make us comfortable, and it was for this reason that the latter had ordered the gate to be shut upon us, for, as the man who did it told us, the hacienda was overrun with women and children, and there was no room for another hammock. He conducted us to the church, standing in a fine situation, and offered us the sacristia, or vestryroom, which was new, clean, and had plastered walls, but it was small, and had only knobs for two hammocks.

Our alternative was a house directly opposite the gate of the hacienda, to which there was no objection on the score of size, for as yet its dimensions were unlimited, as it was merely a frame of poles supporting a thatched roof, with a great pile of lime and sand in the centre, intended to be made into walls.

The next morning, under the guidance of an Indian of the hacienda, we prepared for a preliminary survey. The ruins of Chichen lie on a hacienda, called by the name of the ancient city. It is the property of Don Juan Sosa, and was set off to him, on the decease of his father and an apportionment of his estate, with cattle, horses, and mules, at a valuation of between five and six thousand dollars.

The ruins are nine leagues from Valladolid, the camino real to which passes directly through the field. The great buildings tower on both sides of the road in full sight of all passers-by, and from the fact that the road is much travelled, the ruins of Chichen are perhaps more generally known to the people of the country than any other in Yucatan.

From the door of our hut some of the principal buildings were in sight. We went first to those on the opposite side of the camino real. The path led through the cattle - yard of the hacienda, from which we passed out at one end by a range of bars into the field of ruins, partially wooded, but the greater part open and intersected by cattle-paths. Garrapatas were as abundant as ever, and perhaps more so from the numerous cattle running over the plain, but the luxuries of an open country, and the facility of moving from place to place, were so great, that these could not mar our satisfaction, which was raised to the highest pitch by the ruins themselves.

All the principal building were within a comparatively small compass; in fact, they were in such proximity, and the facilities for moving among them were so great, that by one o'clock we had visited every building, examined every apartment, and arranged the whole plan and order of work.

The name of Chichen is another instance added to those already given, showing the importance attached in that dry country to the possession of water.

It is compounded of the two Maya words *chi*, mouth, and *chen*, well, and signifies the mouth of the well. Among the ruins are two great senotes, which, beyond doubt, furnished water to the inhabitants of the ancient city. Since the establishment of a hacienda and the construction of a well, these had fallen into disuse.

On our journey from Peto, the particulars of which I was obliged to omit, we had entered a region where the sources of the supply of water again formed a new and distinctive feature in the face of the country, wilder, and, at first sight, perhaps creating a stronger feeling of admiration and wonder than even the extraordinary cuevas, aguadas, and senotes we had formerly encountered. These, too, are called senotes, but they differ materially from those before presented, being immense circular holes, from sixty to two hundred feet in

FIG. 10

diameter, with broken, rocky, perpendicular sides from fifty to one hundred feet deep, and having at the bottom a great body of water, of an unknown depth, always about the same level, supposed to be supplied by subterranean rivers.

Figure 10 represents this senote among the ruins of Chichen.

We returned to the hut well satisfied with our first day at Chichen; and there was another circumstance which, though painful in itself, added materially to the spirit with which we commenced our labours at this place. The danger apprehended from the rainy season was coming to pass, and under the anticipation of a failure of the next crop, corn had risen from two reales to a dollar the load. At the time of our arrival, the criados, or servants, of the hacienda, always improvident, had consumed their small stock, and, with no hope from their milpas, with the permission of the master were about moving away to regions where the pressure would be less severe. Our arrival, as the major domo told us, arrested this movement; instead of our being obliged to hunt them up, the poor Indians crowded round the door of our hut, begging employment, and scrambling for the reales which Albino distributed among them.

CHAPTER XVII

Plan of the Ruins — An Edifice called Akatzeeb — Majestic Pile
of Building called the Monjas — The Eglesia or Church — Circular
Edifice called the Caracol — Building called Chichanchob —
Extraordinary Edifice, to which the Name Gymnasium or Tennis-
court is Given — The Castillo — Colossal Serpents' Heads

Plate XXVI represents the general plan of the ruins of Chichen. This plan is made from bearings taken with the compass, and the distances were all measured with a line. The buildings are laid down on the plan according to their exterior form. All now standing are comprehended, and the whole circumference occupied by them is about two miles, which is equal to the diameter of two thirds of a mile, though ruined buildings appear beyond these limits.

By referring to the plan the reader will see the position of the hut in which we lived, and, following the path from our door through the cattle-yard of the hacienda, at the distance of two hundred and fifty yards he will reach the building represented in Plate XXVII. It does not stand on an artificial terrace, but the earth seems to have been excavated for some distance before it, so as to give it elevation of position. It faces the east, and measures one hundred and forty-nine feet in front by forty-eight feet deep. The whole exterior is rude, and without ornament of any kind. A grand staircase, forty-five feet wide, now entirely in ruins, rises in the centre to the roof of the building. On each side of the staircase are two doorways; at each end is a single doorway, and the front facing the west has seven. The whole number of apartments is eighteen.

At the south end the doorway opens into a chamber, round which hangs a greater and more impenetrable mystery. This chamber is nineteen feet wide by eight feet six inches deep; and in the back wall a low, narrow doorway communicates with another chamber in the rear, of the same dimensions, but having its floor one step higher. The lintel of this doorway is of stone, and on the soffite, or under part, is sculptured the subject represented in Plate XXVIII. This tablet, and the position in which it exists, have given the name to the building, which the Indians call Akatzeeb, signifying the writing in the dark; for, as no light enters except from the single doorway, the chamber was so dark that the drawing could with difficulty be copied. The sitting figure seems performing some act of incantation, or some religious or idolatrous rite, which the "writing in the dark" undoubtedly explains, if one could but read it.

PLATE XXVI

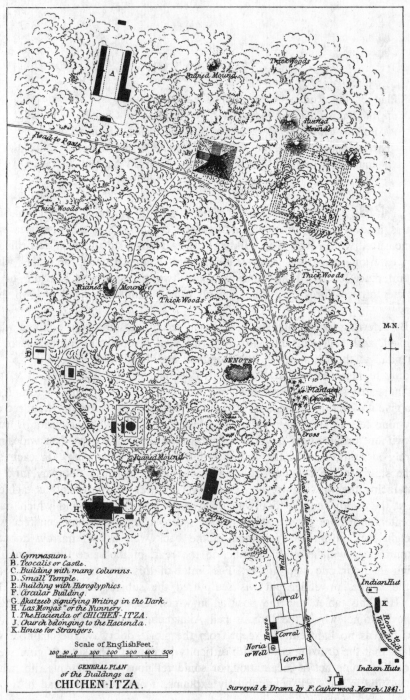

A. Gymnasium.
B. Teocalis or Castle.
C. Building with many Columns.
D. Small Temple.
E. Building with Hieroglyphics.
F. Circular Building.
G. Akatzeeb signifying Writing in the Dark.
H. "Las Monjas" or the Nunnery.
I. The Hacienda of CHICHEN-ITZA.
J. Church belonging to the Hacienda.
K. House for Strangers.

Scale of English Feet.

100 50 0   100   200   300   400   500

GENERAL PLAN
of the Buildings at
CHICHEN-ITZA.

Surveyed & Drawn by F. Catherwood. March, 1841.

PLATE XXVII

CHICHEN ITZA
Building called Akatzeeb

PLATE XXVIII

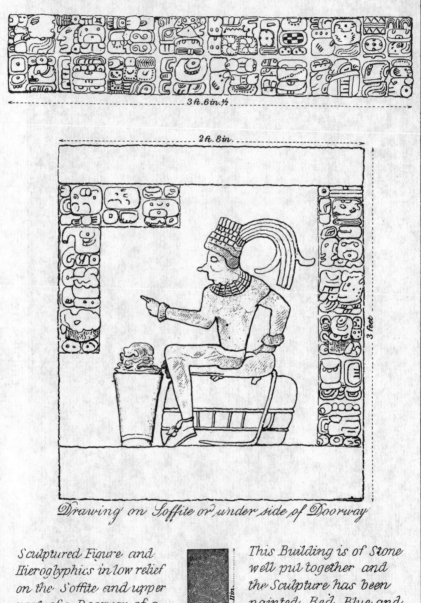

3 ft. 6 in. ½

2 ft. 8 in.

3 Feet

Drawing on Soffite or under side of Doorway

Sculptured Figure and Hieroglyphics in low relief on the Soffite and upper part of a Doorway of a Building called AKATZEEB. at CHICHEN-ITZA

This Building is of Stone well put together and the Sculpture has been painted. Red. Blue and Yellow. are still visible.

5 ft. 11 in.

2 ft. 8.
Step

Level of Floor

DOORWAY

F. Catherwood

J. N. Gimbrede

The Akabdzib, *dating from the Classic period, is divided into three sections. The overall style is plain, but the façade is topped by a roof comb of stone mosaic. The stone lintel of the doorway on the south side has a carving of a priest with a brazier in front of him and is surrounded by hieroglyphs, most of which have not been deciphered. This explains another translation of the name as 'obscure writing'.*

Leaving this building, and following the path indicated in the map, at the distance of one hundred and fifty yards westward we reach a modern stone fence, dividing the cattle-field of the hacienda, on the other side of which appears through the trees, between two other buildings, the end façade of a long, majestic pile, called, like one of the principal edifices at Uxmal, the Monjas, or Nuns; it is remarkable for its good state of preservation, and the richness and beauty of its ornaments, as represented in Plate XXIX. The view comprehends the corner of a building on the right, at a short distance, called the Eglesia, or Church. The height of this façade is twenty-five feet, and its width thirty-five. It has two cornices of tasteful and elaborate design. Over the doorway are twenty small cartouches of hieroglyphics in four rows, five in a row, barely indicated in the engraving, and to make room for which the lower cornice is carried up. Over these stand out in a line six bold projecting curved ornaments, like that presented from the House of the Governor at Uxmal, resembling an elephant's trunk, and the upper centre space over the doorway is an irregular circular niche, in which portions of a seated figure, with a head-dress of feathers, still remain.

Plate XXX represents the front of the same building. It is composed of two structures entirely different from each other, one of which forms a sort of wing to the principal edifice, and has at the end the façade before presented. The whole length is two hundred and twenty-eight feet, and the depth of the principal structure is one hundred and twelve feet. The only portion containing interior chambers is that which I have called the wing. This has two doorways opening into chambers twenty-six feet long and eight feet deep, behind each of which is another of corresponding dimensions, now filled up several feet with mortar and stones, and appearing to have been originally filled up solid to the ceiling, making again casas cerradas, or closed houses. The whole number of chambers in this wing is nine, and these are all the apartments on the ground floor.

A grand staircase fifty-six feet wide, the largest we saw in the country, rises to the top. The grand staircase is thirty-two feet high, and has thirty-nine steps. On the top of the structure stands a range of buildings, with a platform of fourteen feet in front extending all round.

From the back of this platform the grand staircase rises again, having the same width, fifteen steps to the roof of the second range, which forms a platform in front of the third range; this last is, unfortunately, in a ruinous condition.

PLATE XXIX

F. Catherwood.

Gambrede.

CHICHEN ITZA
Monjas

PLATE XXX

CHICHEN ITZA
Casa de las Monjas

The Nunnery Annex, Chichén Itzá.

The Nunnery Complex, Chichén Itzá.

The circumference of this building is six hundred and thirty-eight feet, and its height, when entire, was sixty-five feet. It seems to have been constructed only with reference to the second range of apartments, upon which the art and skill of the builders have been lavishly expended. It is one hundred and four feet long and thirty feet wide, and the broad platform around it, though overgrown with grass several feet high, formed a noble promenade, commanding a magnificent view of the whole surrounding country.

On the side of the staircase are five doorways, of which the three centre ones are what are usually called false doors, appearing to be merely recesses in the wall. The compartments between the doorways contained combinations of ornaments of unusual taste and elegance, both in arrangement and design. The two extreme doorways open into chambers, in each of which are three long recesses in the back wall, extending from the floor to the ceiling, all of which, from the remains still visible, were once ornamented with paintings. At each end of the building was another chamber, with three niches or recesses, and on the other side, facing the south, the three centre doorways, corresponding with the false doors on the north side, opened into an apartment forty-seven feet long and nine deep, having nine long niches in the back wall; all the walls from the floor to the peak of the arch had been covered with painted designs, now wantonly defaced, but the remains of which present colours in some places still bright and vivid; and among these remains detached portions of human figures continually recur, well drawn, the heads adorned with plumes of feathers, and the hands bearing shields and spears.

The Nunnery was built and added to at various periods, but the most extensive construction dates from the Classic period. The name comes from the fact that it reminded the Spaniards of a convent and because, according to Bishop Landa, it was where Maya priestesses lived.

First to be built was the base that ends in a frieze with two moldings. A stairway leads to the second platform were there is a later building with a frieze decorated with masks of Chaac, the god of rain, alternating with panels of latticework.

Finally a third addition was made that includes a narrower stairway with vertical rings on the sides. This leads to a second floor where there is a dilapidated one-roomed building whose façade is decorated with a frieze of small columns.

On the terrace stands a temple with two galleries of six rooms each. The south façade is decorated with Greek frets, small columns and square figures while the north façade has latticework, small columns and squares.

Against the east side of the base is the Nunnery Annex, *one of the finest Chenes style buildings on this site. The north and south faces are decorated with panels of latticework, and masks of Chaac at the corners. A writhing serpent is carved between the upper moldings.*

On the west face there are also masks of Chaac and figures with up-curving noses. Above the entrance is a sort of medallion showing a human figure seated on a throne and wearing a headdress of feathers. Over the doorway is a lintel with a glyph that has been deciphered as corresponding to 880 A.D.

Descending again to the ground, at the end of the wing stands what is called the Eglesia, or Church, a corner of which was comprehended in a previous view, and the front of which is represented in Plate XXXI. It is twenty-six feet long, fourteen deep, and thirty-one high, its comparatively great height adding very much to the effect of its appearance. It has three cornices, and the spaces between are richly ornamented. The sculpture is rude but grand. The principal ornament is over the doorway, and on each side are two human figures in a sitting posture, but, unfortunately, much mutilated. The portion of the façade above the second cornice is merely an ornamented wall, like those before mentioned at Zayi and Labnà.

PLATE XXXI

CHICHEN ITZA
Iglesia

The Church,
Chichén Itzá.

The whole of this building is in a good state of preservation. The interior consists of a single apartment, once covered with plaster, and along the top of the wall under the arch are seen the traces of a line of medallions or cartouches in plaster, which once contained hieroglyphics. The Indians have no superstitious feelings about these ruins, except in regard to this building; and in this they say that on Good Friday of every year music is heard sounding; but this illusion, brought with us from Santa Cruz del Quiché, was here destined to be broken. In this chamber we opened our Daguerreotype apparatus, and on Good Friday were at work all day, but heard no music.

This building was named The Church *simply because it stands near the Nunnery. It has one, vaulted room and one entrance. The decoration consists of stone mosaics, and on the frieze are three large masks of Chaac with the characteristic hooked nose. Similar masks can be seen the roof comb.*

Leaving this pile of buildings, and passing on northward from the Monjas, at the distance of four hundred feet we reach the edifice represented in Plate XXXII, conspicuous among the ruins of Chichen for its picturesque appearance, and unlike any other we had seen, except one at Mayapan much ruined. It is circular in form, and is known by the name of the Caracol, or winding staircase, on account of its interior arrangements. It stands on the upper of two terraces. The lower one measures in front from north to south two hundred and twenty-three feet, and in depth from east to west one hundred and fifty feet, and is still in good preservation. A grand staircase forty-five feet wide, and containing twenty steps, rises to the platform of this terrace. On each side of this staircase,

PLATE XXXII

CHICHEN ITZA
Circular Building

The Caracol or Observatory, Chichén Itzá.

forming a sort of balustrade, were the entwined bodies of two gigantic serpents, three feet wide, portions of which are still in place; and among the ruins of the staircase we saw a gigantic head, which had terminated at one side the foot of the steps.

The platform of the second terrace measures eighty feet in front and fifty-five in depth, and is reached by another staircase forty-two feet wide, and having sixteen steps. In the centre of the steps, and against the wall of the terrace, are the remains of a pedestal six feet high, on which probably once stood an idol. On the platform, fifteen feet from the last step, stands the building. It is twenty-two feet in diameter, and has four small doorways facing the cardinal points. A great portion of the upper part and one of the sides have fallen. Above the cornice the roof sloped so as almost to form an apex. The height, including the terraces, is little short of sixty feet, and, when entire, even among the great buildings around, this structure must have presented a striking appearance. The doorways give entrance to a circular corridor five feet wide. The inner wall has also four doorways, smaller than the others, and standing at intermediate points of the compass, facing northeast, northwest, southwest, and southeast. These doors give entrance to a second circular corridor, four feet wide; and in the centre is a circular mass, apparently of solid stone, seven feet six inches in diameter; but in one place, at the height of eight feet from the ground, was a small square opening choked up with stones, which I endeavoured to clear out; but the stones falling into the narrow corridor made it dangerous to continue. The plan of the building was new, but, instead of unfolding secrets, it drew closer the curtain that already shrouded, with almost impenetrable folds, these mysterious structures.

The Caracol *or* Observatory, *built in the Transitional period, between 900 and 1000 A.D. approximately, is a cylindrical structure with a spiral staircase ('caracol') leading up to the room from which the skies were observed. A complex building, it stands on three distinct bases with decorated stairways and terraces.*

At the distance of four hundred and twenty feet northwest from the Caracol stands the building represented in Figure 11. It is called by the Indians Chichanchob, meaning in Spanish, Casa Colorada, and in English, Red House. The terrace is sixty-two feet long and fifty-five wide, and is still in good preservation; the staircase is twenty feet wide, and as we approached it on our first visit, a cow was coming quietly down the steps.

The building measures forty-three feet front and twenty-three feet deep, and is still strong and substantial. Above the cornice it was richly ornamented, but the ornaments are now much decayed. It has three doorways, which open into a corridor running the whole width of the building; and along the top of the back wall was a stone tablet, with a row of hieroglyphics extending all along the wall. Many of them were defaced, and, from their height, in an awkward position to copy; but we had a scaffold erected, and obtained copies of the whole. Plate XXXIII represents these hieroglyphics, so far as they could be made out. It has a back corridor, consisting of three chambers, all of which retain the marks of painting; and, from the convenience of its arrangements, with the platform of the terrace for a promenade, and the view of a fine open country in front, but for the greater convenience of being near the hacienda we should have been tempted to take up our abode in it.

Fig. 11

*Chichánchob
or Red House,
Chichén Itzá.*

*This building dates from the Classic Period, between 600 and 900 A.D.
and is now known as the* Red House *because of the red border painted
around the portico. Another name for it is Chichánchob, meaning 'Little
Holes' in Maya, and refers to the pierced stonework of its roof comb.
The temple stands on a platform with rounded corners and a stairway
on the east side. On the façade is a plain frieze between two cornices
and stone lintels over the doorways. The roof comb is double, the first
decorated with pierced Greek frets and the second, added at a later
period, with frets and masks of the god Chaac above the doorways.*

At the short distance of two hundred feet is the building represented in
Figure 12. The platform of the terrace was sixty-four feet square, the building
had three rooms, but both terrace and building are ruined, and the view is
presented only because it was so picturesque that Mr. Catherwood could not
resist the temptation to draw it.

These are only buildings on the west side of the camino real which are
still standing; but great vestiges exist of mounds with remains of buildings upon
them, and colossal stones and fragments of sculpture at their feet, which it
would be impossible to present in detail.

Passing among these vestiges, we come out upon the camino real, and,
crossing it, again enter an open field, containing the extraordinary edifice
represented in Plate XXXIV, which, on first reaching the field of ruins, we
rode in on horseback to examine. It consists of two immense parallel walls, each
two hundred and seventy-four feet long, thirty feet thick, and one hundred and
twenty feet apart.

In the centre of the great stone walls, exactly opposite each other, and at
the height of twenty feet from the ground, are two massive stone rings, four
feet in diameter, and one foot one inch thick; the diameter of the hole is one

PLATE XXXIII

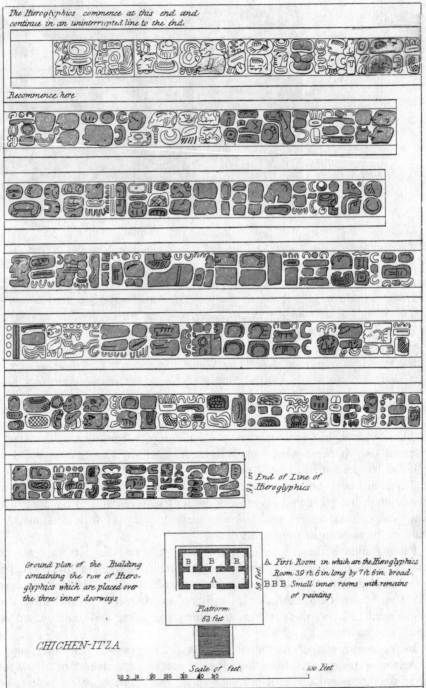

The Hieroglyphics commence at this end and continue in an uninterrupted line to the end.

Recommence here

9¼ in. End of Line of Hieroglyphics

Ground plan of the Building containing the row of Hieroglyphics which are placed over the three inner doorways

A. *First Room in which are the Hieroglyphics Room 39 ft. 6 in. long by 7 ft. 6 in. broad.*
B B B *Small inner rooms with remains of painting.*

Platform 62 feet

56 feet

CHICHEN-ITZA

Scale of feet.   *100 Feet*

FIG. 12

foot seven inches. On the rim and border were two sculptured entwined serpents, one of which is represented in Figure 13.

I have in all cases adopted the names of buildings which I found assigned to them on the spot, where any existed, and where there were none I have not attempted to give any. At Chichen all the principal buildings have names; this is called an Eglesia, or Church, of the antiguos, which was begun, but not finished, and the great open walls present not a bad idea of one of their gigantic churches before the roof is put on; but as we have already one Eglesia, and there is historical authority which, in my opinion, shows clearly the object and uses of this extraordinary structure, I shall call it, as occasion requires, the Gymnasium or Tennis-court.

In the account of the diversions of Montezuma, given by Herrera, we have the following:

"The King took much Delight in seeing Sport at Ball, which the Spaniards have since prohibited, because of the Mischief that often hapned at it; and

PLATE XXXIV

F. Catherwood.

Gombreat.

CHICHEN ITZA

Gymnasium

was by them call'd *Tlachtli*, being like our Tennis. The Ball was made of the Gum of a Tree that grows in hot Countries, which, having Holes made in it, distils great white Drops, that soon harden, and, being work'd and moulded together, turn as black as Pitch.* The Balls made thereof, tho' hard and heavy

The Ballcourt, Chichén Itzá.

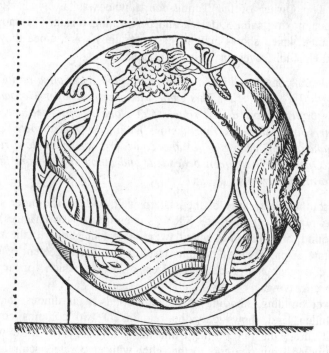

Fig. 13

* Undoubtedly caoutchouc, or India-rubber.

to the Hand, did bound and fly as well as our Foot-balls, there being no need to blow them; nor did they use Chaces, but vy'd to drive the adverse Party that is to hit the Wall, the others were to make good, or strike it over. They struck is with any Part of their Body, as it hapned, or they could most conveniently; and sometimes he lost that touched it with any other Part but his Hip, which was look'd upon among them as the greatest Dexterity; and to this Effect, that the Ball might rebound the better, they fastned a Piece of stiff Leather on their Hips. They might strike it every time it rebounded, which it would do several Times one after another, in so much that it look'd as if it had been alive. They play'd in Parties, so many on a Side, for a Load of Mantles, or what the Gamesters could afford, at so many Scores. They also play'd for Gold, and Feather-work, and sometimes play'd themselves away, as has been said before. The Place where play'd was a ground Room, long, narrow, and high, but wider above than below, and higher on the Sides than at the Ends, and they kept it very well plaster'd and smooth, both the Walls and the Floor. *On the side Walls they fix'd certain Stones, like those of a Mill, with a Hole quite through the Middle,* just as big as the Ball, and he that could strike it through there won the Game. The Owner of the Tennis-court, who was always a Lord, never play'd without making some Offering and performing certain Ceremonies to the Idol of Gaming, which shows how superstitious they were, since they had such Regard to their Idols, even in their Diversions.

The great Ballcourt *at Chichén dates from the Maya-Toltec period, from around 1000 to 1250 A.D. This game was played all over Mesoamerica, and was both a sport and a ritual. The stone hoops here are carved with intertwined serpents representing Kukulcán-Quetzalcóatl, and on the benches along each side of the court are scenes in low relief of players. One player has been beheaded, and blood spurts from his neck in the form of serpents.*

At the southern extremity of the eastern wall, and on the outer side, stands the building represented in Plate XXXV, consisting of two ranges, one even with the ground, and the other about twenty-five feet above it, the latter being in a good state of preservation, simple, tasteful in its arrangement of ornaments, and having conspicuous a procesion of tigers or lynxes, which appear on a small scale in the engraving.

The lower building, standing on the ground, is in a ruinous condition: the front has fallen, and shows only the remains of two columns covered with sculptured figures; the fall of the front has laid bare the entire wall of the chamber, covered from one end to the other with elaborately-sculptured figures in bas-relief.

Plate XXXVI represents a portion of these figures. Exposed for ages to a long succession of winds and rains, the characters were faded and worn; under

PLATE XXXV

Catherwood

S. H. Gimber.

CHICHEN ITZA

PLATE XXXVI

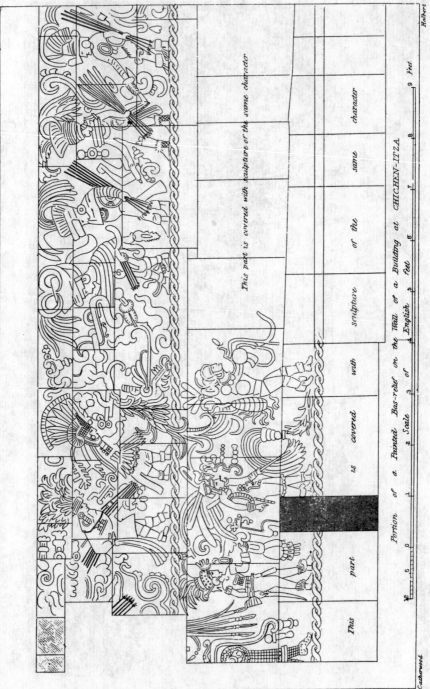

This part is covered with sculpture of the same character

This part is covered with sculpture of the same character

Catherwood

Halbert

Portion of a Painted Bas-relief on the Wall of a Building at CHICHEN-ITZA.

Scale of English feet

0 1 2 3 4 5 6 7 8 9 Feet.

the glare of a tropical sun the lines were confused and indistinct, and the reflection of the heat was so intense that is was impossible to work before it except for an hour or two in the afternoon, when the building was in the shade. The head-dress of the figures is, as usual, a plume of feathers, and in the upper row each figure carries a bundle of spears or a quiver of arrows. All these figures were painted, and the reader may imagine what the effect must have been when all was entire.

The steps or other means of access to this building are gone, and we reached it by clambering over fallen stones. The door opens upon the platform of the wall, overlooking the Tennis-court. The front corridor was supported by massive pillars, portions of which still remain, covered with elaborate sculptured ornaments. The lintel of the inner doorway is a beam of sapote richly carved. The jambs are partly buried, and above the rubbish appear sculptured figures with rich head-dresses, which anywhere else we should have considered it necessary to bring to light and copy; but between these jambs we enter an inner chamber, the walls and ceiling of which are covered, from the floor to the peak of the arch, with designs in painting, representing, in bright and vivid colours, human figures, battles, houses, trees, and scenes of domestic life, and conspicuous on one of the walls is a large canoe; but the first feeling of gratified surprise was followed by heavy disappointment, for the whole was mutilated and disfigured. Plate XXXVII represents detached portions of these paintings.

Here Stephens is describing the Temple of the Jaguars, *attached to the east side of the Ballcourt. A base and a stairway leading up to the platform on the south side were built. On top of this another, short stairway with ramps carved in relief leads up to the temple. This building contains an entrance chamber and a room with an altar, and the door jambs are decorated with warriors. Inside are the murals described above that impressed the explorers so much, since they saw them as proof that Maya art reached a very high standard.*

At the distance of five hundred feet southeast from this rises the Castillo, represented in Plate XXXVIII, the first building which we saw, and from every point of view the grandest and most conspicuous object that towers above the plain. Every Sunday the ruins are resorted to as a promenade by the villagers of Pisté, and nothing can surpass the picturesque appearance of this lofty building while women, dressed in white, with red shawls, are moving on the platform, and passing in and out at the doors. The mound measures at the base on the north and south sides one hundred and ninety-six feet ten inches, and on the east and west sides two hundred and two feet. It does not face the cardinal points exactly, though probably so intended; and in all the buildings, from some cause not easily accounted for, while one varies ten degrees one way, that immediately adjoining varies twelve or thirteen degrees in another.

PLATE XXXVII

Nº 1.

Nº 2.

Nº 3.

Nº 4.

Outlines from paintings on the walls of a Room at CHICHEN-ITZA. The colors are vivid and well preserved, and consist of Green, Yellow, Red, Blue and a Reddish brown, which last color is invariably used for the color of flesh, the color of the women is somewhat lighter than that of the men. On the line marked Nº 1. the figures follow as shewn in the drawing. On line Nº 2. the figures are all on the same line but some figures occur between the first two and last two which are omitted from being much defaced. Line Nº 3 represents figures taken from various groups. Nº 4 the same. Figures 9ᵗʰ high.

PLATE XXXVIII

P. Catherwood.

Gladwin.

CHICHEN ITZA
Castillo

Mural from the Temple of the Warriors, Chichén Itzá. Copy in the National Museum of Anthropology, Mexico City.

The Castle, Chichén Itzá.

It is built up apparently solid from the plain to the height of seventy-five feet. On the west side is a staircase thirty-seven feet wide; on the north, being that presented in the engraving, the staircase is forty-four feet wide, and contains ninety steps. On the ground at the foot of the staircase, forming a bold, striking, and well conceived commencement to this lofty range, are two colossal serpents' heads, ten feet in length, with mouths wide open and tongues protruding, as represented in Figure 14.

The platform on the top of the mound measures sixty-one feet from north to south, and sixty-four from east to west; and the building measures in the same directions forty-three feet and forty-nine. Single doorways face the east, south, and west, having massive lintels of sapote wood covered with elaborate carvings, and the jambs are ornamented with sculptured figures, one of which is represented in Plate XXXIX. The sculpture is much worn, but the head-dress, ornamented with a plume of feathers, and portions of the rich attire still remain. The face is well preserved, and has a dignified appearance. It has, too, earrings, and the nose bored.

FIG. 14

All the other jambs are decorated with sculpture of the same general character, and all open into a corridor six feet wide, extending round three sides of the building.

The doorway facing the north, represented in the engraving, presents a grander appearance, being twenty feet wide, and having two short massive columns, eight feet eight inches high, with two large projections at the base,

Serpent Head at the foot of the North Stairway. Castle, Chichén Itzá.

entirely covered with elaborate sculpture. This doorway gives access to a corridor forty feet long by six feet four inches wide and seventeen feet high. In the back wall this corridor is a single doorway, having sculptured jambs, over which is a richly-carved sapote beam, and giving entrance to an apartment represented in Plate XL, nineteen feet eight inches long, twelve feet nine inches wide, and seventeen feet high. In this apartment are two square pillars nine feet four inches high and one foot ten inches on each side, having sculptured figures on all their sides, and supporting massive sapote beams covered with the most elaborate carving of curious and intricate designs, but so defaced and timeworn that, in the obscurity of the room, lighted only from the door, it was extremely difficult to make them out.

> *The Castle, also called the* Pyramid of Kukulkán, *stands out both because of its grandeur and its position. It is one of the buildings that clearly shows the Toltec influence in Yucatán, present between 1000 and 1250 A.D. approximately. Each tier of the pyramid has sloping walls decorated with raised rectangles. There is a flight of steps on each side and, at the bottom of the north one, two large heads of plumed serpents. The temple has a main entrance separated into three bays by two columns in the shape of serpents. The heads are on the ground, the bodies form the shafts, and the tails support the wooden lintel over the doorway. There is also a mask of the god of rain. The roof is decorated with merlons in the shape of sections of conch shell, and on the doorposts are warriors and priests.*
>
> *It was later discovered that there is a smaller pyramid inside, with its temple intact, that contains a throne in the shape of a jaguar, painted red, and a statue of Chac-Mool.*

And from this lofty height we saw for the first time groups of small columns, which, on examination, proved to be among the most remarkable and

PLATE XXXIX

4 feet 8 in.

Figure in Bas-relief on Stone on one of the Jaumbs of the
TEOCALLIS at CHICHEN-ITZA.

Catherwood

Hibbet

PLATE XL

unintelligible remains we had yet met with. They stood in rows of three, four, and five abreast many rows continuing in the same direction, when they changed and pursued another. They were very low, many of them only three feet high, while the highest were not more than six feet, and consisted of several separate pieces, like millstones. Many of them had fallen, and in some places they lie prostrate in rows, all in the same direction, as if thrown down intentionally. I had a large number of Indians at work clearing them, and endeavouring to trace their direction to the end. In some places they extended to the bases of large mounds, on which were ruins of buildings and colossal fragments of sculpture, while in others they branched off and terminated abruptly. I counted three hundred and eighty, and there were many more; but so many were broken, and they lay so irregularly, that I gave up counting them. They were entirely too low to have supported a roof under which persons could walk. The idea at times suggested itself that they had upheld a raised walk of cement, but there were no remains visible. Plate XLI will give some idea of these columns. They enclose an area nearly four hundred feet square; and, incomprehensible as they are in their uses and object, add largely to the interest and wonder connected with these ruins.

Stephens is describing the Group *of the Thousand Columns, located on the Maya-Toltec part of the site. The name comes from the large number of columns and pillars that surround the plaza, which has not been fully investigated. These columns, with capitals, once supported the beams holding up vaults. The complex is divided into the North, East, Southeast, West and Northwest subgroups.*

I have now closed my brief description of the ruins of Chichen, having presented, with as little detail as possible, all the principal buildings of this ancient city. Ruined mounds exist, and detached portions of sculpture strew the ground, exhibiting curious devices, which often arrested us in wandering among them, but which I shall not attempt to give. They were the ruins which we had had longest in prospect, of which we had formed the largest expectations, and these expectations were not disappointed, but more than realized. And they had additional interest in our eyes from the fact that the broad light of day beams upon their history. The first settlement of the Spaniards in the interior was made at this very spot.

Stephen's books excited interest in other explorers, travelers and archeologists, and he was followed at Chichén Itzá by Augustin LePlongeon, Desiré Charnay, the naturalist Alfred P. Maudsley, and Teobert Maler, who photographed the ruined buildings between 1891 and 1892.

At the beginning of this century the American consul in Merida, Edward H. Thompson, bought the hacienda whose land included the

PLATE XLI

*Temple of the Warriors
and part of the
Thousand Columns
Group, Chichén Itzá.*

*ruins. He explored the Sacred Cenote and brought out a huge quantity
of objects, most of which are now in the Peabody Museum of Harvard
University.*

*Later, the Mexican government became the owner of the site, and
between 1923 and 1933, with the collaboration of the Carnegie Institution, work of exploration and restoration was carried out. More recent
work was done by the Mexican government alone.*

I shall close with one general remark. These cities were, of course, not all
built at one time, but are the remains of different epochs. Chichen, though in
a better state of preservation than most of the others, has a greater appearance
of antiquity; some of the buildings are no doubt older than others, and long
intervals may have elapsed between the times of their construction.

The Maya manuscript places the first discovery of Chichen within the
epochs corresponding with the time between A.D. 360 and A.D. 432. From
the words used, it may be understood that the discovery was then made of an
actual existing city, but it is a fair construction of these words to suppose that
nothing more is meant than a discovery of what the words Chi-chen import,
viz., the mouths of wells, having reference to the two great senotes, the discovery
of wells being, among all primitive people, and particularly in the dry region of
Yucatan, an event worthy to be noted in their history.

One of these senotes I have already mentioned; the other I did not visit
till the afternoon preceding our departure from Chichen. Setting out from the
Castillo, at some distance we ascended a wooded elevation, which seemed an
artificial causeway leading to the senote. The senote was the largest and wildest
we had seen; in the midst of a thick forest, an immense circular hole, with
cragged, perpendicular sides, trees growing out of them and overhanging the
brink, and still as if the genius of silence reigned within. A hawk was sailing
around it, looking down into the water, but without once flapping its wings.

The water was of a greenish hue. A mysterious influence seemed to pervade it, in unison with the historical account that the well of Chichen was a place of pilgrimage, and that human victims were thrown into it in sacrifice. In one place, on the very brink, were the remains of a stone structure, probably connected with ancient superstitious rites; perhaps the place from which the victims were thrown into the dark well beneath.

CHAPTER XVIII

Departure from Chichen — Arrival at Valladolid — Village of
Chemax — Ruins of Coba

On Tuesday, the twenty-ninth of March, we left Chichen. It was still
in the gray of the morning when we caught our last view of the great buildings,
and as we turned away we felt that the few short months of our journey had
been a time of interest and wonder, such as rarely occurs in life. At nine o'clock
we reached the village of Kaua, six leagues distant, and at half past eleven the
small village of Cuncunul, within an hour's ride of Valladolid, and there we
determined to dine, and wait for the servants and carriers.

We remained till four o'clock, and then set out for Valladolid. As far as the
suburbs the road was broken and stony. We entered by the great Church of
Sisal, with convent and cloisters by its side, and a square in front, which, as
we rode across it, sounded hollow under our horses' feet, and underneath was
an immense senote. We passed up the Calle de Sisal, a long street with straggling
houses on each side, and were directed to the house of Don Pedro Baranda, one
of the largest and best in the place. This gentleman had received advices of
our intended visit, and had engaged for us a house. As our luggage did not
arrive, he furnished us with hammocks, and in an hour we were comfortable as
in our house at Merida. About midnight Albino came clattering to the door,
accompanied by only one horse, carrying our hammocks, and bringing the
disastrous intelligence that the horse carrying the Daguerreotype apparatus had
run away, and made a general crash.

The next morning we were in no hurry. From Valladolid it was our purpose to prosecute our exploration through a region of which less was known
than of any we had yet visited. In our short voyage with Captain Fensley from
the Laguna to Sisal, he had told us of stone buildings on the coast, near Cape
Catoche, which he called old Spanish forts. These accounts were confirmed by
others, and we at length ascertained what we supposed to be the fact, that in
two places on the coast called Tancar and Tuloom, what were taken for Spanish
forts were aboriginal buildings.

In the mean time, a few days did not hang heavy on our hands in Valladolid. The city, which was founded at an early period of the conquest, contains
about fifteen thousand inhabitants, and is distinguished as the residence of the
vicar-general of the church of Yucatan.

It was built in a style commensurate with the lofty pretensions of the conquerors, and, like other cities of Spanish America, bears the marks of ancient grandeur, but is now going to decay.

In the mean time we were making inquiries and arrangements for our journey to the coast. It is almost impossible to conceive what difficulty we had in learning anything definite concerning the road we ought to take. Don Pedro Baranda had a manuscript map, made by himself, which, however, he did not represent as very correct; and the place on the coast which we wished to visit was not laid down on it at all. There were but two persons in the town who could give us any information, and what they gave was most unsatisfactory. Upon the information we received, we determined on going to the village of Chemax, from which, we were advised, there was a direct road to Tancah, where a boat was on the stocks, and probably then finished, which we could procure for a voyage down the coast.

Before our departure Doctor Cabot performed an operation for strabismus, under circumstances peculiarly gratifying to us, and, with the satisfaction arising from its complete success, on Saturday, after an early dinner, we mounted for our journey to the coast, going first to the house of Don Pedro Baranda, and to the factory to bid farewell to Mr. Burke. The road was broad, and had been lately opened for carretas and calesas. On the way we met a large straggling party of Indians, returning from a hunting expedition in the forests along the seacoast. Naked, armed with long guns, and with deer and wild boars slung on their backs, their aspect was the most truculent of any people we had seen.

It was some time after dark when we reached the village. The outline of the church was visible through the darkness, and beside it was the convent, with a light streaming from the door. The cura was sitting at a table surrounded by the officials of the village, who started at the clatter of our horses; and when we appeared in the doorway, if a firebrand had been thrown among them they could not have been more astounded. The village was the Ultima Thule of population, the last between Valladolid and Tancah, and the surprise caused by our appearance did not subside when we told them that we were on our way to the latter. They all told us that it was impossible. Tancah was a mere rancho, seventy miles distant, and the whole intermediate country was a dense forest. There was no road to it, and no communication except by an overgrown footpath.

The rancho was established by one Molas, a smuggler and pirate, who, while under sentence of death in Merida, escaped from prison, and established himself at this lonely point, out of the reach of justice. Soldiers had been sent from Merida to arrest him, who, after advancing as far as Chemax, turned back.

The news of the difficulties involved in the journey made them change their plans. However, they had no intention of returning to Valladolid, so their only alternative was to reach the small port of Yalahau and then take a 'canoa'. This meant making two journeys along the coast instead of one, and it would take them about two weeks to reach Tancáh.

In the midst of the vexation attending this derangement of our plan, we were cheered by the comfortable appearance of the convent, and the warm reception given us by the cura Garcia.

The village of Chemax contains nearly ten thousand inhabitants, and was in existence at the time of the conquest. Four years after the foundation of Merida the Indians in the neighbourhood of Valladolid formed a conspiracy to destroy the Spaniards, and the first blow was struck at Chemax, where they caught two brothers, whom they put upon crosses, and shot at from a distance till they were covered with arrows. At sunset they took down the bodies, dismembered them, and sent the heads and limbs to different places, to show that vengeance was begun.

The curacy of Chemax comprehended within its jurisdiction all between it and the sea. The cura had drawn up a report, by order of the government, of the condition and character of the region under his charge, and its objects of curiosity and interest, from which I copied the following notice in regard to ruins known by the name of Coba.

"In the eastern part of this village, at eight leagues' distance, and fourteen from the head of the district, near one of the three lagunas, is a building that the indigenes call Monjas. It consists of various ranges of two stories, all covered with arches, closed with masonry of rude stone, and each piece is of six square yards. Its interior pavement is preserved entire, and on the walls of one, in the second story, are some painted figures in different attitudes, showing, without doubt, according to the supposition of the natives, that these are the remains of that detestable worship so commonly found. From this edifice there is a calzada, or paved road, of ten or twelve yards in width, running to the southeast to a limit that has not been discovered with certainty, but some aver that it goes in the direction of Chichen Itza."

But the cura had much more interesting information. On his own hacienda of Kantunile, sixteen leagues nearer the coast, were several mounds, in one of which, while excavating for stone to be used in building, the Indians had discovered a sepulchre containing three skeletons, which, according to the cura, were those of a man, a woman, and a child, but all, unfortunately, so much decayed that in attempting to remove them they fell to pieces.

At the head of the skeletons were two large vases of terra cotta, with covers of the same material. In one of these was a large collection of Indian ornaments, beads, stone, and two carved shells, which are represented in Figure 15.

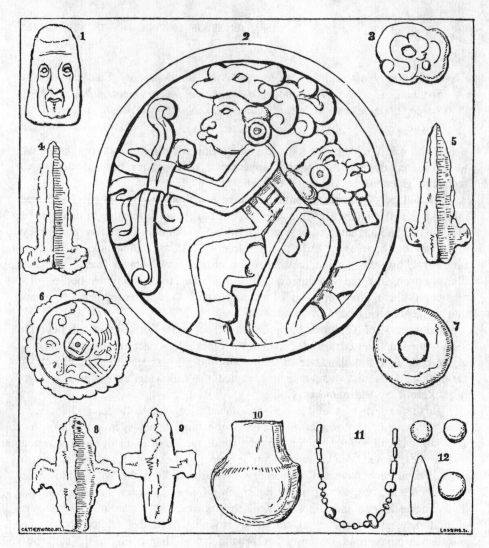

FIG. 15

CHAPTER XIX

Journey to Yalahao — The Canoa El Sol — Cape Catoche — Island of Contoy — Island of Mugeres — Island of Kancune — Point of Nesuc — Island of Cozumel

On Monday, the fourth of April, we took leave of the warm-hearted cura, and set out for our new point of destination, the port of Yalahao.

I am obliged to hurry over our journey to the coast. The road was lonely and rugged, mostly a complete crust of stone, broken and sharp pointed, which severely tried and almost wore out our horses. It was desperately hot; we had no view except the narrow path before us, and we stumbled along, wondering that such a stony surface could support such a teeming vegetation.

In the afternoon of the third day we were approaching the port. When within about a league of it, we came out upon a low, swampy plain, with a grove of cocoanut trees at a long distance before us, the only objects rising above the level surface, indicating, and, at the same time, hiding, the port of Yalahao. With a satisfaction perhaps greater than we had experienced in our whole journey, we reached the port, and, after a long absence, came down once more upon the shore of the sea.

We rode on to the house of Don Juan Bautista, to whom we had a letter from the cura of Chemax, but he had gone to his rancho. His house and one other were the only two in the place built of stone, and the materials had been obtained from the ruins of Zuza, standing on his rancho, two leagues distant on the coast.

We returned through the village to a house belonging to our friend the cura, better than any except the two stone houses, and in situation finer than these. It stood on the very edge of the bank, so near the sea that the waves had undermined part of the long piazza in front; but the interior was in good condition, and a woman tenant in possession. We were about negotiating with her for the occupation of a part; but wherever we went we seemed to be the terror of the sex, and before we had fairly made a beginning, she abandoned the house and left us in quiet possession. In an hour we were completely domesticated, and toward evening we sat in the doorway and looked out upon the sea. The waves were rolling almost to our door, and Doctor Cabot found a new field opened to him in flocks of large seafowl strutting along the shore and screaming over our heads.

Plate XLII represents this place as taken from the shore.

In our journey to the coast we had entered a region of novel and exciting interest. On the road we had heard of quondam pirates, having small sugar ranchos, and enjoying reputations but little the worse for wear, in fact, much respected, and looked upon with a sort of compassion, as men who had been unfortunate and broken up in business. We had now reached the focus of their operations.

It is not many years since the coast of Cuba and the adjacent continent were infested by bands of desperadoes, the common enemies of mankind, and doomed to be hung and shot without trial, wherever caught.

We found one great deficiency at this place: there was no ramon for the horses. At night we turned them loose in the village; but the barren plain furnished them no grazing, and they returned to the house. Early in the morning we despatched Dimas to a ramon tree two leagues distant, that being the nearest point at which any could be procured; and in the mean time I set about searching for a canoa, and succeeded in engaging one, but not of the best class, and the patron and sailors could not be ready in less than two or three days.

The next morning, when we opened our door, we saw a sloop lying at anchor, which we soon understood was the balandra of Don Vicente Albino. Don Vicente was already on shore, and, before we had time to make many inquiries, he called upon us. We had heard of him before, but never expected to see him in person, for our accounts were that he had established a rancho on the island of Cozumel, and had been murdered by his Indians. The first part of the story was true, but Don Vicente himself assured us that the last was not, though he told us that he had had a narrow escape, and showed us a machete cut in the arm as a token.

Don Vicente was the person of all others whom we wished to see, as he was the only one who could give us any information about the island of Cozumel.

The next day we completed laying in our stock of provisions, to wit, chocolate, sweetened bread, beef and pork in strings, two turtles, three bushels of corn, and implements for making tortillas. We had one other important arrangement to make, which was the disposition of our horses; and, according to our previous plan, to avoid the long journey back through the interior we determined to send Dimas with them to Vallodolid, and thence to the port of Silan, a journey of two hundred and fifty miles, while we should, on our return, continue down the coast with the canoa, and meet him there.

Our canoa was known in the port of Yalahao by the name of El Sol, or the Sun. It was thirty-five feet long and six feet wide at the top, but curving toward the bottom. It carried two large sails, with the peaks held up by heavy poles

PLATE XLII

R.Batheman.

M.Osborne

YALAHAO

secured at the masts; had a space of eight or ten feet clear in the stern, and all the rest was filled with luggage, provisions, and water-casks. We had not been on board till the moment of embarcation, and prospects seemed rather unpromising for a month's cruise. There was no wind; the sails were flapping against the mast; the sun beat down upon us, and we had no mat or awning of any kind, although the agent had promised one. Our captain was a middle-aged Mestizo, a fisherman, hired for the occasion.

Under these circumstances we set out on our voyage. It was one which we had determined upon before leaving home, and to which we had always looked forward with interest; and the precise object we had in view was, in following the track of the Spaniards along this coast, to discover vestiges or remains of the great buildings of lime and stone which, according to the historical accounts, surprised and astonished them.

At eleven o'clock the breeze set in. At twelve the patron asked if the should run ashore for us to dine, and at half past one the breeze was so strong against us that we were obliged to come to anchor under the lee of Point Moscheto. This was an island about two leagues distant from Yalahao, with a projecting point, which we had to double.

The next morning, with the rising of her great namesake, El Sol was under way. The prevalent wind along the coast was southeast, adverse for us; but, as the captain said, on our return it would be in our favour. At one o'clock another bold point intercepted us. It was a great object to get round it, for the wind would then be fair. El Sol made a vigorous effort, but by this time the breeze had become strong, and we were fain to come to anchor under the lee of Point Frances, which was on the same island with Point Moscheto. The island itself has no name, and is a mere sand-bank covered with scrub bushes, having a passage between it and the mainland, navigable for small canoas.

Toward evening the breeze again died away, we slowly got round the point, and at half past eight came to anchor, having made six leagues on our voyage. Our captain told us that this desolate point was Cape Catoche, the memorable spot on the Continent of America at which the Spaniards first landed, and approaching which, says Bernal Dias, we saw at the distance of two leagues a large town, which, from its size, it exceeding any town in Cuba, we named Grand Cairo. The Spaniards set out for it, and passing by some thick woods, were attacked by Indians in ambuscade. Near the place of this ambuscade, he adds, were three buildings of lime and stone, wherein were idols of clay, with diabolical countenances, &c.

Navigators and geographers, however, have assigned different localities to this memorable point, and its true position is, perhaps, uncertain.

At daylight we were again under way, and soon were opposite Boca Nueva, being the entrance to a passage between the island and the main, better known to the fishermen as the Boca de Iglesia, from the ruins of a church visible at a great distance. This church was one of the objects I intended to visit; and one reason for preferring the canoa, when we had the chance of Don Vicente's sloop, was that we might do so; but our captain told us that even with our draught of water we could not approach nearer than a league; that a long muddy flat intervened; and that we could not reach the shore by wading. The wind was ahead, but we could make a good stretch from the coast, and, anxious to lose no advantage, we made sail for the island of Contoy. It was dark when we came to anchor, and we were already distressed for water. Our casks were impregnated with the flavour of agua ardiente, and the water was sickening. Through the darkness we saw the outline of a desolate rancho. Our men went ashore, and, moving round it with torches, made a fine piratical appearance; but they found no water.

Before daylight we were roused by the screaming of seabirds; in the gray of the morning, the island seemed covered with a moving canopy, and the air was noisy with their clamour; but, unfortunately for Doctor Cabot, we had a fine breeze, and he had no opportunity of getting at their nests. The coast was wild and rugged, indented occasionally by small picturesque bays. Below the point of the island Doctor Cabot shot two pelicans, and getting the canoa about to take them on board was like manœuvring a seventy-four gun-ship.

At eleven o'clock we reached the island of Mugeres, notorious in that region as the resort of Lafitte the pirate. Monsieur Lafitta, as our skipper called him, bore a good character in these parts; he was always good to the fishermen, and paid them well for all he took from them. At a short distance beyond the point we passed a small bay, in which he moored his little navy. The mouth was narrow, and protected by ledges of broken rocks, on which, as the patron told us, he had batteries constantly manned. On the farther point of the island we had a distant view of one of those stone buildings which were our inducement to this voyage along the coast. While looking at it from the prow of the canoa, with the patron by my side, he broke from me, seized a harpoon, and pointing with it to indicate the direction to the helmsman, we came silently upon a large turtle, apparently asleep, which must have been somewhat surprised on waking up with three or four inches of cold steel in his back. The patron and sailors looked upon him as upon a bag of dollars snatched from the deep.

In the afternoon we steered for the mainland, passing the island of Kancune, a barren strip of land, with sand hills and stone buildings visible upon it. The whole of this coast is lined with reefs of rocks, having narrow passages which enable a canoa to enter and find shelter; but it is dangerous to attempt the passage at night. We had a good wind, but as the next harbour was at some distance, the patron came to anchor at about four o'clock under the lee of the point of Nesuc. Immediately we went ashore in search of water, but found only a dirty pool, in which the water was so salt that we could scarcely drink it, but still it was an agreeable change from that we had on board.

We had time for a bath, and while preparing to take it saw two large sharks moving along the shore in water four or five feet deep, and so clear that their ugly eyes were visible. We hesitated, but, from the heat and confinement of the canoa, we were in real need; and stationing Albino on the prow to keep a look out, we accomplished our purpose. Afterward we rambled along the shore to pick up shells; but toward dark we were all hurrying back, flying before the natives, swarms of moschetoes, which pursued us with the same bloodthirsty spirit that animated the Indians along this coast when they pursued the Spaniards. We heaved upon our cable, hauled up our big stone, and dropped off to some distance from the shore, with horrible apprehensions for the night, but, fortunately, we escaped.

At daylight the next morning we were again under way, and, with a strong and favourable wind, steered from the coast for the island of Cozumel. Very soon, in the comparatively open sea, we felt the discomfort and even insecurity of our little vessel. The waves broke over us, wetting our luggage and ourselves, and interfering materially with Bernaldo's cooking. At about four o'clock in the afternoon we were upon the coast of Cozumel, and here for the first time we made a discovery, at the moment sufficiently annoying, viz., that our patron was not familiar with the coast of this island; it was bound with reefs; there were only certain places where it was practicable to run in, and he was afraid to make the attempt.

Our plan was to disembark at the rancho of Don Vicente Albino, and the patron did not know where it was. It was too late to look for it, and, sailing along till he saw a passage among the reefs, he laid the old canoa into it, and then threw out the big stone, but at some distance from the shore. On the outer reef was the wreck of a brig; her naked ribs were above the water, and the fate of her mariners no one knew.

The next morning, after some hours spent in groping about, we discovered the rancho of Don Vicente, distant about three miles. Here we encountered a strong current of perhaps four miles an hour; and, taking the wind close hauled, in a little while found that El Sol was not likely to have a very brilliant career that day. At length we went close in, furled sails, and betook ourselves to poles, by means of which, after two hours' hard work, we reached the little Bay of San Miguel, on which stood the rancho of Don Vicente.

This rancho was established by the pirate Molas, who, escaping from death in Merida made his way hither. He succeeded in getting to him his wife and children and a few Indians, and for several years nothing was heard of him.

Our act of taking possession was unusually exciting. It was an immense relief to escape from the confinement of the canoa. The situation commanded a a view of the sea, and, barely distinguishable, in the distance was the coast of Yucatan. The place, had a sort of piratical aspect. In the hut were doors and green blinds from the cabin of some unlucky vessel, and reeving blocks, tar

PLATE XLIII

F. Catherwood   J.N. Gimbrede

ISLAND OF COZUMEL
San Miguel

buckets, halliards, drinking gourds, fragments of rope, fishing nets, and two old hatches were scattered on the ground. Above all, the first object we discovered, which would have given a charm to a barren sand bank, was a well of pure and abundant water, which we fell upon at the moment of landing, and were almost like the Spanish soldier in the expedition of Cordova, who drank till he swelled and died.

This well was shaded by a large cocoanut tree. We hauled up under it one of the hatches, and, sitting around it on blocks, had served up the turtle which had been accomplishing its destiny on board the canoa. With our guns resting against the trees, long beards, and canoa costume, we were, perhaps, as piratical-seeming a trio as ever scuttled a ship at sea. Toward evening we strolled for a great distance along the shore, picking up shells, and at night we had a luxurious swing in our hammocks.

CHAPTER XX

Island of Cozumel known to the Natives by the Name of Cuzamil —
Discovered by Juan de Grijalva — Towers seen by the Spaniards
— A Sudden Storm — The Canoa in a Strait

The island of Cozumel, as it is now called, was known to the natives by the name of Cuzamil, signifying in their language the Island of Swallows. Before setting out from home I had fixed upon this island an one of the points of our journey. My attention was directed to it by the historical accounts of its condition when it first became known to the Spaniards. It was discovered accidentally in 1518 by Juan de Grijalva, who, in attempting to follow in the track of Cordova, was driven in sight of it. The itinerary of this voyage was kept by the chaplain-chief of the fleet, under the direction of Grijalva, and, with a collection of original narratives and memoirs, was published for the first time in 1838 at Paris. The itinerary opens thus:

"Saturday, the first of March of the year 1518, the commandant of the said fleet sailed from the island of Cuba. On the fourth of March we saw upon a promontory a white house. * * * * * All the coast was lined with reefs and shoals. We directed ourselves upon the opposite shore, when we distinguished the house more easily. It was in the form of a small tower, and appeared to be eight palms in length and the height of a man. The fleet came to anchor about six miles from the coast. Two little barks called canoes approached us, each manned by three Indians, which came to within a cannon shot of the vessel. We could not speak to them nor learn anything from them, except that in the morning the cacique, *i. e.*, the chief of that place, would come on board our vessel. The next morning we set sail to reconnoiter a cape which we saw at a distance, and which the piloto told us was the island of Yucatan. Between it and the point of *Cucuniel*, where we were, we found a gulf, into which we entered, and came near the shore of Cuzamil, which we coasted. Besides the tower which we had seen, we discovered fourteen others of the same form. Before leaving the first, the two canoes of Indians returned; the chief of the village was in one of them, and came on board the vessel of the admiral, and spoke to us by means of an interpreter (one of the two Indians carried off from Yucatan on the previous voyage of Cordova), and prayed the commander to come to his village, saying that it would be a great honour to him.

"We set sail, following the coast at the distance of a stone's throw, for the sea is very deep upon the borders. The country appeared very agreeable; we counted, on leaving this point, *fourteen towers* of the form indicated. At sunset we saw a large white tower, which appeared very high. We approached, and saw near it a multitude of Indians, men and women, who were looking at us, and remained until the fleet stopped within musket shot of the tower. The Indians, who are *very numerous* in this island, made a great noise with their drums.

"On Friday, the sixth of May, the commandant ordered one hundred men to arm themselves. They embarked in the boats, and landed. They were accompanied by a priest, and expected to be attacked by a great number of Indians. Being prepared for defence, they arranged themselves in good order, and came to the tower, where they found no one; and in all the environs they did not see a single man. The commandant mounted upon the tower with the standard bearer, the flag unfurled. He planted this standard upon one of the façades of the tower, took possession in the name of the king, in presence of witnesses, and drew up a declaration of said taking possession.

"The ascent to this tower was by eighteen steps; the base was very massive, one hundred and eighty feet in circumference. At the top rose a small tower of *the height of two men placed* one upon the other. Within were figures, bones, and idols that they adored. From these marks we supposed that they were idolaters. While the commandant was at the top of the tower with many of our people, an Indian, followed by three others who kept the doors, put in the interior a vase with very odoriferous perfumes, which seemed of storax. This Indian was old; he burned many perfumes before the idols which were in the tower, and sang in a loud voice a song, which was always in the same tone. We supposed that he was invoking his idols. ✳ ✳ ✳ ✳ These Indians carried our commandant with ten or twelve Spaniards, and gave them to eat in a hall constructed of stones very close together, and covered with straw. Before the hall was a large well, from which everybody drank. ✳ ✳ ✳ ✳ ✳ They then left us alone, and we entered the village, where all the houses were built of stone. Among others, we saw five very well made, and commanded by small towers. The *base* of these edifices is *very large* and *massive*; the *building is very small at the top*. They appeared to have been built a long time, but there are also *modern ones*.

"That village, or bourg, was paved with concave stones. The streets, elevated at the sides, descended, inclining toward the middle, which was paved entirely with large stones. The sides were occupied by the houses of the inhabitants. They are constructed of stone from the foundation to half the height of the walls, and covered with straw. To *judge by the edifices and houses, these Indians appear to be very ingenious*; and if we had not seen a number of recent constructions, we should have thought that these buildings were the works of the Spaniards. This island appears to me very handsome. ✳ ✳ ✳ ✳ We penetrated, to the number of ten men, three or four miles in the interior. We saw there edifices and habitations separated one from another, and very well constructed."

On the tenth of February, 1519, the armament of Cortez rendezvoused at this island. Bernal Dias was again a companion, and was an actor in a scene which he describes as follows: "There was on the island of Cozumel a temple containing some hideous idols, to which all the Indians of the neighbouring districts used to go frequently in solemn procession. One morning the courts of this temple were filled with Indians, and curiosity having also drawn many of us thither, we found them burning odoriferous resins like our incense, and shortly after an old man in a large loose mantle ascended to the top of the temple, and harangued or preached to the multitude for a considerable time. Cortez, who was present, at length called to him Melchorejo, an Indian prisoner taken on a previous voyage to Yucatan, to question him concerning the evil doctrines which the old man was delivering. He then summoned all the caciques and chief persons to come before him, and as well as he could, by signs and interpretations, explained to them that the idols which they worshipped were not gods, but evil things, which would draw their souls down to hell, and that, if they wished to remain in brotherly connexion with us, they must pull them down, and place in their stead the crucifix of our Lord, by whose assistance they would obtain good harvests and the salvation of their souls, with many other good and holy reasons, which he expressed very well. The priests and chiefs replied that they worshipped these gods as their ancestors had done, because they were kind to them, and that, if we attempted to molest them, the gods would convince us of their power by destroying us in the sea. Cortez then ordered the idols to be prostrated, which we immediately did, rolling them down some steps. He next sent for lime, of which there was abundance in the place, and Indian masons, by whom, under our direction, a very handsome altar was constructed, whereon we placed an image of the Holy Virgin; and the carpenters having made a crucifix, which was erected in a small chapel close to the altar, mass was said by the reverend father Juan Dias, and listened to by the priests, chiefs, and the rest of the natives with great attention."

These are the accounts given by eyewitnesses of what they saw on the first visits of the Spaniards. The later historians are more explicit, and speak of Cozumel as a place containing many adoratorios and temples, as a principal sanctuary and place of pilgrimage, standing to Yucatan in the same relation as Rome to the Catholic world.

By these accounts I had been induced to visit the island of Cozumel; and an incidental notice in the Modern Traveller, speaking of existing ruins as remains of Spanish buildings, led me to suspect that their character had been mistaken, and that they were really vestiges of the original population; but on the ground we asked ourselves where to look for them. The whole island was

FIG. 16

overgrown with trees, and, except along the shore or within the clearing around the hut, it was impossible to move in any direction without cutting a path. Fortunately, however, on the borders of the clearing there were vestiges of ancient population, which, from the directions of Don Vicente Albino, we had no difficulty in finding. One of them, standing about two hundred feet distant from the sea, and even now visible above the tops of the trees to vessels sailing by, is represented in Figure 16. It stands on a terrace, and has steps on all four of its sides.

The exterior is of plain stone, but was formerly stuccoed and painted, traces of which are still visible.

South-southeast from this, near an opposite angle of the clearing, and five or six hundred feet from the sea, stands another building raised upon a terrace, consisting of a single apartment, twenty feet front and six feet ten inches deep, having two doorways and a back wall seven feet thick.

At the rear of the last building, buried in the woods, so that we should never have found it but for our patron, is another memorial, perhaps equal in interest to any now existing on the island of Cozumel. It is the ruins of a Spanish church, sixty or seventy feet front and two hundred deep. The front wall has almost wholly fallen, but the side walls are standing to the height of about twenty feet. The plastering remains, and along the base is a line of painted ornaments. The interior is encumbered with the ruins of the fallen roof, overgrown with bushes; a tree is growing out of the great altar, and the whole is a scene of irrecoverable destruction.

At noon we had finished all our work, but there was a charm about our absolute proprietorship of this desolate island which made us regret that there was not more to give us occupation. Doctor Cabot found in it a rich field for his ornithological pursuits, but he was rather unfortunate. Two specimens of rare birds, which he had dissected and put away to dry, were destroyed by ants.

In the afternoon we picked up shells along the shore, and toward evening we again took a bath; while we were in the water black clouds gathered suddenly, thunder rolled, lightning flashed, and sea-birds flew screaming over our heads. Rain following quickly, we snatched up our clothing and ran for the hut. Looking back for a moment, we saw our canoa under way, with scarcely a yard of mainsail, and seeming like a great bird flying over the water. As she turned the point of the island and disappeared our fears were roused. The patron was not familiar with the coast, there was but one place in which he could find shelter, a narrow passage, difficult to enter even by daylight, and night was almost upon him; Mr. Catherwood had timed the precise moment when he turned the point, and we knew that the canoa would not be able to reach the cove before dark, but would have to ride through the storm, and, perhaps, be driven to sea. It was fearful to think of the danger of the poor patron and sailors; and mingled with these fears was some little uneasiness on our own account.

CHAPTER XXI

Departure from Cozumel — Coast of Yucatan — Rancho of Tancar
— Visit to the Ruins of Tuloom

Very early in the morning we were moving. The rain had ceased, but the wind was still high, and the waves exhibited its power. Passing round the point which had cut off our view of the canoa, we came upon what might well be called an iron-bound coast, being a table of rock rising but a few feet above the level of the sea, washed by every storm, until it had become porous and full of holes, and the edges stuck up like points of rusted iron. The waves were still dashing over them, forming great whirlpools in the hollow spaces, and suggesting a frightful picture of the fate of any unhappy voyagers who might have been thrown upon them; and the rocks were strewed with staves and planks from some wrecked vessel. We went on, and after three hours' painful walking reached the cove. It was a wild, abrupt, and narrow opening between the rocks, about fifty feet wide, with perpendicular sides, and leading into a sheltered basin, which, while the sea outside was raging, was calm and quiet as a pond. At the head of this lay the canoa, which came down and took me on board.

From the simple and unaffected account of the patron, his entry into the cove must have been sublime. Night had overtaken him, and he supposed that he had run by, when a flash of lightning disclosed the narrow passage, and he turned the old canoa short into the very middle of it. In passing through he struck upon a sunken rock, lost one man overboard, caught him by the light of another flash, and in a moment was in still water. Sails, luggage, Doctor Cabot's birds, and my copy of Cogolludo, were spread out to dry, and, after dining upon turtles' eggs laid a few minutes on the coals, I set out on my return, gathering on the way an unusual harvest of shells.

On the third day, at twelve o'clock, the canoa again hove in sight, working her way round the point, and in a short time was at her old anchorage ground. The wind was still so high that the patron was afraid to remain; we filled our water casks, in an hour were on board, and left, solitary as we found it, the once populous island of Cozumel.

From the point at which we left the island, the opposite coast of Yucatan was dimly visible, and I would remark, that, from our own observation and from information given to us by others, it is the only point from which the opposite coast can be seen at all, whence it is a conclusion almost unquestionable that it was from this same point Grijalva steered for Yucatan. The wind was high, the sea rough, and a strong current was sweeping us down toward the point of Cape Catoche.

Saling close to the coast, they saw three small buildings but could not land because the sea was so rough. Stephens supposed that these must have been the buildings sighted by members of Grijalva's expedition.

We ran on till after dark, and came to anchor under a projecting point, behind a reef of rocks. In the edge of the water was a square enclosure for turtle, and on the shore a deserted fisherman's hut.

At daylight we were again under way. We passed three more square buildings; but as the coast was rocky we could not land without endangering the safety of our precious canoa; and far off, on a high cliff, stood the Castillo of Tuloom, the extreme point at which we were aiming. At twelve o'clock we turned a point, and came upon a long, sandy beach, forming a bay, at the head of which was a small collection of huts, composing the rancho of Tancar.

It was this point which we expected to reach by land direct from Chemax. The moment the stone was thrown out we were in the water, wading ashore. The sun was intensely hot, and the sand burning. In front of the principal hut, beside the sloop, was a thatched arbour to protect the carpenter who occasionally worked upon it. Near by was a ruined hut, which we had cleared out, and for the third time took up our abode in a habitation erected by Molas. On leaving the island of Cozumel it was only to this desolate point on the coast that he dared venture.

Molas, old and sick, decided to go to Chemax, accompanied by one Indian, and died on the return journey.

It was but a year since he died, and his two sons were in possession of the rancho, both young men, who paid us a visit soon after our arrival.

Our first inquiries were upon the subject of ruins. A short path through the woods leads to a milpa, in which are numerous remains of ancient buildings standing on terraces, but all small and dilapidated. These buildings once stood erect in full view from the sea, but now the stranger sails along the coast unconscious that among the trees lie shrouded the ruins of an aboriginal town.

In the afternoon we set out for the ruins of Tuloom, a league distant on the coast, and with the Castillo on a high cliff in full sight. Our road lay for a mile and a half along the shore. At the end of the beach was a high rocky promontory, standing out into the sea, and cutting off all progress along the shore. This we ascended, and continued along the cliff, which sloped toward the sea, in some places forming a perpendicular wall, and on our right rose great masses of rock, cutting off entirely the view of the Castillo. In half an hour we came unexpectedly upon a low building, apparently an adoratorio, or altar, climbing to the top of which, we again saw the Castillo. By this time it was late, and, afraid of being overtaken by darkness on this wild range, we turned back. Night was upon us when we again reached the shore. The sandy beach was now a welcome relief, and at a late hour we again reached the hut, having come to a rapid conclusion that a frequent repetition of this walk would be neither pleasant nor profitable, and that, in order to get through our work with the celerity we aimed at, it would be necessary again to take up our abode among the ruins.

The next morning we set out for that purpose, escorted by the younger Molas, a fine lad of about twenty, who considered our arrival the greatest incident that had ever occurred at Tancar, and before we reached the end of the beach be wanted to go travelling with us.

We had undertaken our long journey to this place in utter uncertainty as to what we should meet with; impediments and difficulties had accumulated upon us, but already we felt indemnified for all our labour. We were amid the wildest scenery we had yet found in Yucatan; and, besides the deep and exciting interest of the ruins themselves, we had around us what we wanted at all the other places, the magnificence of nature. Clearing away the platform in front, we looked over an immense forest; walking around the moulding of the wall, we looked out upon the boundless ocean, and deep in the clear water at the foot of the cliff we saw gliding quietly by a great fish eight or ten feet long.

Plate XLIV represents the front of the Castillo. The building, including the wings, measures at its base one hundred feet in length. The grand staircase is thirty feet wide, with twenty-four steps, and a substantial balustrade on each side, still in good preservation, gives it an unusually imposing character. In the doorway are two columns, making three entrances, with square recesses above them, all of which once contained ornaments, and in the centre one fragments of a statue still remain. The interior is divided into two corridors, each twenty-six feet long; the one in front is six feet six inches wide, and had at each end a stone bench, or divan; and again on the walls we found the mysterious prints of the red hand.

A single doorway leads to the back corridor, which is nine feet wide, and has a stone bench extending along the foot of the wall. On each side of the doorway are stone rings, intended for the support of the door, and in the back wall are oblong openings, which admit breezes from the sea. Both apartments have the triangular-arched ceiling, and both had a convenience and pleasantness of arrangement that suited us well as tenants.

The wings are much lower than the principal building. Each consists of two ranges, the lower standing on a low platform, from which are steps leading to the upper. The latter consists of two chambers, of which the one in front is twenty-four feet wide and twenty deep, having two columns in the doorway, and

PLATE XLIV

TULOOM
Front of the Castillo

Façade of the Castle, Tulum.

two in the middle of the chamber corresponding with those in the doorway. The centre columns were ornamented with devices in stucco, one of which seemed a masked face, and the other the head of a rabbit. The walls were entire, but the roof had fallen. There were holes along the top of the wall, as if beams had been laid in them, all which induced us to believe that the roofs had been flat, and supported by wooden beams resting upon the two columns in the centre. From this apartment a doorway three feet wide, close to the wall of the principal building, leads to a chamber twenty-four feet wide and nine feet deep, also roofless, and having the same indications that the roof had been flat and supported by wooden beams.

Pate XLV represents the back or sea wall of the Castillo. It rises on the brink of a high, broken, precipitous cliff, commanding a magnificent ocean view, and a picturesque line of coast, being itself visible from a great distance at sea. The wall is solid, and has no doorways or entrances of any kind, nor even a platform around it. At evening, when the work of the day was ended and our men returned to the hut, we sat down on the moulding of the wall, and regretted that the doorways of our lofty habitation had not opened upon the sea. Night, however, wrought a great change in our feelings. An easterly storm came on, and the rain beat heavily against the sea wall. We were obliged to stop up the oblong openings, and congratulated ourselves upon the wisdom of the ancient builders. The darkness, the howling of the winds, the cracking of branches in the forest, and the dashing of angry waves against the cliff, gave a romantic interest, almost a sublimity to our occupation of this desolate building.

Our first day did not suffice to finish the clearing of the area in front of the Castillo. Within this area were several small ruined buildings, which seemed intended for altars. Opposite the foot of the steps was a square terrace, with steps on all four of its sides, but the platform had no structure of any kind upon it, and was overgrown with trees, under the shade of which Mr. Catherwood set up his camera to make his drawing.

PLATE XLV

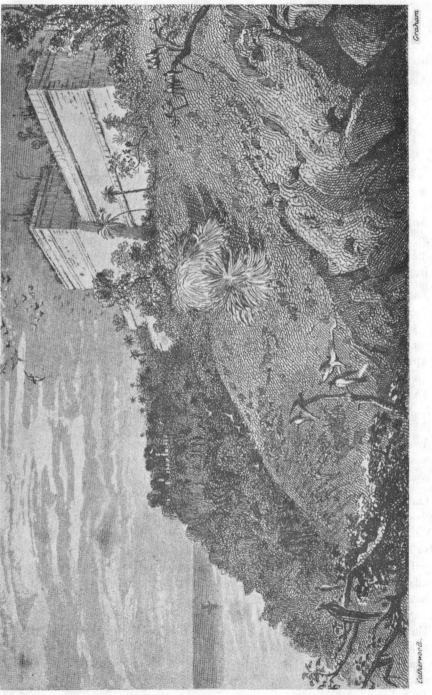

Catherwood.   Graham.

TULOOM

The Castle, viewed from the sea, Tulum.

Adjoining the lower room of the south wing were extensive remains, one of which contained a chamber forty feet wide and nineteen deep, with four columns that had probably supported a flat roof. In another, lying on the ground, were the fragments of two tablets, of the same character with those at Labphak.

The Castle is the tallest building in Tulum and must be the one that the Spaniards of Grijalva's expedition described as a tower when they saw it from out at sea. It was built in three stages and part of the original construction can still be seen on the north and south sides. The central part was covered by the buildings of the second stage, whose temple stands on the new stairway and the rear buttress and has two corridors. The frieze has two borders forming three niches above the columns. In the central one is part of the figure of the Descending God, and in the north one, the remains of a human figure. Stucco masks with feather headdresses decorate the corners of the main façade. Finally, in the third stage, two small oratories were added to what remained of the original façade.

On the north side, at the distance of about forty feet from the Castillo, stands a small isolated building, a side view of which is represented in Plate XLVI. It stands on a terrace, and has a staircase eight feet wide, with ten or twelve broken steps. The platform is twenty-four feet front and eighteen deep. The building contains a single room, having, like the Castillo, a triangular-arched roof. Over the doorway is the same curious figure we saw at Sayi, with the head down and the legs and arms spread out; and along the cornice were other curious and peculiar ornaments.

The interior of this building consisted of a single chamber, twelve feet by seven, having the triangular-arched ceiling, and at each end a raised step of divan. The wall and ceiling were stuccoed and covered with paintings, the subjects of which were almost entirely effaced.

PLATE XLVI

Catherwood

Graham

TULOOM

*Temple of the
Descending God.
Tulum.*

The building described here is the one now known as the Temple of the
Descending God, *standing on top of another flat-roofed structure that
was filled in to make a base. A small flight of steps leads up to the
temple, whose vault is similar to the one in the* Castle. *Above the entrance is a niche holding the stucco figure of a god head downward as
if descending from the sky. Paintings, some of which were restored in
the 1930's by Miguel Angel Fernández, decorate the façade and the
interior. These show scenes of offerings, stars and serpents.*

The day ended without our making any advances beyond this immediate
nieghbourhood, but the next was made memorable by the unexpected discovery
that this forest-buried city was encompassed by a wall, which had resisted all
the elements of destruction at work upon it, and was still erect and in good
preservation. Since the beginning of our exploration we had heard of city walls,
but all vestiges of them elsewhere had been uncertain, and our attempts to trace
them unsatisfactory. Young Molas had told us of these, and was on the ground
early to guide us to them. We set out without much expectation of any decided
result, and, following him through the woods, all at once found ourselves
confronted by a massive stone structure running at right angles to the sea; and,
following its direction, we soon came to a gateway and watch-tower. We passed
through the gateway, and followed the wall outside, keeping as close to it as the
trees and bushes would permit, down to the sea.

Figure 17 represents the plan of this wall. The sun beat upon us, móschetoes,
flies, and other insects pestered us, but, under all annoyances, the day employed
on the summit of this wall was one of the most interesting we passed among
ruins.

The wall is of rude construction, and composed of rough, flat stones, laid
upon each other without mortar or cement of any kind, and it varies from
eight to thirteen feet in thickness. The south side has two gateways, each

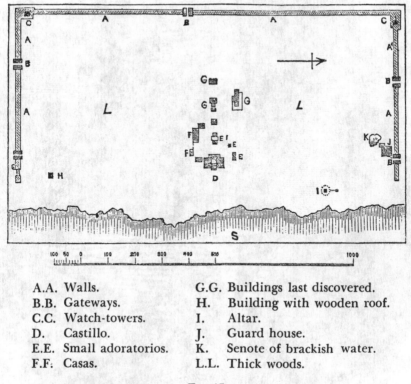

A.A. Walls.
B.B. Gateways.
C.C. Watch-towers.
D. Castillo.
E.E. Small adoratorios.
F.F: Casas.

G.G. Buildings last discovered.
H. Building with wooden roof.
I. Altar.
J. Guard house.
K. Senote of brackish water.
L.L. Thick woods.

FIG. 17

about five feet wide. At the distance of six hundred and fifty feet the wall turns at right angles, and runs parallel to the sea. At the angle, elevated so as to give a commanding view, and reached by ascending a few steps, is the watch-tower represented in Figure 18. It is twelve feet square, and has two doorways. The interior is plain, and against the back wall is a small altar, at which the guard might offer up prayers for the preservation of the city.

The Great Wall *or* Outer Precinct *was built to defend the city. At the northwest and southwest corners are small temples that might have been used as watchtowers. The wall was reconstructed in 1974 and 1975 by the Southeastern Regional Center of the National Institute of Anthropology and History.*

On the north side of the wall, near the east gateway, is a building thirty-six feet in front and thirty-four deep, divided into two principal and two smaller rooms, the ceilings of which had entirely fallen. At one corner is a senote, with the remains of steps leading down to it, and containing brackish water. Near this was a hollow rock, which furnished us with our supply.

FIG. 18

View of Tulum showing the city wall.

This building, which has four corridors or galleries, is the House of the Cenote, *so called because it stands over an old natural well, reached through the southeast room.*

Toward the southeast corner of the wall, on the brow of the cliff, stands a building fifteen feet front and ten deep. The interior is about seven feet high, and the ceiling is flat, and discloses an entirely new principle of construction. It has four principal beams of wood, about six inches in diameter, laid on the top of the wall from end to end of the chamber, with smaller beams, about three inches in diameter, laid across the larger so closely as to touch; and on these crossbeams is a thick mass of mortar and large pebbles, which was laid on moist, and now forms a solid crust, being the same materials which we had seen in ruins on the floors of other rooms. Against the back wall was an altar, with a rude triangular stone upon it, which seemed to bear marks of not very distant use. On each side of the doorway were large sea-shells fixed in the wall for the support of the doors.

This must be the Temple of the Sea, *a one-roomed building that over-looks the Caribbean. The roof is made of a mixture of lime, pieces of shell and shards and used to have wooden beams supporting it.*

These were all the buildings to which young Molas conducted us, and he said there were no others within the area of the walls, but there many vestiges without; and it was our belief that the walls enclosed only the principal, perhaps the sacred buildings, and that ruins existed to great distance beyond; but, with only young Molas and one boatman, being all that the patron could spare at a time, we did not consider it worth while to attempt any exploration. A legion of fierce usurpers, already in possession, were determined to drive us out, and after hard work by day, we had no rest at night;

> "There was never yet philosopher
> That could endure the toothache patiently;"

and I will venture to say that a philosopher would final the moschetoes of Tuloom worse than the toothache.

CHAPTER XXII

Discovery of a Building — Two others — Adoratorios — Return
Voyage — Island of Mugeres

The next morning we finished what remained to be done, and, after an early dinner, prepared to leave the ruins. While the men were arranging their loads I gave Doctor Cabot a direction to a point in the wall, where, in measuring around it, Mr. Catherwood and I had started two ocellated turkeys. He set out to cut his way in a straight line with his hunting knife, and very soon, while sitting on the steps of the Castillo, I heard him calling to me that he had come upon another building which we had not seen. He was so near that we comunicated without any particular effort of voice, but I could see nothing of him or of the building. Following his path, I found him standing before it; and while working our way around it we discovered two others near by, almost invisible, so dense was the foliage of the trees, but the largest, except the Castillo, and most important of any we had seen. Our plans were all deranged, for we could not go away without drawings of these buildings. We returned to the steps of the Castillo, and summoned all hands to council. The men had their back-loads ready, Bernaldo reported two tortillas as the stock of provisions on hand, and the idea of another night in the Castillo struck us with dismay. We had been so long accustomed to sleep that it had become part of our nature; a night's rest was indispensable, and we determined to break up and return the next day.

Before daylight the next morning Albino set off with Molas and the sailors, and by the time Mr. Catherwood arrived on the ground the clearing of the first building was made.

Plate XLVII represents the front of this building. It faces the west, measures twenty-seven feet in length and nineteen in depth, and consists of two stories. The exterior had been richly decorated, and above the cornice were fragments of rich ornaments in stucco. The lower story has four columns, making five doorways opening into a narrow corridor, which runs round and encloses on three sides a chamber in the centre. The walls of the corridor on both sides were covered with paintings, but green and mildewed from the rankness of vegetation in which the building is smothered. A small doorway in front opens into the chamber, which measures eleven feet by seven; of this, too, the walls were covered with paintings, decayed and effaced, and against the back wall was an altar for burning copal.

PLATE XLVII

Catherwood

Hoogh

TULOOM

*Temple of the Frescoes
and fragment of mural
painting inside.*

The building on the top stands directly over the lower chamber, and corresponds with it in dimensions, this being the only instance we met with in which one room was placed directly over another. There was no staircase or other visible means of communication between the lower and upper stories.

At the rear of this building were others attached to it, or connected with it, but uprooted and thrown by trees.

They had found the Temple of the Frescos, *now considered by experts to be the most important building on the site since it provides information on the Maya picture of the universe. It stands almost at the center of the city and was added to several times. The original structure was a room at ground level that was later surrounded on three sides by a gallery, with entrances on the west front formed by four columns. This building was reinforced at a third stage to support the weight of a temple built on top.*

The paintings in the first temple, done in bluish-green on a black background, are the best preserved because they are protected by the gallery that was added. The second building has stucco decoration, and the main façade has a frieze with three niches in it. The two side ones contain seated figures wearing feather headdresses, while the center one holds an image of the Descending God. On the northwest and southwest corners are two large masks, perhaps of Itzamná, the giver of life. The upper temple, built at the third stage, has simple moldings and a niche at the center with traces of a god.

On a base in front of this temple stands stele number 2 of Tulum, with glyphs that are so worn that no date has yet been deciphered.

At the short distance of fifty-three feet is the building represented in Plate XLVIII. It stands on a terrace six feet high, with a staircase in the centre, measures forty-five feet by twenty-six, has two pillars in the doorway, and over the centre is the head of a multilated figure. The interior is divided into two principal and parallel apartments, and at the north extremity of the inner one is a smaller apartment, containing an enclosed altar five feet long, and three feet six inches deep, for burning copal. The roof had fallen, and trees were growing out of the floor.

This building now has the name House of the Chultún. *Some years ago the wooden lintel over the entrance broke and central part of the façade collapsed. Until then it had stood as shown in Catherwood's engraving. The stucco head was recovered, but in very bad condition.*

Near this is another building, larger than the last, constructed on the same plan, but more ruined. These buildings were all within about two hundred feet of the steps of the Castillo.

It will be borne in mind that when this city was inhabited and clear of trees, the buildings were all visible from the sea; the Spaniards are known to have sailed along this coast, and the reader will ask if they have given us no accounts of its existence. The narrative of the expedition of Grijalva, taken up at the point at which we left it, after crossing from Cozumel, continues: "We ran along day and night, and the next day toward sunset we saw a burg, or village, so large that Seville would not have appeared larger or better. We saw there a very high tower. There was upon the bank a crowd of Indians, who carried two standards, which they raised and lowered as signs to us to come and join them. The same day we arrived at a bay, near which was a tower, the highest we had seen. We remarked a very considerable village; the country was watered by many rivers. We discovered a bay *where a fleet would have been able to enter.*" This account is certainly not so accurate as a coast survey would be at this day, but it is more minute than most accounts of the early voyages of the Spaniards, and, in my opinion, it is all sufficient to identify this now desolate city.

PLATE XLVIII

Catherwood.

Johnson.

TULOOM

Outside of the walls are several small buildings, no doubt intended for adoratorios, or altars, one of which is represented in Figure 19. It stands on a terrace, having a circular platform, on the brow of the cliff, overlooking the sea, and measures fifteen feet front by twelve deep. The doorway faces the north. The interior consists of a single chamber, and against the back wall is an altar in such a state of preservation as to be fit for its original uses. Near the foot of the steps, overgrown by the scrubby wild palm which covers the whole cliff, is a small altar, with ornaments in stucco, one of which seems intended to represent a pineapple. These wanted entirely the massive character of the buildings, and are so slight that they could almost be pushed over with the foot. They stand in the open air, exposed to strong easterly winds, and almost to the spray of the sea. It was impossible to believe that the altar had

FIG. 19

been abandoned three hundred years; within that time some guardian eye had watched over it, some pious hand had repaired it, and long since the arrival of the Spaniards the Indian had performed before it his idolatrous rites.

The Temple of the Wind *stands on a cliff overlooking the small bay north of the main complex.*

Tulum, meaning 'enclosure' or 'wall' is the modern name for the site, given to it because of the wall surrounding it on three sides. The original name seems to have been Zamá, 'Dawn'.

Between 1916 and 1922, the Carnegie Institution of Washington carried out the first scientific investigations, in which Morley, Howe and Prince William of Sweden participated. In 1937 a team of Mexican experts visited and recorded the archeological sites on the east coast of Yucatán. A year later, the National Institute of Anthropology and History commissioned Miguel Angel Fernández to do conservation and restoration work at Tulum. The Southeast Regional Center of the same Institute continued the investigation and restoration of this important site in 1974 and 1975.

Our journey in this direction is now ended, and our course is homeward. We were detained one day at Tancar by a storm, and on Tuesday morning the patron came to us in a hurry with a summons on board; the wind had veered so that he could get out of the harbour; and, bidding good-by to the carpenter and Molas, we were soon under way. We had a strong wind and fair, and late in the afternoon put in at Nesuc, where we had stopped before, distinguished by its solitary palm tree.

Early in the morning we were again under way, and coasted to the point of Kancune, where we landed in front of a rancho then occupied by a party of fishermen. Near by was another great pile of the skeletons of turtles. The fishermen were busy within the hut mending their nets, and seemed to be leading a hardy, independent, and social life, entirely different from anything seen in the interior. A short walk brought us to the point, on which stood two dilapidated buildings, one entirely fallen, and the other having dimensions like the smallest of those seen at Tuloom. It was so intensely hot, and we were so annoyed by millions of sand-flies, that we did not think it worth while to stay, but returned to the hut, embarked, and, crossing over, in two hours reached the island of Mugeres. In wading ashore we stuck in a mud-bank, and had time to contemplate the picturesque beauty of the scene before us. It was a small sandy beach, with a rocky coast on each side, and trees growing down to the water, broken only by a small clearing opposite the beach, in which were two palm leaf huts, and an arbour covered with palm leaves. Under the arbour hung three small hammocks, and a hardy, sun-dried fisherman sat repairing a net, with two Indian boys engaged in weaving a new one. The old fisherman, without desisting from his work, invited us to the hammocks, and, to satisfy our invariable first want on this coast, sent a boy for water, which, though not good, was better than that on board.

The island was famed among the fishermen as the rendezvous of Lafitte the pirate, and the patron told us that our host had been his prisoner two years.

The fisherman, about fifty-five years old, told them he did not know whether what people said about Lafitte was true, but assured them that he had never harmed the fishermen.

Early in the morning, under the guidance of two of the fisherman, we set out to visit the ruins. The island of Mugeres is between four and five miles long, half a mile wide, and four miles distant from the mainland. The ruins were at the north end. For a short distance we kept along the shore, and then struck into a path cut straight across the island. About half way across we came to a santa cruz, or holy cross, set up by the fishermen, at which place we heard distinctly the sound of the breakers on the opposite shore. To the right a faint track was perceptible, which soon disappeared altogether; but our guides knew the direction, and, cutting a way with the machete, we came out upon a high, rocky, perpendicular cliff, which commanded an immense expanse of ocean, and against which the waves, roused by the storm of the night before, were dashing grandly. We followed along the brink of the cliff and around the edges of great perpendicular chasms, the ground being bare of trees and covered with a scrubby plant, called the uba, with gnarled roots spreading like the branches of a grape-vine. At the point terminating the island, standing boldly upon the sea, was the lonely edifice represented in Plate XLIX. Below, rocking on the waves, was a small canoa, with our host then in the act of getting on board a turtle. It was the wildest and grandest scene we had looked upon in our whole journey.

The steps which led to the building are in good preservation, and at the foot is a platform, with the ruins of an altar. The front, on one side of the doorway, has fallen. When entire it measured twenty-eight feet, and it is fifteen feet deep.

The ceiling had the triangular arch, and throughout the hand of the builders on the mainland could not be mistaken, but on the walls were writings which seemed strangely familiar in an aboriginal building. These inscriptions were,

D. Doyle, 1842.   A. C. Goodall, 1842.

H. M. Ship Blossom.

11th October, 1811. Corsaire Françes (Chebek) le Vengeur,

Capt. Pierre Liovet;

PLATE XLIX

ISLAND OF MUGERES
Ancient Building.

and wafered on the wall on separate cards were the names of the officers of the Texan schooners of war San Bernard and San Antonio.

In the account given by Bernal Dias of the expedition of Cortez, he says that, after leaving the island of Cozumel, the fleet was separated by a gale of wind, but the next day all the ships joined company except one, which, according to the surmise of the pilot, was found in certain bay on the coast wind bound. "Here", says Bernal Dias, "several of our companions went on shore, and found in the town hard by, four temples, the idols in which represented human female figures of large size, for which reason we named this place *Punta* de las Mugeres," or the Point of the Women.

The island does in fact owe its name to the numbers of female figurines discovered there by the first Spaniards to visit it. In the south of the island there is a small site with a shrine standing on a square base, dedicated to Ixchel, *goddess of the moon, divination and procreation.*

We returned to the hut ready to embark, and at twelve o'clock we took leave of the fishermen, and were again on board our canoa.

The wind was fair and strong, and very soon we reached the point of the island. Toward dark we doubled Catoche, and, for the first time coasting all night, day broke upon us in the harbour of Yalahao. After the desolate regions we had been visiting, the old pirates' haunt seemed a metropolis.

At seven o'clock we were again under way, with the wind directly astern, and as much as we could carry, the canoa rolling so that we were compelled to take in the mainsail. The coast was low, barren, and monotonous. At three o'clock we passed an ancient mound, towering above the huts that constituted the port of El Cuyo, a landmark for sailors, visible at sea three leagues distant; but our patron told us that there were no buildings or vestiges of ruins.

CHAPTER XXIII

Port of Silan — Shooting Excursion to Punta Arenas — Village of
Silan — Gigantic Mound — Temax — Izamal — Fiesta of Santa
Cruz — Gigantic Head — Church and Convent

At daylight the next morning we crawled out from the bottom of the
canoa, and found her anchored off the port of Silan, which consisted of a few
huts built around a sandy square on a low, barren coast. We gave portions of
our tattered garments to the waves, and waded ashore. It was three weeks since
we had embarked; our coast voyage had been more interesting than we expected,
but there was no part of it so agreeable as the end; we were but too happy to
get rid of the discomfort and confinement to the canoa. The patron went to find
lodgings for us, and I followed with one of the boatmen, carrying a load. A
man just opening the door of a sort of warehouse called to me, and offered
it for our accommodation, which, on looking within, I did not hesitate to accept.

Silan is the port of Izamal, which is eleven leagues distant. According to
our arrangement, Dimas was to meet us here with the horses, but he had not
arrived or been heard of. We learned, however, that there was no green food to
be procured at this place, which Dimas had probably learned at the village, three
leagues distant, and had therefore remained at that place; yet we had some
uneasiness, as he had to make a journey of two hundred and fifty miles, and
our first business was to despatch Albino for information. Next we had a great
enterpise in procuring breakfast, and after this in providing for dinner, which
we determined should be the best the country afforded, to consist of fish and
fowl, each of which had to be bought separately, and, with separate portions
of lard, sent to different houses to be cooked.

During the interval of preparation I took a walk along the shore. Toward
the end of a sandy beach was a projecting point, on a line with which I noticed
on the water what seemed to be a red cloud of singular brilliancy, and, at the
same time, delicacy of colour, which, on drawing nearer, I found to be a flat
covered with flamingoes. On my return I reported the discovery to Doctor
Cabot, when our host gave us such a glowing account of flamingoes, scarlet
ibises, and roseate spoonbills at Punta Arenas, about two leagues distant, that
my imagination was excited by the idea of such clouds of beautiful plumage. In
good time our horses arrived with Dimas, in fine order; and as he had had some
days' rest, we took him and an Indian procured by our host, and at about four

o'clock set out. For the first league our road lay directly along the shore, but farther on there were projecting points, to cut off which a footpath led among mangrove trees, with shoots growing from the branches into the ground, forming what seemed a naked and impenetrable canebrake, surmounted by thick green foliage. In many places it was difficult to advance on horseback; from time to time we came out upon a broken, stony shore, and, considering that we had set out merely for a short ride, we found ourselves travelling on one of the wildest roads we had met with in the country. At dusk we reached a hut in a beautifully picturesque position, imbosomed in a small bay, with a frail bridge, about two feet wide, running out some distance from the shore, and a canoa floating at the end. We swung our hammocks, kindled a fire, and when the occupant arrived had a cup of chocolate ready for him, and endeavoured to make him feel himsef at home; but this was no easy matter. He was a lad of about sixteen, the son of the proprietor, who had gone away that day, the fishing season being nearly over.

In the gray of the morning we heard a loud quacking of ducks, which almost lifted us out of our hammocks, and carried us out of doors. Beyond the point of the little dock was a long sand-bank, covered with immense flocks of these birds. Below us the shore formed a large bay, with the Punta de Arenas, or Point of Sand, projecting toward us, bordered down to the water's edge with trees, and all over the bay were sand-banks, barely appearing above water, and covered with wild fowl of every description known, in numbers almost exceeding the powers of conception. In recurring to them afterward, Doctor Cabot enumerated of ducks, the mallard, pin-tail, blooming teal, widgeon, and gadwall; of bitterns, the American bittern, least bittern, great and lesser egret, blue crane, great blue heron, Louisiana heron, night heron, two kinds of rail, one clapper rail, white ibis, willets, snipes, red-breasted snipe, least snipe, semi-palmated sandpiper, black-breasted plover, marble godwit, longbilled curlew, osprey or fish-hawk, black hawk, and other smaller birds, of which we took no note, and all together, with their brilliant plumage and varied notes, forming, as we passed among them, an animated and exciting scene, but it was no field for sporting. It would have been slaughter to shoot among them.

For mere sporting, such a ground is not often seen, and the idea of a shooting lodge, or rather hut, on the shores of Punta de Arenas for a few months in the season, with a party large enough to consume the game, presented itself almost as attractively as that of exploring ruined cities. On our return, each of us made a single shot, from which we picked up between thirty and forty birds, leaving others crippled and hopping on the beach. We got back to the hut, and tumbled them all into a dry pot (the feathers being, of course, taken off), and sat down ourselves to the business of dissection.

At four o'clock we took leave of our young host, and at dark reached the port, and rode across the sandy plaza. The door which had opened to us with so much alacrity was now shut, but not by the hand of inhospitality. Mr. Catherwood and the owner had left for the village, and the house was locked up. Some of the villagers, however, came to us, and conducted us to the quartel, which was garrisoned by two women, who surrendered at discretion, provided us with chocolate, and, although the hut was abundantly large for all of us, unexpectedly bade us good-night, and withdrew to a neighbour's to sleep. If they had remained, not being worn down by fatigue as we were, and, consequently, more wakeful, a sad catastrophe might have been prevented. We laid our birds carefully on a table to dry; during the night a cat entered, and we were awaked to see the fruits of our hard day's labour dragged along the floor, and the cat bounding from them, and escaping through a hole in the side of the hut.

Before daylight the next morning we were again in the saddle. For some distance back from the port the ground had been washed or overflowed by the sea, and was a sandy, barren mangrove brake. Beyond commenced the same broken, stony surface, and before we had proceeded far we discovered that Doctor Cabot's horse was lame. Not to lose time, I rode on to procure another, and at eight o'clock reached the village of Silan. In the suburbs I discovered unexpectedly the towering memorial of another ruined city, and riding into the plaza, saw at one angle, near the wall of the church, the gigantic mound represented in Plate L., the grandest we had seen in the country. Much as we had seen of ruins, the unexpected sight of this added immensely to the interest of our long journeying among the remains of aboriginal grandeur. Leaving my horse at the casa real, and directing the alcalde to see about getting one for Doctor Cabot, I walked over to the mound. At the base, and inside of the wall of the church, were five large orange trees, loaded with fruit. A group of Indians were engaged in getting stone out of the mound to repair the wall, and a young man was superintending them, whom I immediately recognised as the padre. He accompanied me to the top of the mound; it was one of the largest we had seen, being about fifty feet and four hundred feet long. There was no building or structure of any kind visible; whatever had been upon it had fallen or been pulled down. The church, the wall of the yard, and the few stone houses in the village, had been built of materials taken from it.

Silan was known to us as the scene of a modern and minor event. Our ambiguous friend on the island of Mugeres had told us that at this place Lafitte died and was buried, and I inquired for his grave. The padre was not in the village at the time, and did not know whether he was buried in the campo santo or the church, but supposed that, as Lafitte was a distinguished man, it was in the latter. We went thither, and examined the graves in the floor, and the padre drew out from amid some rubbish a cross, with a name on it, which he supposed to that of Lafitte, but it was not. The sexton who officiated at the burial was dead; the padre sent for several of the inhabitants, but a cloud hung

PLATE L

Ancient Mound, Village of Silan.

over the memory of the pirate: all knew of this death and burial, but none knew or cared to tell where he was laid.

The cura also managed to find a horse for Dr. Cabot.

At ten o'clock we set out, and at half past twelve reached Temax, two and a half leagues distant. It had a fine plaza, with a great church and convent, and a stone casa real, with a broad corridor in front, under which the guarda were swinging in hammocks.

We were but six leagues from Izamal, at which place, we learned, a fiesta was then going on, and there was to be a ball in the evening; but we could neither push our horses through, nor procure a calesa, thought the road was good for wheel carriages.

Early in the evening we took to our hammocks, but had hardly lain down, when one of the guarda came to inform us that a caricoche had just arrived from Izamal, and wanted a return freight. We had it brought down to the casa real, and at two o'clock, by a bright moonlight, we started, leaving Dimas to follow with the horses. The caricoche was drawn by three mules, and had in it a bed, on which we reclined at full length.

At nine o'clock we entered the suburbs of Izamal, but fifteen leagues from Merida. In the centre of the plaza our driver stopped for instructions. We directed him to the casa real, and as we were moving on, our English saddles, strapped on behind, caught the eye of Albino, who conducted us to the house in which Mr. Catherwood was already domiciled.

It was the last day of the fiesta of Santa Cruz. By the grace of a beneficent government, the village of Izamal had been erected into a city, and the jubilee on account of this accession of political dignity was added to the festival of the holy cross. From desolation and solitude we had come into the midst of gayeties, festivities, and rejoicings. But amid this gay scene the eye turned involuntarily to immense mounds rising grandly above the tops of the houses, from which the whole city had been built, without seeming to diminish their colossal proportions.

One of these great mounds, having at that time benches upon it, commanding a view of the bull-fight in the plaza, blocked up the yard of the house we occupied, and extended into the adjoining yard of the Señora Mendez, who was the owner of both. It is, perhaps, two hundred feet long and thirty high. The part in our yard was entirely ruined, but in that of the señora it appeared that its vast sides had been covered from one end to the other with colossal ornaments in stucco, most of which had fallen, but among the fragments is the gigantic head represented in Plate LI. It is seven feet eight inches in height and seven feet in width. The ground-work is of projecting stones, which are covered with tucco. A stone one foot six inches long protrudes from the chin, intended, perhaps, for burning copal on, as a sort of altar.

PLATE LI

Lindevienti.   S.H.Gimber.

IZAMAL
Gigantic Head.

Two or three streets distant from the plaza, but visible in all its huge proportions, was the most stupendous mound we had seen in the country, being, perhaps, six or seven hundred feet long and sixty feet high, which, we ascertained beyond all doubt, had interior chambers.

On the north side of the plaza is the great church and convent of Franciscan monks, standing on an elevation, and giving a character to the plaza that no other in Yucatan possesses. Two fights of stone steps lead up to it, and the area upon which they open is probably two hundred feet square; on three sides is a colonnade, forming a noble promenade, overlooking the city and the surrounding country to a great distance.

According to the account of the padre Lizana, in the year 1553, at the second chapter held in the province, the padre Fr. Diego de Landa was elected guardian of the convent of Izamal, and charged to erect the building, the monks having lived until that time in houses of straw. He selected as the place for the foundation one of the cerros, or mounds, which then existed, "made by hand,' and called by the natives Phapphol-chac, which, says the padre Lizana, "signifies the habitation or residence of the priests of the god; this place was selected in order that the devil might be driven away by the divine presence of Christ sacrificed, and that the place in which the priests of the idol lived, and which had been the place of abomination and idolatry might become that of sanctification, where the ministers of the true God should offer sacrifices and adoration due to his Divine Majesty."

In Izamal there are remains of Maya buildings and examples of Colonial architecture. The pre-Hispanic city was founded around 500 B.C. by a legendary figure called Zamná or Itzamná, which means Dew of Heaven. It became the sacred city of the Mayas, and pilgrims arrived there from all over the peninsula.

Later the city was abandoned for some reason and the pryamids were gradually covered by vegetation until they just looked like hills. In 1968 the largest of these structures, that of Kinich-Kakmó, House of the Sun or House of the Fire Macaw was uncovered. This consistis of a large platform with rounded corners, which used to have a stairway up to the ceremonial platform.

CHAPTER XXIV

Departure for Merida — Hacienda of Aké — The Ruins — Number
of Cities discovered

The next morning we started for Merida, with the intention of diverging
for the last time to visit the ruins of Aké. The road was one of the best in the
country, made for carriages, but rough, stony, and uninteresting. At Cacalchen,
five leagues distant, we stopped to dine and procure a guide to Aké.

In the afternoon we proceeded, taking with us only our hammocks, and
leaving Dimas to go on direct with the luggage to Merida. Turning off immediately from the main road, we entered the woods, and following a narrow path,
a little before dark we reached the hacienda of Aké, and for the last time were
among the towering and colossal memorials of an aboriginal city.

*The major domo was away and the main building locked, so they settled
into a dirty hut. At ten o'clock the major domo arrived and lodged them
in the house.*

Plate LII represents a great mound towering in full sight from the door of
the hacienda, and called El Palacio, or the Palace. The ascent is on the south
side, by an immense staircase, one hundred and thirty-seven feet wide, forming
an approach of rude grandeur, perhaps equal to any that ever existed in .the
country. The platform on the top is two hundred and twenty-five feet in length,
and fifty in breadth. On this great platform stand thirty-six shafts, or columns,
in three parallel rows of twelve, about ten feet apart from north to south, and
fifteen from east to west. They are from fourteen to sixteen feet in height, four
feet on each side, and are comopsed of separate stones, from one to two feet
in thickness. But few have fallen, through some have lost their upper layer of
stones. There are no remains of any structure or of a roof. If there ever was
one, it must have been of wood, which would seem most incongruous and inap-
propriate for such a solid structure of stones.

In the same vicinity are other mounds of colossal dimensions, one of which
is also called the Palace, but of a different construction and without pillars. On
another, at the head of the ruined staircase, is an opening under the top of a
doorway, nearly filled up, crawling through which, by means of the crotch of
a tree I descended into a dark chamber fifteen feet long and ten wide, of rude
construction, and of which some of the stones in the wall measured seven feet

PLATE LII

AKE
Ruined Structure on Mound.

in length. This is called Akabna, casa obscura, or dark house. Near this is a senote, with the remains of steps leading down to water, which once supplied the ancient city. The ruins cover a great extent, but all were overgrown, and in a condition too ruinous to be presented in a drawing. They were ruder and more massive than all the others we had seen, bore the stamp of an older era, and more than any others, in fact, for the first time in the country, suggested the idea of Cyclopean remains.

> *The site of Aké, a few miles east of Merida, has been explored very little. It was built near a cenote and the remains cover a wide area. Among them are a carved monolith that has not been deciphered, a sort of labyrinth of columns, and the* Castle, *which has simply been cleared of the vegetation that covered it.*

I have now finished my journey among ruined cities. I know that it is impossible by any narrative to convey to the reader a true idea of the powerful and exciting interest of wandering among them, and I have avoided as much as possible all detailed descriptions, but I trust that these pages will serve to give some general idea of the appearance which this country once presented. In our long, irregular, and devious route we have discovered the crumbling remains of forty-four ancient cities, most of them but a short distance apart, though, from the great change that has taken place in the country, and the breaking up of the old roads, having no direct communication with each other; with but few exceptions, all were lost, buried, and unknown, never before visited by a stranger, and some of them, perhaps, never looked upon by the eyes of a white man.

CHAPTER XXV

Departure — Arrival at Merida — Embarcation for Havana —
Passage Home

At two o'clock we mounted for Merida, nine leagues distant. We did not expect to reach it till night, and, from the unfortunate condition of our travelling costume, did not care to enter the capital by daylight; but, pushing on, and miscalculating the pace of our horses, we found ourselves in the suburbs at that unlucky hour when, the excessive heat being over, the inhabitants, in full dress, were sitting in the doorways or along the side-walks, talking over the news of the day, and particularly alive to the appearance of such a spectacle as our party presented. Approaching the plaza, an old acquaintance greeted us, and accompanied us to the Casa de las Diligencias, a new establishment, opened since our departure, opposite the convent, one of the largest and finest in the city, and equal to a good hotel in Italy. Very soon we had the best apartments, and were sitting down to *thé du China,* in English, tea, and *pan Frances,* or bread without sweetening. After our hard journey among Indian ranchos and unwholesome haciendas, at times all prostrated by illness, we had returned to Merida, successful beyond our utmost hopes. Our rough work was all over, and our satisfaction cannot easily be described.

In Merida they learned the latest news and political problems of the State of Yucatan, Mexico, and America. They put their horses up for sale, visited their friends, and made preparations to leave.

A vessel was then at Sisal ready to sail. It was one which we had hoped never to be on board of again, being the old Alexandre, in which we made our former unlucky voyage, but we had now no alternative, being advised that if we lost that opportunity, it was entirely uncertain when another would present itself. At the request of the governor, we delayed our departure a few days, that he might communicate with a relative in Campeachy, who wished a surgical operation perfomed by Doctor Cabot, and had passed two months in Merida awaiting our return. In the mean time the governor procured the detention of the vessel.

On Sunday, the sixteenth of May, early in the morning, we sent off our luggage for the port, and in the afternoon we joined for the last time in a paseo.

In the evening we rode to the house of Doña Joaquina Peon, said farewell to our first, last, and best friends in Merida, and at ten o'clock started for the port.

On Tuesday, the eighteenth, we embarked for Havana. On the second of June we anchored under the walls of the Moro Castle. Before obtaining passports to land, a barque entered, which we immediately recognised as an American, and on landing, learned that she was the Ann Louisa, Captain Clifford, one of a line of packets from Vera Cruz, had put in short of water, and was to sail the next day for New-York. The yellow fever had already broken out; there was no other vessel in port, and we determined, if possible, to get on board, but we were met with a difficulty, which at first threatened to be insuperable. By the regulation of the port, it was necessary for all luggage to be carried to the custom-house for inspection, and a list furnished beforehand of every article. The last was utterly impossible, as we had on board the whole miscellaneous collection made on our journey, with no such thing as a memmorandum of the items. But by the active kindness of our late consul, Mr. Calhoun, and the courtesy of his excellency the governor, a special order was procured for transferring the whole without inspection from one vessel to the other. The next day was occupied in the details of this business and in the afternoon we joined in a paseo, the style and show of which, for the moment, made us think slightingly of the simple exhibition at Merida; and after dark, by the light of a single candle, with heads uncovered, we stood before the marble slab enclosing the bones of Columbus.

On the fourth we embarked on board the Ann Louisa. She was full of passengers, principally Spaniards escaping from the convulsions of Mexico, but Captain Clifford contrived to give us accommodations much better than we were used to, and we found on board the comforts and conveniences of Atlantic packets. On the seventeenth we reached New-York. The reader and I must again part, and trusting that he will find nothing in these pages to disturb the friendship that has hitherto existed between us, I again return him my thanks for his kindness, and bid him farewell.

CONCLUSION

The journeys and adventures in Yucatan end here. But what became of Stephens and Catherwood?

On arriving in New York, Stephens set to work putting his notes in order and reading through the accounts of the Spanish chroniclers to write *Incidents of Travel in Yucatan*. Meanwhile, the carved wooden beams and other Maya sculptures and artifacts were being exhibited in Catherwood's Panorama. As mentioned earlier, these were destroyed in a fire on the night of July 31, 1844.

Stephen's book, with 120 engravings, was published in two volumes in March 1843, and was an immediate success. It was reprinted several times and later translated into French, German, Spanish and other languages.

Stephens and Catherwood planned another book on American archeology and antiquities, to contain engravings made from Catherwood's drawings and texts by Alexander von Humboldt, William Prescott, Albert Gallatin and Stephens. However, they were unable to find the necessary 300 subscribers and so Catherwood decided to bring the book out himself.

With this in mind, he returned to England with his family and went to see various publishers, but they showed little interest. Stephens, for some unknown reason, withdrew from the project and the book, *Views of Ancient Monuments in Central America, Chiapas and Yucatan,* was reduced to a publication of only 25 engravings, maps and an introduction written by Catherwood. Dedicated to Stephens, it appeared in London in April 1844: the first and only publication of this splendid draughtsman.

Some time later Catherwood was in British Guiana, working on the construction of a railroad. Meanwhile, Stephens invested money in a shipping line, made a trip to Europe, and met Alexander von Humboldt.

Stephens was one of the founders of the Panama Railroad Company, that planned to run a line across the isthmus from the Atlantic to the Pacific. Catherwood worked on this project for some time then went to California to invest in mining.

For reasons of health, Stephens spent some time in New York and, when the railroad shares rose, returned to Panama to finish the work. By this time he was very sick as a result of suffering from malaria so many times.

From California Catherwood tried to revive Stephen's interest in archeology again, writing about the antiquities of Baja California. He set out for London, crossing Panama by the railroad he had helped to build, and joined Stephens for the last time. Shortly afterward, the American was found unconscious under a ceiba tree and taken to New York, where he died on October 13, 1852.

In 1854, Catherwood reedited *Incidents of Travel in Yucatan* adding a short biographical sketch of Stephens. In September of the same year he left England for New York on the *S.S. Arctic*, intending to go on to California. In the dense dog off Newfoundland the ship collided with a French vessel, the *S.S. Vesta*, and Catherwood was one of the 300 passengers drowned.

GLOSSARY

Proper names used by Stephens and the corresponding modern name or spelling.

Stephens	Modern
Akahba	Akab-há
Akatzeeb	Akabdzib
Ba Khalal	Bakhalal
Campeachy	Campeche
Chack	Chaac
Chacka	Chac-há
Chimaisha	Chimez-há
Conil	Aconil
Hiokowitz	Yokoluitz
Huncuma	Hunucmá
Jalacho	Halachó
Jalal	Halal
Jalasac	Halalsak
Kancune	Cancún
Kantunile	Kantunil
Kewick	Kiuic
Kuepak	Kupak
Labpak	Xlabpak
Mankeesh	Manküx
Moona	Muna
Mucuyché	Mukuiché
Mugeres (Isla)	Mujeres (Isla)
Nesuc	Nizuc
Noyaxche	Nohyaxché
Ociha	Ocil-há
Ocosingo	Ococingo
Opocheque	Opichén
Pucuelha	Pucul-há

Stephens	Modern
Sabachshé	Sabacché
Sacbey	Saché
St. Jago (de Cuba)	Santiago (de Cuba)
Sallab	Sayab
Salli	Sayil
Sannacté	Sacnicté
Schawill	Chaví
Schoolhoke	Xchonlok
Sijoh	Sihó
Silan	Cilam
Tancar	Tancáh
Tankuché	Tankuiche
Tekoh	Tecoh
Timucui	Timucuy
Tixmeach	Tixmeuac
Tobasco	Tabasco
Tuloom	Tulum
Vayalquex	Uayalceh
Xcoch	Xkoch
Xtacumbi Xunan	Xtacumbil-Xunaan
Yakatzib	Akabcib
Yalahao	Yalahau
Ytsimpte	Itzimté
Yzamal	Izamal
Zayil	Sayil